AN OBJECTIVE PSYCHOLOGY OF MUSIC

By

ROBERT W. LUNDIN

Assistant Professor of Psychology
Hamilton College

THE RONALD PRESS COMPANY · NEW YORK

Library of Congress Catalog Card Number: 53–5710
PRINTED IN THE UNITED STATES OF AMERICA

To

J. R. K.

PREFACE

THIS BOOK is addressed to students of psychology who want to find out more about musical behavior and to students of music whose knowledge of human responses to musical stimuli needs a scientific basis. Although the content will be familiar to musicians with some knowledge of psychology and to psychologists with special interest in music, they will find in the book a fresh approach to the study of musical behavior, a field in which scientific progress has been slower than in other areas of psychology.

The objective approach gives scientific meaning to the voluminous data on the psychology of music. It considers those human reactions to musical stimuli which are observable and can be measured and evaluated experimentally, and demonstrates that human responses to musical objects or experiences are as amenable to psychological investigation as any other human activity. Objective investigation gives a better understanding of the factors operating in musical responses and greater ability to predict these responses.

In this book we shall attempt to analyze many kinds of human reactions to musical stimuli. During the past generation, much scientific work has been done on the psychological aspects of music, including musical tests and measurements, and the most fruitful of these investigations are discussed within a systematic frame of reference. There is still much to be learned about reactions to musical stimuli, leaving aside such factors in musical behavior as cannot yet be measured. By further development of the objective approach, a body of facts and principles can be evolved that will stand up with the findings in other areas of psychology.

The viewpoint from which the book is written is that of interbehaviorism, because the theoretical structure of this school is most useful in fitting together the findings of various investigators of musical behavior. However, no objective finding known to the author has been omitted because it supported some point of view other than interbehaviorism. Interbehaviorism considers a psychological event as the interaction of a responding organism with a stimulus and gives equal significance to both. The interaction that takes place in musical behavior is considered in the light of (*a*) the kind of stimulus involved, (*b*) the biological equipment of the person responding, (*c*) the immediate environment, and (*d*) the person's life history of previous musical responses.

The different aesthetic responses to music that play so great a part in the development of critical judgment (why some people enjoy music that others find boring) are analyzed in Chapters 9 and 10. Other chapters deal with the measurement and prediction of musical talent, methods of learning music, and the improvement of musical performance. Music has proved its worth in industrial plants as an aid to production and morale, and in hospitals as a method of therapy with the mentally and physically ill. Significant findings in both of these areas are fully reviewed in the last two chapters.

I am indebted to many people for their kind cooperation in the preparation of this work, particularly to Dr. J. R. Kantor, professor of psychology at Indiana University, who read the manuscript and offered helpful suggestions. Professor Berrian Shute, head of the Music Department at Hamilton College, and Professor G. Howard Williams, of the English Department at Hamilton, also made constructive criticisms. For typing the manuscript and reading the proof I am grateful to my wife and to my mother.

R. W. Lundin

Clinton, New York
February, 1953

CONTENTS

ILLUSTRATIONS

AN OBJECTIVE PSYCHOLOGY OF MUSIC

Chapter 1

A POINT OF VIEW

IN GENERAL, interest in a psychology of music may be said to have had its experimental foundations in the nineteenth century acoustic studies of Helmholtz [1] and later of Stumpf.[2] Helmholtz was mainly concerned with problems relating to the perception of individual and combination tones and the nature of harmony and discord. He came to the conclusion that there is in the ear a mechanism capable of receiving individual variations in pitch which the subject can discriminate. These studies led to the formulation of the Helmholtz theory of hearing well known to the student of psychology. Stumpf's studies on music placed him second only to Helmholtz in the realm of acoustics. His theory of consonance and dissonance, which we will consider in a later chapter, won him special favor.

More specifically, the first attempt at a psychology of music had its beginnings with Seashore's studies in the early part of the twentieth century.[3] Contributions to the field have been largely of a subjective sort. Textbooks such as those by Seashore,[4] Mursell,[5] and Schoen [6] have approached the psychology of music from the mentalistic point of view. Such mentalism, with its ref-

[1] H. L. F. von Helmholtz, *On the sensations of tone* (1862), trans. Ellis (4th ed.; London: Longmans, Green & Co., 1912).

[2] C. Stumpf, *Tonpsychologie,* 2 vols. (Leipzig: S. Hirzel, 1883–90).

[3] C. E. Seashore, *The psychology of musical talent* (New York: Silver Burdett Co., 1919).

[4] C. E. Seashore, *Psychology of music* (New York: McGraw-Hill Book Co., Inc., 1938).

[5] J. L. Mursell, *The psychology of music* (New York: W. W. Norton & Co., Inc., 1937).

[6] M. Schoen, *The psychology of music* (New York: The Ronald Press Co., 1940).

erence to psychology as the study of the mind and its workings rather than the investigation of observable behavior is highly out of keeping with current thinking in psychology.

For examples of what we mean by the mentalistic or dualistic approach to psychology of music, let us consider two of our foremost authorities in the field.

Concerning musical talent, Seashore writes:

> Musical talent is not one, but a hierarchy of talents branching out along certain trunk lines into the rich arborization, foliage, and fruitage of the tree which we call the "musical mind." The normal musical mind is first of all a normal mind. What makes it musical is the possession, in a serviceable degree, of those capacities which are essential for the hearing, the feeling, the understanding, and ordinarily, for some form of expression of music, with a resulting drive or urge toward music.[7]

Seashore, like most mentalists, supposes the mind to be some sort of nonspatial entity which governs our musical actions, a place where our talents are stored.

And concerning the relation of the physical to the spiritual, Seashore writes:

> While all music is objectively due to physical sound waves, we must bear in mind that we can never be directly aware of the rate of vibration as such. . . . This is one of the wondrous transformations "from matter to mind." [8]

Although Mursell and Seashore are at variance in their views toward musical talent and the musical personality, they are on common ground when they support a dualistic doctrine.

> For music depends essentially not on the stimuli which reach the external ear, nor even upon the responses which the structures of the inner ear make to those stimuli, but rather upon the organizing and transforming operation of the mind upon them. . . .
>
> Musical effects depend upon an intricate selective activity carried on by the mind. . . .

[7] Seashore, *Psychology of music,* p. 2.
[8] *Ibid,* p. 53.

> Musical effects depend also upon a whole array of organizing and synthesizing activities carried on by the mind. . . .
> Musical effects depend upon an array of organizing activities, by which the mind determines the patterns and relationships in which we shall hear what comes to the ear. . . .[9]

With the growth and recognition of psychology as an objective science, a need has arisen, in that area of human behavior which we may term "musical," to take stock of our accomplishments in light of present-day objective analyses. Our aim in this book is to give students of both psychology and music a point of view toward musical behavior, stripped of mentalistic concepts, which will be in keeping with the trend of other current psychological thought.

Many musicians have taken the attitude of "hands off" toward psychological investigations in their field. This attitude is based on the false assumption that musical responses are of a spiritual, unmeasurable sort coming directly from the soul of man, that the field of music is an area which, by its very nature, does not lend itself to scientific investigation with, of course, the exception of physical sound waves.

Our approach must be critical in nature. In those circumstances where we no longer find valid conclusions heretofore rendered, we will attempt to substitute a more objective alternative.

Musical stimuli and responses.—Just what is the subject matter of psychology of music? What areas of music are the legitimate domain of the student of the psychology of music? We know that psychology as the science of behavior deals with the responses of organisms to things. These things with which we interact are conventionally called "stimuli."[10] We are essentially concerned with those responses which are of a musical sort. For example, we play the piano, sing a song, beat out a tune, listen to a concert, or compose a piece of music for the violin: all these

[9] Mursell, *op. cit.*, pp. 50–53.
[10] J. R. Kantor, *A survey of the science of psychology* (Bloomington, Ind.: The Principia Press, Inc., 1933), chap. i.

and many others are musical responses. We must not leave out the stimuli, however, because they interact with organisms and they are as important psychologically as the responses. Stimuli can also be many things: a sheet of music, an orchestra playing, a trombone, an accordion. In short, any object or event which serves a musical function is a stimulus. This all seems very simple and obvious. And yet, we have already seen how psychologists interested in this subject have tried to describe these simple musical interactions in a vague and unrealistic way.

Musical responses, like other kinds of psychological action, have special characteristics which help distinguish them from other biological and physical phenomena.[11] Psychological responses are *discriminative, integrative, variable, modifiable, delayable, inhibitive*, and of a *cultural nature*. How do these characteristics fit musical responses? These days we hear a lot about musical aptitude and music tests which are devised to measure how well we can discriminate differences in pitch (high or low), loudness (strong or weak), timbre, rhythm, and so forth. As musicians we are expected to be able to distinguish good from poor compositions, proficient from mediocre performances. Indeed, musical responses are *discriminative*.

The *integrative* aspect of our musical actions may be illustrated by the process of learning to play the piano. We practice hands alone, then together, then with the use of the pedals and finally the eye-hand coordination of reading and playing music at sight. These separate behaviors have been combined into one series of well-coordinated acts. When we play in concert, the integrative aspect of our playing with our fellow-musicians is obvious.

That musical responses are *variable* is illustrated by the fact that we do not always interpret a composition the same way each time we play it. Our performance may depend on the particular mood we are in at the time. We are also able to change the tempo of our performance, and we exhibit different emotions

[11] *Ibid.*

and feelings toward music. Indeed, some musicians have been called temperamental. This illustrates how *variable* our musical actions may be.

In practicing a particular piece for the cello, we make mistakes. But these mistakes can be corrected so that finally our performance of the piece is without error. Here we have demonstrated the fact that musical responses are *modifiable*. One does not continue to make the same mistake over and over again, but modifies his behavior by correcting the mistakes and playing the right notes.

Musical responses are *delayable* and *inhibitive*. This further characterizes them as a form of psychological activity. We are able to restrain our musical impulses to play or listen until appropriate times for their expression. We only perform them when the setting is favorable, as in a music room or a concert hall, and only under direction during a period of silent prayer or when people are trying to sleep.

Finally, the musical stimuli and responses are of a *cultural nature*. That is, they may serve the same function for more than one person. True, all do not respond to musical stimuli in the same way. But these responses are shared. Some of us are pleased and relaxed when we listen to a composition; others are bored and displeased. Why? The answer lies in the fact that the same musical stimuli function differently for separate groups of us. This function that musical stimuli have will depend on the previous contacts that we have had with them, or whether we have ever had any contact with them at all. Some people like music because they have been trained to appreciate it, others because they have associated it with pleasant things. Thus, our attitudes have been acquired from the group to which we belong. They are learned, so there is no inherited disposition to like or dislike music, be attracted or repelled by it.

The term "cultural" may be used to include whole civilizations. At other times, it refers to groups of individuals. Either use of the term still applies to our statement that musical stimuli are largely cultural. The function these musical stimuli have for us and the responses we make to them arise out of our group interactions. We generally appreciate certain music, such as that of the national anthem, and more definitively, our special study group as a cultural collectivity also has special shared preferential responses perhaps for quartet music or opera. Of course, we are going to respond partially to certain natural properties of the object such as highness or lowness of a pitch or loudness or softness of a sound. But even discrimination in this area is influenced by training.[12] The acuity of our discrimination is at least in part a function of our previous contacts with the stimulus. There is nothing inherent in the music which makes us predisposed to respond to it in one way or another. The music in different civilizations illustrates this well. What seems consonant to the Chinese or inhabitants of Pago Pago may seem dissonant to us. Even within our Western culture the hillbilly band and the symphony orchestra may have audiences that are miles apart in their reactions to the same music.

The fact that musical responses are shared is also illustrated in our tastes or preferences for music. Surveys have indicated that we generally agree on the composers we call eminent. This applies not only to classical but to jazz composers as well. Further, our symphony orchestra conductors tend to arrange similar programs. Yet, there are no absolutes in music. Occidental people love simple rhythms, careful tuning, fixed tonal steps, and harmonies. But these tastes are not shared the world over. Africans prefer a complicated rhythm, whereas the Chinese appear oblivious to mistunings. However, Orientals can learn to love Western music and we can appreciate their music as well,[13] because there is nothing inherent in the stimuli which predisposes us to act toward or against any musical stimulus. We will have more to say about the cultural aspects of consonance and musical

[12] R. F. Wyatt, The improvability of pitch discrimination, *Psychol. Monogr.*, 1945, 58:267, 1–58.

[13] P. R. Farnsworth, *Musical taste: its measurement and cultural nature* (Stanford, Calif.: Stanford University Press, 1950).

taste in later chapters. Suffice it to say here that there is good experimental evidence to support this view.

Musical responses, then, are acquired. Their acquisition may occur through casual contact with the various musical stimuli, or they may be learned quite deliberately, through training by qualified instructors. It is my belief that no one is born gifted with any "powers" which will destine him to be a genius, musically speaking. This is not to deny that some persons are more biologically predisposed to respond to musical stimuli than others. But we must be careful in our definition of a biological predisposition or potential. Here we mean merely any structure which may facilitate the acquisition of relative behavior. Obvious examples occur in the field of athletics. The successful basketball player is biologically predisposed by his height, or the football star by his large build and weight. As yet we do not have complete agreement on what may predispose to musicianship, but it is recognized that successful performance on certain wind instruments is facilitated by certain lip and mouth structure, piano playing by shape and size of the hands, and singing by the structure of the vocal cords. These physical structures are inherited, but no psychic "gifts" or "powers" are. Musical success is a function of many factors, always provided that one has a sound biological equipment. These may include the particular stimuli with which one comes in contact—musical ones. The contact may be rather incidental, both at the beginning and later, or quite deliberate. Other musical surroundings and the attitude of parents and friends toward music are important.

The existence of alternate stimuli, which may command one's attention even though the musical stimuli are present, may have a more important function. Thus, one may never develop adequate responses to musical stimuli even though they are present. All these factors must be considered in determining the extent and kind of one's musical actions. Musical responses are subject to the same kind of conditions as any other type of psychological action.

Kinds of musical responses.—What kinds of psychological responses are most important in the psychology of music? All are involved, but some are more important than others. Intelligence, for example may serve as a necessary factor, but its influence is largely indirect. It has been demonstrated that, given average intellectual ability, there is little relation between musical ability and intelligence.[14] However, such psychological processes as perceiving, learning, remembering, and feeling are of special importance to us because they constitute a large part of what we call musical behavior.

Our first task in the next three chapters is to consider the perceptual responses to music. In so doing we consider the various psychological dimensions of tone: pitch, loudness, volume, timbre, density, and brightness. We will relate them to the physical attributes of the sound wave. Tones usually come in combinations, so we must consider the perceptual aspects of melody and harmony, consonance and dissonance. One interested in the psychology of music must have a thorough understanding of the perceptual nature of tone. Another area of musical responses includes the feeling and emotional responses. Musical stimuli have brought a wide variety of feeling responses, pleasant, unpleasant, excited, relaxed, happy, and sad.

When we perform, we are operating on musical stimuli. Performing musical compositions involves learning, learning to play the instrument as well as possibly memorizing the piece of music. Since we have noted that musical responses are acquired (i.e., learned), this aspect of psychological responses is important to us. We also consider preferential reactions as well as what is beautiful in music.

Next, we want to apply some of our principles to various fields of applied psychology. The most widely talked about is, undoubtedly, the matter of musical aptitudes. The measurement of musical ability and an understanding of its development and nature

[14] R. W. Lundin, The development and validation of a set of musical ability tests, *Psychol. Monogr.*, 1949, **63**:305, 1–20.

are very important factors in selecting those who may be potential musicians. Finally, in recent years music has been used in industry to improve production and in both mental and general hospitals as an aid in therapy. These last two applications serve to round out our discussion.

We have made no attempt to be all-inclusive in our coverage of the experiments on music that have been reported or the theories that have been expounded to account for musical behavior. This book is merely an attempt to untangle some of the snarls in which musicians and psychologists alike have become caught. It is an attempt to put the field of musical behavior on the same footing as other fields of objective psychology. The position taken is that musical responses, though supposed to be largely subjective, are actually objective facts as are other kinds of psychological action.

Chapter 2

THE DIMENSIONS OF TONE: PITCH

As PSYCHOLOGICAL organisms we are constantly responding to sound stimuli. As a stimulus, sound has two aspects or sets of qualities, the *vibrational* or physical, and the *tonal,* often referred to as the psychological. However, to characterize sound as having physical and psychological attributes is dangerous because we may unwittingly fall into a psychophysical parallelism, a dualistic dichotomy so typical of mentalistic thinking. A division such as that between psychological and physical implies that physical and psychic qualities exist which characterize the same thing. Objective psychologists prefer to consider what have been formerly called the physical and psychological aspects of the sound stimulus as the *vibrational* and the *tonal.* Both of these attributes characterize the same stimulus object, sound. They are both sets of qualities which serve to describe it as a stimulus object. The *tonal* attributes include such qualities as *pitch, loudness, timbre, time,* and *density* or *volume* and refer to one set of properties of the stimulus. *Frequency, intensity, duration,* and *form* are another set of characteristics applying to the *vibrational* aspect of the same stimulus. Both sets of properties refer to the stimulus side of the psychological event.

On the other side is the organism which is responding to these sound stimuli. The kinds of reactions we have will depend on what aspects of the stimulus we are considering, the tonal or the vibrational. The physicist might be particularly interested in studying the vibrational aspects of the stimulus, measuring the frequency or intensity of the sound wave, while the psychologist would be more interested in examining how people react to the tonal aspects, as in the determination of an individual's sensitivity to differences in pitch or loudness. In order to be objective psychologists, we must constantly remind ourselves that the tonal and vibrational dimensions of sound are properties or relative qualities of the stimulus, and our reactions to these qualities complete the psychological event.

The vibrational attributes of sound can readily be distinguished and studied apart from the tonal, but the two kinds of qualities are often confused. It is the purpose of this and the following two chapters to describe some of the tonal dimensions of the stimulus and, whenever necessary, to distinguish them from the vibrational attributes.

Both aspects of sound can be measured. The difference between the two kinds of measurements lies in the fact that in the vibrational, an observer responds by making a judgment about a scale reading, whereas in the tonal, a more direct judgment is made about the tone as a stimulus object.[1]

The physical sound wave.—All sounding bodies are in a state of vibration. In the most obvious cases such as a vibrating stretched string, the motion can be seen as a blurred outline.

That these vibrating objects need some medium of contact between their source and the receiver in order for sound to be heard is simply demonstrated by the well-known experiment of Boyle in which a bell is placed in a jar where it can be heard ringing. As air is withdrawn from the jar, making it a vacuum, the ringing becomes fainter and fainter until finally the bell continues to vibrate, but we sense nothing. Sound is produced by setting in motion some object, for example, a bell. When these vibrations are set up in an elastic medium such as air, sound waves are the inevitable result. These waves consist of the alternations of condensation and rarefaction, corresponding to the forward and backward movements of the vibrating object. As

[1] S. S. Stevens and H. Davis, *Hearing: its psychology and physiology* (New York: John Wiley & Sons, Inc., 1938).

the metal of the bell vibrates, moving back and forth, neighboring air molecules become condensed and then rarefied. Thus, a state of compression is passed on through the air medium, followed by a rarefaction, another compression and so on, as long as the bell continues to vibrate.

All vibratory motion has four properties: *frequency, intensity, form,* and *duration*. The first of these, *frequency,* refers to the number of times the motion occurs in any particular interval of time, usually a second. Thus, sound waves may have many different frequencies corresponding to the rate of the vibrating medium. When an object vibrates rapidly, we designate the motion as having a high frequency, while only a few vibrations per second would be considered a low frequency.

Frequency is, then, a measure of the number of times a vibrating particle executes a completed cycle. A cycle is two single vibrations or one double vibration (dvb.) measured from the crest of one wave to the crest of the next. The terms "frequency," "double vibrations," "number of vibrations," "cycles," and "waves" are used interchangeably and refer to the rate of motion.

Contrary to popular belief, frequency as a vibrational attribute of sound is *not* synonymous with pitch. This latter term refers to the tonal aspect of the stimulus. Frequency must be measured by some instrument such as a tonometer or frequency meter.

Intensity is the energy or pressure exerted by the vibrating object. It is measured at any particular place in dynes per square centimeter. Described in terms of the sound wave, the intensity of the sound will be proportional to the *amplitude squared* of the wave, where amplitude is the height of the wave from the top to the center axis. Figure 1 illustrates the vibrational qualities of frequency and amplitude. A simple or pure wave, such as that illustrated, might be emitted by an oscillator or tuning fork and has the dimensions of frequency, amplitude, intensity, and duration. The waves from the fork will be regular in occurrence and will remain at the same frequency so long as this particular object remains in motion. As the vibration continues, the energy gradually dies out, so that the amplitude of the wave becomes less and less until the vibrating fork comes to rest.

Obviously, all sounds do not come from tuning forks which emit pure waves free from overtones. Therefore, each sound wave has a characteristic *form*. Such sources of sound as the

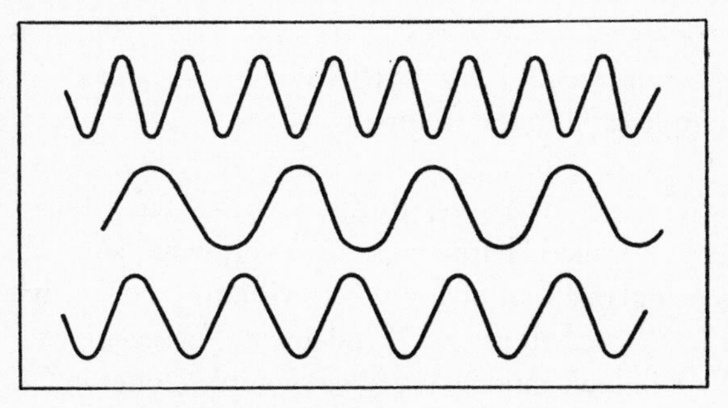

Sound Waves of the Same Amplitude but of Different Frequencies

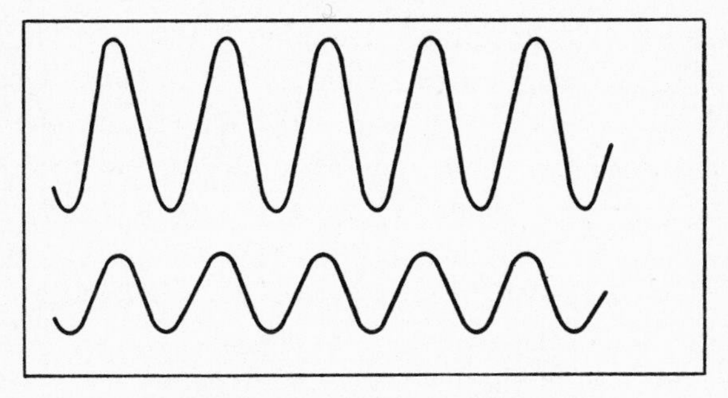

Sound Waves of the Same Frequency but Differing in Amplitude

Fig. 1.–Differences in sound waves.

piano, violin, flute, or human voice each will produce a different form of wave. It is possible for two sound waves to have the same frequency and intensity but to differ in form. We realize that when middle C at a frequency of 256 cps. (cycles per second) is sounded on the piano and clarinet, the form of the two sound waves differs, while the other characteristics might be the same. In discussing frequency and intensity, we were referring to simple sound waves set up by a single vibration. When the wave form becomes complex because a number of different vibrations occur simultaneously, the resulting sound is usually called a "complex tone." This is produced because the object is not only vibrating as a whole (as in a simple tone), but it is vibrating in parts as well. These partial vibrations (called "partials") bear a simple ratio to the frequency of the whole vibrating object of 1:2:3:4, etc. This means that the object vibrating as a whole is also vibrating in halves, thirds, fourths, etc. These partial tones are also called "harmonics" or "overtones," since they have a frequency above that of the whole vibrating object, whose frequency is referred to as the "fundamental" (see Figure 8, page 47). We will have more to say about complex tones in Chapter 4.

A last physical attribute of the sound wave is its *duration,* which refers to the length of time the sound wave lasts. When we make a judgment of the length or duration of the sound wave, we speak of its "time." Duration is then the vibrational aspect of the sound stimulus, while time is the tonal characteristic. The duration of sound is also the substratum for rhythm, since the latter refers to the number, duration, and arrangement in time of the sound stimuli. Of course, rhythm also depends on the duration of the time intervals between the sound stimuli.

Our discussion so far has centered largely around a description of the vibrational aspects of the stimulus. Before beginning our consideration of the tonal aspects of sound, one distinction should be made, namely between *tone* and *noise*. In some of our more modern compositions, we will agree, the distinction is sometimes a difficult one to make. In general, however, tone is correlated with regular or periodic vibrations of the sound wave regardless of the complexity or quality of the wave. In noise, the vibrations are irregular or aperiodic. This is only a practical distinction which does not completely apply, because any musical tone may have some amount of noise in it.

The attribute of pitch.—We are now ready to consider the first of our *tonal* attributes of sound, which is called "pitch." As a tonal quality, pitch refers to the highness or lowness of a tone. It is a property of the stimulus and not a product of the individual's reaction, as is so often implied by our mentalistic thinkers. True, one may *report* a pitch as being high or low. That is the individual's response to a quality of the sound which exists. But the pitch quality of highness or lowness exists as an attribute of the stimulus regardless of whether or not there is someone around to tell us that. The chief vibrational correlate of pitch is frequency of the sound. Sounds of many or high frequencies are reported as having high pitch, while those of few cycles are reported as having low pitch. Despite the fact that pitch and frequency as different attributes of the sound stimulus do correlate in a positive way, this relationship is not a perfect one. Let us examine some of the evidence to demonstrate this fact.

The scale on which we arrange our various degrees of pitch has upper and lower limits. These are biologically set by the responding mechanism, the ear. The range of audible frequencies in humans is from about 20 to 20,000 cycles per second. However, the lower limit of auditory responses is not the lowest heard pitch, as evidenced by the fact that objects may be heard vibrating without pitch. These emit sound waves and the subjects report merely vibrating thumping sounds with no definite pitch. Also, objects may vibrate so rapidly that they cannot be heard by the human ear. That is, they are above the threshold of perception in the human. The limits of our auditory perception will be discussed in more detail in the chapter following, but an example of the individual differences between animal and man in upper thresholds for pitch is illustrated by blowing a Galton whistle, often used to call dogs. This gives frequencies too high for human perception. When blown, the whistle can produce a frequency above the range of human perception but within the range of the animal's. He hears it and responds by coming to his master. We hear nothing.

Pitch and intensity.—Although pitch is related in a positive way to frequency, it also depends on intensity (amplitude). This is demonstrated by studies in which reported *changes in pitch* occur while frequency is *held constant* and intensity is varied.

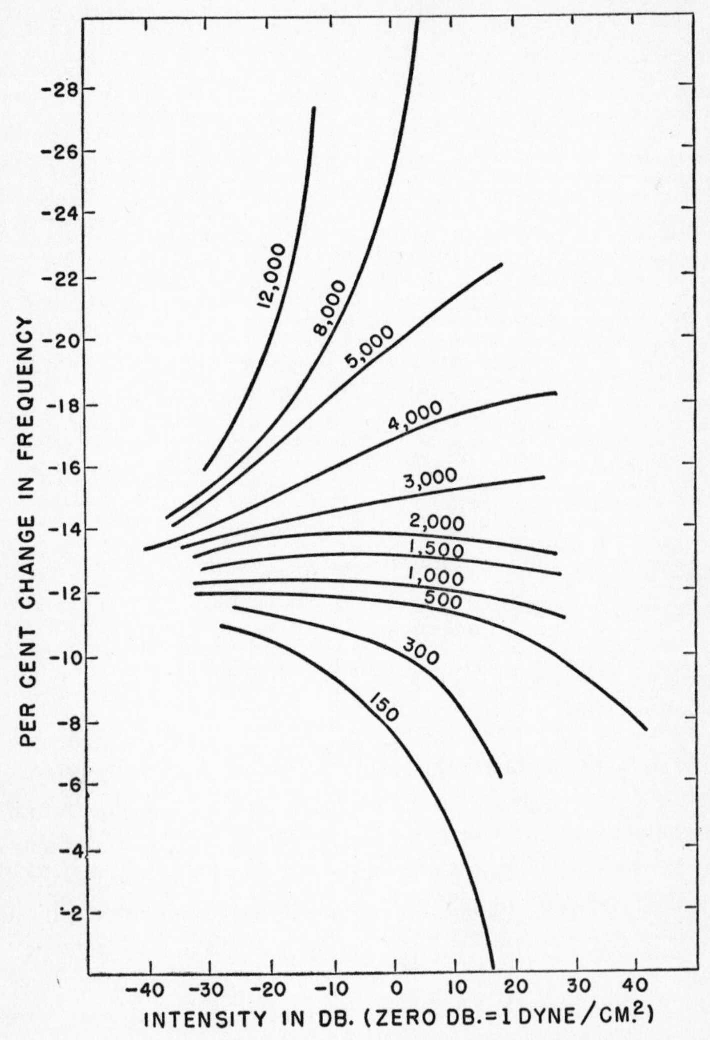

FIG. 2.—Equal pitch contours. (From Stevens—see footnote 3.)

An early illustration of this effect is reported by Miles.[2] Subjects were asked to reproduce middle C vocally after hearing a tuning fork. When the fork was held close to the ear so that the intensity was greater, the pitch of the singer's voice was lowered slightly. The subject heard the louder tone as lower.

Probably the most complete investigation reporting the relationship between pitch and intensity was made by Stevens.[3] In this study a survey of eleven different frequencies ranging from 150 to 12,000 cycles were made. Two tones of slightly different frequency were presented alternately to the subject in each trial. He was asked to adjust the intensity of one of the tones until the pitch of the two tones appeared equal. As a result, what are called *equal pitch contours* (see Figure 2) were plotted, showing a relation between pitch and intensity which must be maintained to keep a tone at a constant level of pitch. These contours indicate that *for low tones the pitch decreases with intensity,* but *for high tones the pitch increases with intensity.* In general, the higher the frequency, the higher the intensity at which the reversal takes place. Throughout the middle range of frequencies, there will be the least change (see Figure 2). In summary, if one increases the physical intensity of tone below 3,000 cps. (holding the frequency constant), he will report a lower pitch. This is greatest for 150–300 cps. and if one increases the pitch of a high frequency, say above 3,000 cps., an increase in the intensity will *raise* the pitch. The greatest increase occurs for the highest pitches (8,000–12,000).

Pitch discrimination.—The matter of discrimination of pitch has played a large role in the psychology of music. Psychologists and musicians have both placed great emphasis on such an ability as a necessary attribute for musicianship. Common sense tells us that one will not be a successful singer, regardless of the fine

[2] W. R. Miles, Accuracy of the voice in simple pitch singing, *Psychol. Rev. Monogr.,* 1914, **16**:69, 13–66.

[3] S. S. Stevens, The relation of pitch to intensity, *J. acoust. Soc. Amer.,* 1935, **6**, 150–54.

quality of his voice, if he cannot sing "in tune" with his accompaniment, or that a violinist who cannot distinguish A from C might do better by selecting another occupation unless, of course, he has some other source of private income.

In discrimination of pitch, we must take into consideration, as we do with other kinds of psychological action, the individual making the response. We remember that the tone is the stimulus and that we must consider the various factors which will effect the interaction of the organism and this stimulus.

Individuals differ in their ability to discriminate differences in pitch. How are we able to find out how acute an individual's pitch discrimination is? The answer is by determining his *difference limen* for various pitches. This difference limen (DL) is the frequency (f.) change in a tone which he is just able to perceive 50 per cent of the time. Let us take a tone, A (the one usually played as a reference in tuning an instrument). This has a frequency of 435 cps. The *average* individual is able to distinguish it from another tone which is plus or minus three cycles from this standard. So, when the frequency of the tone drops from 435 to 432 cps. or rises to 438, he can *just perceive* that it has changed. By means of the *method of constant stimuli,*[4] a common psychophysical method of measurement discussed in most introductory books in experimental psychology, a subject is given two tones in immediate succession and asked to tell whether the pitch of the first is higher or lower than that of the second. In this type of experiment one must take care that the duration of the two tones (standard and comparison tone) is at least 0.5 second or over and that the interval between the tones is short, because the longer this interval, the poorer the discrimination; also the intensity of the stimuli must be kept constant. By comparing various frequencies with the standard, we are able to determine a minimum point in frequency which is just detectable at any particular frequency level. This DL will differ from indi-

[4] B. J. Underwood, *Experimental psychology* (New York: Appleton-Century-Crofts, Inc., 1949).

vidual to individual for any particular frequency. It will also differ for the same individual at various frequencies. For our standard of 435 cps. frequency, let us suppose that the Δf or DL is 3 cps. (this is the absolute DL, the smallest difference the average observer can detect). The relation of these quantities, DL to standard ($\Delta f./f.$ or 3/435), gives us a *relative* difference *limen.* It has been found by Shower and Biddulph that this ratio remains fairly constant throughout the middle range of frequencies for most people. However, we realize that this ratio will not be the same for all persons. For one with excellent discrimination it might be 1/435, and for one with poor discrimination it could be 20/435. In the former case, the person can detect a change in pitch with only one cycle difference in frequency at 435 cps., whereas in the latter case the frequency must change twenty cycles before there would be any recognizable difference in pitch.

Shower and Biddulph [5] have demonstrated that for monaural listening (one ear) the DL's are larger than for binaural (both ears). Generally speaking, they found that the DL's at low frequencies and intensities are the largest. At frequencies above 500 cycles, the relative DL's ($\Delta f./f.$) are fairly constant for any one individual. Below 500 cycles, the absolute DL's ($\Delta f.$) are approximately constant. This study used a frequency range from 31 to 11,700 cycles with various intensities. A rotary condenser in a tuning circuit of an oscillator was arranged so the listener could hear a tone of unvarying pitch for a short interval at a time. The frequency was then changed to a new value so that there was a smooth transition from one frequency to another.

How many different pitches can the average individual discriminate? According to Stevens and Davis,[6] at a 40-db. (see Chapter 3) level of loudness between the limits of 20 and 20,000 cycles there are about 1,500 possible different pitches. Again we hasten to add that there are many individuals who can dis-

[5] E. G. Shower and R. Biddulph, Differential pitch sensitivity of the ear, *J. acoust. Soc. Amer.*, 1931, **3**, 275–87.

[6] Stevens and Davis, *op. cit.*, p. 94.

criminate more pitches than the average and many who can discriminate a smaller number. At a loudness level of 60 db., the number of discriminable differences (between 20 and 20,000 cps.) is about 1,800. At 60 db., the number seems to be the maximum and is about three times as large as the number at a very low level of 5 db.

So far we have been dealing with the pitches of pure tones (single frequencies). How do we judge the pitch of complex frequencies? The pitch of a complex sound will depend on the frequencies of its dominant components.[7] When we ask listeners to designate the pitch of a tonal mass composed of numerous frequencies, they usually name a pitch close to the center of the band of frequencies. Of course, when the number of frequencies is small, the trained person can analyze this complex into its individual frequencies, as for example, the upper partials of a vibrating piano string.

Pitch and duration.—We have thus far indicated the relationship between pitch and frequency and pitch and amplitude (intensity) of the sound wave. What relationship exists between pitch and the *duration* of the wave? Our studies so far have been based on pitches which last one second or more. What happens when the duration of a wave is reduced to less than that? As the duration of the tone is decreased, several things happen. If we take a tone of a standard frequency and start with a very brief period (3 msec.) and then increase the duration of the stimulus, we find the response passes through three stages. First, we hear a toneless click seemingly without pitch. Then the sound begins to acquire a more or less definite pitch, although the click remains as one of the dominant aspects. This pitch differs from the final one perceived when the tone is played over a longer period of time. Finally, a constant pitch is ascertained without the error in judgment typical of the second stage.[8]

[7] *Ibid.*, p. 98.
[8] *Ibid.*, p. 100.

Improvement of pitch discrimination.—It used to be believed that individual differences in the ability to discriminate pitches were innate (inborn) characteristics of the organism.

In 1919, C. E. Seashore wrote,

> Pitch discrimination is not a matter of logical judgment. It is rather an immediate impression, far more primitive than reflective thought, and dependent upon the presence or absence in various degrees of the sensitive mechanisms of the inner ear.[9]

Later, in 1938, he reasserted his belief that after an early age one's ability to discriminate pitch does not vary with age or training.

> It seems probable that just as the physical eye of the child at the age of three is as keen as it will ever be, so the pitch sensitiveness in the ear reaches its maximum very early. . . . The physiological limit for hearing pitch *does not improve with training* [italics mine]. Training, like maturation, results in the conscious recognition of the nature of pitch, its meaning, and the development of habits of use in musical operations. Training probably does not modify the capacity of the sense organ any more than the playing of the good violin may improve the quality of its tone.[10]

The fact that an individual's acuity in discrimination of pitch *might change* would never be accounted for as the result of training or of more subtle forms of learning. The differences probably would be due to the fact that the first test of discrimination was an inaccurate one because of misunderstanding of instructions on the part of the subject or a lack of mental development or poor power of will (motivation). We have taken time to state Seashore's views on this matter because of the profound influence his thinking has had on subsequent attitudes among musicians and psychologists alike.

[9] C. E. Seashore, *The psychology of musical talent* (New York: Silver Burdett Co., 1919), p. 57.

[10] C. E. Seashore, *Psychology of music* (New York: McGraw-Hill Book Co., Inc., 1938), p. 58.

This view, although a common one, must not be taken uncritically. What evidence is there to substantiate such a hypothesis? Actually, the great bulk of experimental work serves to refute this hypothesis and to substantiate another one, namely, that pitch discrimination is subject to improvement. However, let us consider some of the evidence on both sides.

In support of his view, Seashore cites an unpublished study by H. S. Buffum[11] in which pitch thresholds were determined for twenty-five eighth-grade children. They were given "specific and intensive" practice. At the end of the practice period, he found a change in only two cases. Of these, one was a borderline psychotic case and the other suffered from misunderstanding! What kind of training is this? All they did was practice their errors without any kind of remedial training. If I should allow you to practice incorrect responses without giving any clues as to when you are right or wrong, *regardless* of how long you practiced, the chances are good that at the end of your practice period, you would continue to make just as many wrong responses as before.

Further reported evidence which is supposed to support Seashore's view comes from studies done by Stanton and Koerth[12] at the Eastman School of Music. They selected four groups of students and administered the Seashore Measures of Musical Talent[13] (one of which was on pitch discrimination) at the time of entrance and again three years later. Groups I and II consisted of preadolescents in grades 4, 5, and 6 and 7, 8, and 9 respectively. Group III consisted of special students, and Group IV of college students working for music degrees. After three years of study, there was a significant increase in the mean raw

[11] C. E. Seashore, *The psychology of musical talent,* p. 60.

[12] H. Stanton and W. Koerth, *Musical capacity measures in adults repeated after musical education,* Univ. Ia. Stud. Aims Progr. Res., 1930, No. 31; *Musical capacity measures in children repeated after musical training,* Univ. Ia. Stud. Aims Progr. Res., 1933, No. 42 (New Series, No. 259).

[13] C. E. Seashore, *Manual of instructions and interpretations for Measures of Musical Talent* (New York: Columbia Gramophone Co., 1919).

scores on the test for Groups I and II. These improvements were interpreted, not as being due to benefits of the musical training, but as due to the progressive lessening with maturation of the "cognitive" factor (error due to misunderstanding). However, so far as the adults (Group IV) were concerned, the improvement was negligible. This is natural, the authors tell us, since it supports their hypothesis. These people had already reached their physiological limit. That is, they had reached their best level of discrimination and could not improve. This level was determined by heredity.

Our interpretation of these results based on Wyatt's conclusions [14] differs somewhat from those of the investigators. Two factors might easily account for this lack of change in the adults' performance, namely the selection of subjects and the type of training they received. First of all, the students selected for the study already had sufficient musical ability to be chosen; they also had to survive academically for three successive years. These people were already highly skilled and possessed a high degree of discriminative ability as measured by the Seashore test. They were the "cream of the crop," so to speak. Why should we expect much improvement? Secondly, what kind of training did they receive? A generalized one in theory, instrumentation, and history of music. This is certainly not specific training in pitch discrimination, so no one should expect any special improvement.

We next turn to evidence to support an opposing view, that pitch discrimination, like other musical behavior, is acquired and subject to improvement. Since ability to discriminate pitches is included in this category of learned responses, it should be subject to change by training.

In 1932, Wolner and Pyle [15] selected seven children for *training*. They were selected because of their poor ability, manifested

[14] R. F. Wyatt, The improvability of pitch discrimination, *Psychol. Monogr.*, 1945, **58**:267, 1–58.

[15] M. Wolner and W. H. Pyle, An experiment in individual training in pitch-deficient children, *J. educ. Psychol.*, 1933, **24**, 602–8.

by the fact that they could not even discriminate octaves. Each child was given sixteen hours of individual training. In this training procedure, the investigator used tuning forks accompanied by verbal explanations as to rightness or wrongness of each response. At the conclusion of the training period, all seven pitch-deficient children had improved. Before training they were unable to discriminate a difference of 30 cps. After training, four children could distinguish differences as small as one-half cycle, and the others could discriminate differences of two, three, and eight cycles, respectively.

In another study by R. H. Seashore,[16] twelve adults were selected as subjects. An oscillator was used for training, which was given in weekly periods of forty-five minutes each. After training, these pitch-deficient adults were able to discriminate an average threshold of 4.6 cps., whereas before it was 9.2 cps. For the nine who completed the test, the average centile rank on the Seashore pitch test had improved from 6.6 to 45.

Other studies to support the same viewpoint have been reported by Whipple,[17] Smith,[18] and Capurso.[19] Whipple reports one subject who improved with practice in the discrimination on a tone variator, but this did not transfer to piano semitones. Smith demonstrated that after instruction in distinguishing tone qualities and forming right habits of attention, there was considerable improvement in the threshold of discrimination for both boys and girls (106 children were used). Cameron[20] used vocal practice in pitch discrimination with six adults. Four improved at the frequency level at which instruction was

[16] R. H. Seashore, Improvability of pitch discrimination, *Psychol. Bull.*, 1935, **32**, 546.

[17] G. M. Whipple, Studies in pitch discrimination, *Amer. J. Psychol.*, 1903, **14**, 289–309.

[18] F. O. Smith, The effect of training on pitch discrimination, *Psychol. Monogr.*, 1914, **16**:69, 67–103.

[19] A. A. Capurso, The effect of an associative technique in teaching pitch and interval discrimination, *J. appl. Psychol.*, 1934, **18**, 811–18.

[20] E. H. Cameron, Effects of practice in the discrimination and singing of tones, *Psychol. Monogr.*, 1917, **23**:3 (Whole No. 100), 159–80.

given, and two did not. None improved from the group with no practice. After six weeks of training principally in interval recognition, one of Capurso's subjects showed a centile increase on the Seashore test of 6 to 93. The other subject changed from a rank of 3 before to 17 after training.

The most recent and controlled study on the improvement of pitch discrimination has been reported by Ruth Wyatt[21] at Northwestern University. She gave the Seashore test of pitch discrimination (1938 revision, series B) and her own test of pitch discrimination[22] to sixteen college students, eight from the school of music and eight from the college of liberal arts. The test was given twice before and twice after training. Prior to training, both groups were classified as "poor" in their ability to discriminate pitch as measured by the tests. In the nonmusician group, one girl had been told she never could sing because she was a "monotone." The preliminary period was followed by about 12 fifty-minute periods of special individual training in both intonation and pitch discrimination. In the pitch intonation training period, a Conn chromatic stroboscope was used to provide a visual check on the individual's ability to match a standard tone and to sing intervals. In the training in pitch discrimination, an oscillator was used and subjects were informed as to the correctness of their responses. In the nonmusic group, instructions and demonstrations as to the meaning of pitch were also given. Results after training showed that in fifteen cases there was improvement. The average *increase* was 6.1 points on the Seashore test (average 7.75 for musicians and 4.50 for nonmusicians). The average decile rank for music students changed from 7 (low average) to 2 (excellent). For the nonmusicians the rank change was from 7 (low average) to 3.5 (good). The rank of the nonmusic students was, thus, higher after training than the rank of the music students before the beginning of training. On the Wyatt pitch

[21] Wyatt, *op. cit.*

[22] R. F. Wyatt, A new instrument for measuring pitch discrimination, *Amer. J. Psychol.*, 1936, **48**, 335–41.

test, all subjects showed a gain after training, a mean increase of 13.60 points. The maximum possible score on this test was 100 points. Gains on both tests were found to be statistically significant. Although greater improvement was obtained on the tone on which the subjects were trained, there was positive transfer to notes an octave above and below the training level. Wyatt concludes that the deficiencies which a test of pitch discrimination reveals are remediable, that special individualized training can mend the deficiency.

These studies give fairly conclusive evidence that ability to discriminate pitches is not an absolute given trait. Like other forms of behavior, it is subject to change. Pitch discrimination is behavior which is not merely a function of a sense organ as was previously presumed, but behavior of a discriminative sort developed through interaction with stimulus objects. This behavior is subject to change and improvement through casual learning or by means of a contrived situation where a prepared series of training procedures is prescribed.

Absolute pitch.—Many conflicting claims have been made regarding the ability of certain people to name the pitch of a musical note without the aid of a standard of reference and to do so invariably. Some people claim to be able to name any tone anywhere at any time. But most of the evidence for these remarkable skills comes from anecdotal sources.

Generally, the term "absolute pitch" has meant an ability to name correctly some particular tone which may be either sung or played on an instrument without using any other heard tone as a point of reference. Being able to name a tone correctly after another tone is given as a reference point is often called "relative pitch." That is, once you are given a named tone, you are able to name others when played by making a perceptible reference to it. Heretofore, the possession of *absolute pitch* has been considered an all-or-none matter—either you had it or you didn't, and like other musical "gifts" it was an innate quality. Actually, absolute pitch is better defined as a high degree of discrimination and naming of tone, without the aid of other tones. A recent review of the literature by Neu[23] gives us good evidence that such is the case and that so-called absolute pitch is an acquired behavior. For example, white notes are more correctly judged than black ones on the piano and notes in the middle range are more correctly judged than those at extremes. Riker[24] has shown that we judge most accurately notes that we have had most experience with.

The matter of timbre (quality of tone) plays an important part in our judgments. Subjects have found that recognition of correct tones is more difficult when tuning forks are sounded than when a familiar medium like the piano is used. Thus, familiarity with the timbre is an important factor affecting the judgment. Early experiments done by Stumpf[25] showed that a bass player could judge tones in the lower-range frequencies better than the rest of the scale, while a violinist was best in the upper range. Baird[26] has listed various instruments in order of the difficulty in correctly naming their tones, as follows: piano, organ, voice, and tuning fork. This indicates fairly well the role of previous experience in our judgments of absolute pitch. The fact that a piano player is more likely to judge tones correctly on any musical instrument other than the tuning fork or bells, with which he has had little contact, illustrates the point.

Pitch naming, like pitch discrimination, is improved by practice. Mull,[27] using college students as subjects, found that ability to judge notes can be improved with training, but a high degree

[23] D. M. Neu, A critical review of the literature on "absolute pitch," *Psychol. Bull.*, 1947, **44**, 249–66.

[24] B. L. Riker, The ability to judge pitch, *J. exp. Psychol.*, 1946, **36**, 331–46.

[25] C. Stumpf, *Tonpsychologie* (Leipzig: S. Hirzel, 1883–90).

[26] J. W. Baird, Memory for absolute pitch, in *Studies in psychology: Titchener commemorative volume* (Worcester, Mass.: Louis H. Wilson, 1917).

[27] H. K. Mull, Acquisition of absolute pitch, *Amer. J. Psychol.*, 1925, **36**, 469–93.

of attention to the stimulus is absolutely necessary. She further reports that this ability correlates with musical ability. She concludes that the average person can acquire an ability for absolute pitch. Wedell[28] has also demonstrated that relatively unmusical people can learn to improve their ability to assign pitches to *pure tones*. The greatest increase in ability takes place during the first few periods of practice.

However, Bachem[29] reports evidence to the contrary. He describes seven subjects out of ninety studied who "possessed infallible absolute pitch over the whole scale of the piano and for all musical instruments and physical apparatus with which they were tested." Forty-five others had absolute pitch providing we discount such errors as confusion between octaves, constant errors of one-half tone in one direction which may be due to several existing standards of pitch now in use, and errors of one-half tone downward in the highest point of the musical scale and errors of one-half tone upward in the lowest part. However, he admits other factors are operating in this ability beside inheritance. Early training is important. "It seems that attention to musical tones in early youth plays a predominant role in the *development* [italics mine] of absolute pitch." [30]

From his consideration of the available studies of absolute pitch, Neu draws the following conclusions:

1) Absolute pitch and lesser degrees of pitch discrimination can be acquired by some individuals. Thus, it proves false ideas that absolute pitch is some rare power over which we have no control.
2) Behavior which closely entails pitch discrimination such as musical experience and musical training allows a much better opportunity to develop keener pitch discrimination.

[28] C. H. Wedell, The nature of the absolute judgment of pitch, *J. exp. Psychol.*, 1934, **17**, 485–503.

[29] A. Bachem, Various types of absolute pitch, *J. acoust. Soc. Amer.*, 1937, **9**, 146–51.

[30] A. Bachem, Genesis of absolute pitch, *J. acoust. Soc. Amer.*, 1939–40, **11**, 434–39.

3) Pitch discrimination can be acquired readily in early age, which may be an indication that the younger the reactional biography, the easier it is to acquire new reactions.
4) The development of keener attending to stimuli makes for a keener development of pitch discrimination. Obvious examples of this are congenital blind persons and child prodigies.
5) The subtlety of behavioral development is brought out by those individuals who have built up in their lifetime keen pitch discrimination and suddenly realize that they are able to perform such behavior.[31]

From most of the evidence given, we see again that absolute pitch is merely a fine degree of discrimination. No mysterious gift or power is involved, only a highly developed skill which has been the result of a constant and fine stimulus-organism interaction.

> Basically, the interbehavioral explanation of absolute pitch rejects the conception of an inherent faculty or quality. It accounts for absolute pitch and all pitch discrimination in behavior developed within the lifetime of the individual. This means that the discrimination is due to the way in which the individual builds up reactions to sounds, and more specifically to the thoroughness of his development of attending to tone (stimuli). Accordingly, the individual's reactional biography, built up from past experiences, is the important factor in determining what sort of tonal discriminations he will make. It follows then that "absolute pitch" is nothing more than a fine degree of accuracy of pitch discrimination. The pitch of a tone is the sound that the particular individual learns as that particular tone.[32]

Discrimination of pitch, be it relative or very accurate, is no set quality but depends on the behavioral evolution during the individual's life history.

[31] Neu, *op. cit.*, pp. 263–64.
[32] *Ibid.*, p. 264.

Chapter 3

THE DIMENSIONS OF TONE: LOUDNESS

IN THE preceding chapter we considered pitch as a tonal attribute of sound and frequency as the vibrational aspect of the sound stimulus. We noted that these attributes of the stimulus are often confused by being used interchangeably. This difficulty is due to a pre-existing lack of understanding about the two kinds of characteristics of sound, tonal and vibrational. An even greater difficulty arises when we consider the tonal attribute of loudness and the vibrational one of intensity.[1] In the case of pitch and frequency, we made certain comparisons, noting relationships and differences. We are now ready to analyze loudness and intensity. Intensity refers to the vibrational aspect of the stimulus, which is expressed in terms of physical energy or pressure. Loudness, on the other hand, refers to the tonal dimension, which is often expressed as loudness or softness, strength or weakness of a tone.

Intensity: The Vibrational Dimension

The limits of auditory perception.—It is impossible for us to respond to all of the sounds that occur in nature. We are limited in this respect by our biological equipment in the same sense that other behaviors must operate within a biological capacity. This limitation holds for both the frequency and the intensity of sounds which we are able to perceive. For example, our ears are simply incapable of responding to frequencies above a certain point or intensities below a certain point. In considering fre-

[1] The relation of intensity to amplitude was discussed on page 14.

quency, we observed that vibrations of the sound wave may vary from none at all upward to many thousand per second. The human organism, however, can perceive only sounds within a limited range of frequencies. For a child with normal hearing, the upper limit at which he can perceive sound will be about 20,000 cps. Beyond this point there is usually no response. Occasionally, one can respond to sounds up to 23,000 cps. providing the stimulus is a very intense one. As we grow older, our upper limit of frequency perception drops. The average middle-aged person cannot usually hear frequencies above 16,000 cps. This upper limit of sound perception is a function of both frequency and intensity of the sound wave. In order for high frequencies to be heard, the stimulus must be of greater intensity than for frequencies in the middle range. For example, let us suppose that we can just hear a tone at a given intensity and a frequency of 14,000 cps. If we should continue to increase the frequency but keep the intensity level the same, the sound would soon fade out. In an attempt to hear a very high frequency, we need to increase intensity. As we continue to do this, eventually instead of perceiving a sound, our response will be one of pain. This, then, is the upper level of hearing. Should we increase the intensity further, some damage to the mechanism of the ear might result. The upper limit of hearing, being a function of both frequency and intensity of the sound wave, is the highest frequency at which a pitch can be perceived at an intensity that is below the threshold of pain.

In considering the lower limit of hearing, we must find the lowest frequency at which *sound* is heard and the lowest limit at which pitch is actually perceived. These two limits are not the same, since we are dealing with two different aspects of the stimulus, one vibrational, the other tonal. We may respond to sounds (frequencies) which are below the lowest pitch limit. In the neighborhood of 200 cps., sounds will be perceived as rough in quality, regardless of the purity of their vibration. As the frequency is lowered from this point, the roughness increases.

When we perceive a sound with a frequency of about 30 cps., a separateness of wave impulses is noticeable. Although one usually considers 15–20 cps. as the lowest limit at which any perceivable pitch can be heard, many people report hearing some vibrations below this limit. For those with acute auditory perception below this limit, a low, pumping noise is reported.

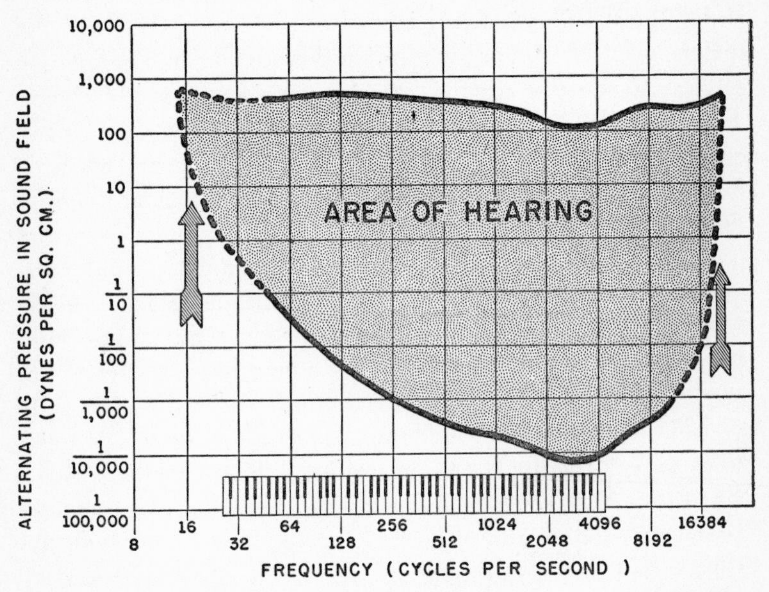

Fig. 3.—The limits of human hearing. (From *Fundamentals of acoustics.* Copyright by The Encyclopaedia Britannica Films, Inc.)

The range of hearing with respect to the vibrational aspects, frequency and intensity, is illustrated in Figure 3. The shaded part represents the area of perceptible sound. The reader will note that at low and high frequencies, a great deal more intensity is necessary to elicit a just perceptible sound than in the middle range.

The decibel.—In studying the vibrational aspect of the sound stimuli, some unit of measurement is useful. Although intensity is measured in dynes per square centimeter, it is often expressed as a ratio instead of an absolute magnitude. The decibel is the unit of a logarithmic scale expressing the ratio of two amounts of power, usually at a standard frequency of 1,000 cps. The number of decibels denoting the ratio of two amounts of power is ten times the logarithm to the base 10 of this ratio. A bel is ten times a decibel. The intensity of sound can then be measured in so many decibels above a certain standard. On the basis of this standard, we may compare various intensities. For example, the rustle of leaves in a strong wind is about one bel or ten decibels. Its energy is ten times that required to make a 1,000-cycle frequency just audible. For example, a whisper is about 12 db., a vacuum cleaner about 50 db., an elevated train about 90 db., and an airplane engine about 110 db.

Audiometry.—The measurement of the threshold for hearing tones relative to their intensity and frequency is called audiometry. The instrument used is an audiometer. This instrument produces pure tones at various levels of frequency in the tonal register. It consists of a vacuum tube oscillator which produces tones of fixed frequencies and definitely measurable intensities. By measuring the amount by which the intensity of a sound must be increased above "normal" for the subject to just hear it, one can measure the amount of loss of hearing for that frequency. Usually the test frequencies are spaced an octave apart throughout the scale range. The technique of measurement thus involves finding the weakest sound that can be perceived at the various frequency levels. A graph is then plotted to show the amount of deviation from the standards of normal hearing. We can then visualize the "hearing loss," if any, that an individual has for different levels of frequency and intensity. This chart, which usually pictures the hearing range, is known as an audiogram (see Figure 4).[2] The abscissa represents the frequency of sound

[2] N. A. Kelley, A comparative study of the response of normal and pathological ears to speech sounds, *J. exp. Psychol.*, 1937, **21**, 342–52.

and the ordinate measures in decibels the degree to which hearing is below normal.

Hearing loss, particularly for higher frequencies, comes on gradually with advancing age, so that the sounds of the human voice and of common musical instruments do not appear any different to the aging person from what they were in youth. This

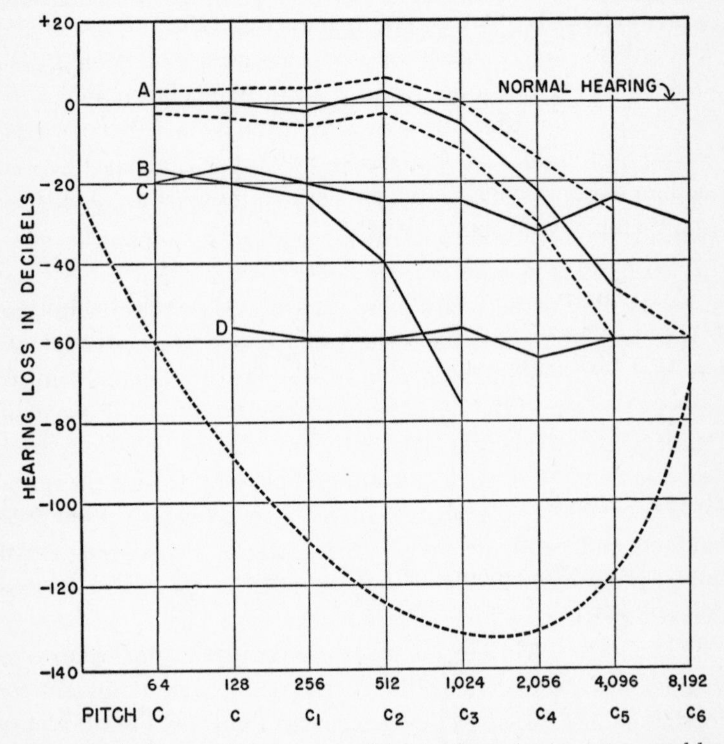

FIG. 4.—Audiogram showing types of hearing loss. *A* represents normal loss due to aging in a subject sixty-five years old. *B* shows a hearing loss due to middle ear impairment, not responsive to treatment. *C* indicates a milder type of loss in a subject hard of hearing who does not require a hearing aid. *D* shows an extreme form of loss where a hearing aid would be a distinct advantage. The broken lines above and below *A* show the range of average deviation from persons of the age of subject *A*. The broken line at the bottom indicates the limits at which sounds are loud enough to cause a pain reaction. (From Kelley—see footnote 2. By permission of the American Psychological Association.)

state of partial deafness is called "presbycousis" and refers to a normal type of hearing loss which occurs with aging and not to that which occurs below the region of 1,000 cps. This latter may be due to some damage or disease.

Tonal lacunae are isolated regions of frequency to which the individual cannot respond. The sensitive regions between the tonal lacunae are called *tonal islands.* Actually, tonal lacunae are areas of relative rather than absolute insensitivity.

Loudness: The Tonal Dimension

As already indicated, loudness is not exclusively dependent on intensity, any more than pitch is on frequency. Loudness increases as intensity and contrariwise; as intensity approaches zero, the loudness of a tone decreases also. Although loudness and intensity have some relationship, loudness also varies with the frequency of the sound wave. In order to be of an equal loudness, low and high frequencies require a great deal more intensity (energy) to sound the same as those within the middle range of frequencies (1,000–5,000 cps.). In another way, it takes a great deal more energy to produce a just audible tone outside the range of 1,000–5,000 cps. than within it. This relationship between loudness and frequency may be demonstrated by mapping equal loudness contours. In so doing we attempt to equate various degrees of loudness for each frequency.

Fletcher and Munson [3] have equated tones in an earphone to a standard frequency of 1,000 cycles, the accepted standard for loudness comparisons. Their results are shown in Figure 5. On the abscissa is plotted frequency, and the ordinate represents level in decibels above the average threshold of the subjects used in the experiment. Thus, all the tones on the contour marked 50 sound equal in loudness to a 1,000-cycle tone 50 db. above the threshold.

[3] H. Fletcher and W. A. Munson, Loudness in definition, measurement and calculation, *J. acoust. Soc. Amer.,* 1933, **5,** 82–108.

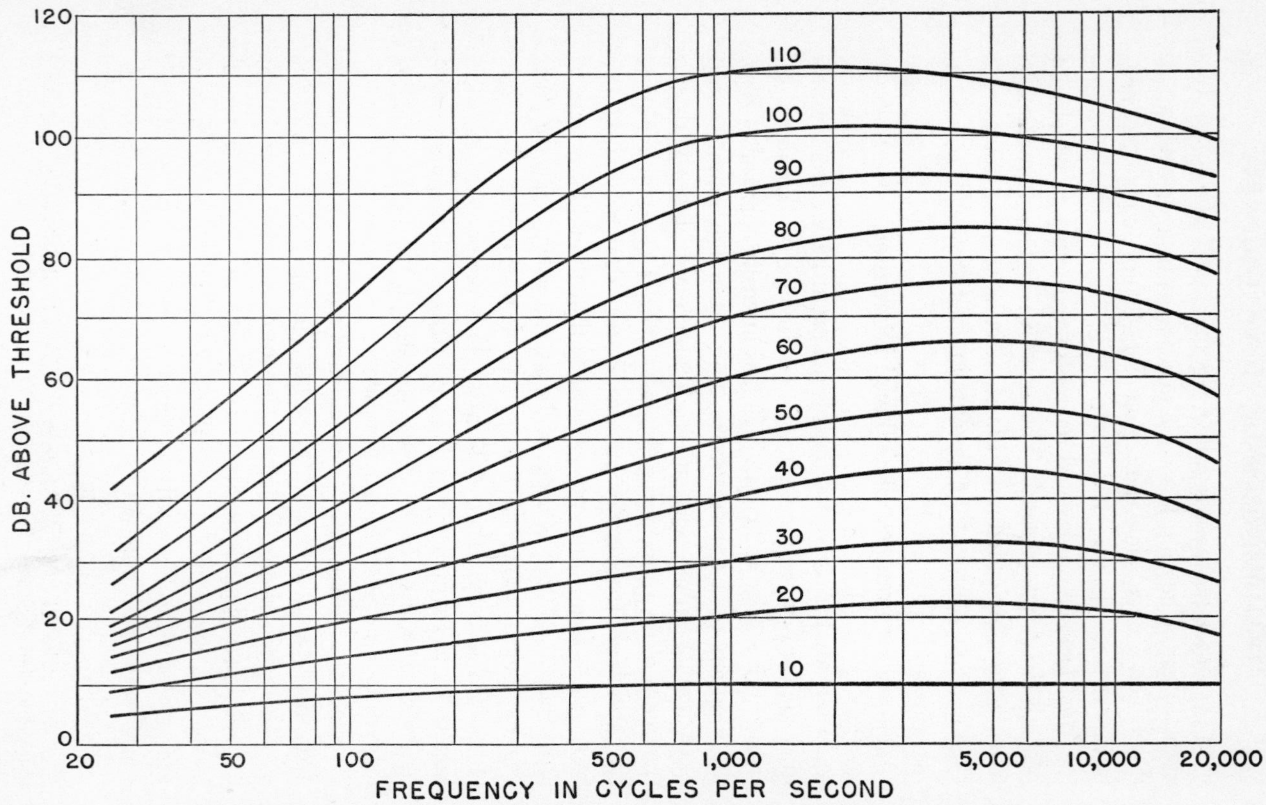

FIG. 5.—Relation of frequency to loudness. (From Fletcher and Munson—see footnote 3.)

Loudness discrimination.—Methods for studying loudness discrimination are much the same as those for pitch.[4] Again two tones of the same frequency but of different loudness may be presented, one of greater intensity than the other. The subject is asked to make a relative judgment just as he did for pitch. Is the second tone louder or softer than the first? Just as for pitch, there are great individual differences in ability to discriminate different degrees of loudness. Seashore[5] has included in his Measures of Musical Talents a test of loudness discrimination. Again, he believes the ability to discriminate small changes in loudness is an important constituent of musical talent. However, the evidence to support this statement is less obvious than that for discrimination of pitch. His test for loudness discrimination has been found to be both less reliable and less valid than that for pitch (see Chapter 13). In the test, subjects are asked to discriminate differences in the loudness of pairs of tones. Two tones are presented in each item, and the listener responds by telling whether the second tone is stronger (louder) or weaker (softer) than the first. Fifty such pairs are included in the test, with discrimination thresholds of 0.5, 1.0, 1.5, 2.0, and 4.0 decibel differences.

In loudness discrimination a number of factors are going to affect the sensitivity of response at different intensities. These will be a function of the individual's biological and psychological equipment.

1. In binaural hearing it is possible to detect a change in intensity 15 to 30 per cent smaller than that perceptible in monaural listening.
2. The difference limen (DL) is smaller when the duration of the tone is greater.

[4] T. G. Andrews, *Methods in psychology* (New York: John Wiley & Sons, Inc., 1949), pp. 230–42.

[5] J. G. Saetveit, D. Lewis, and C. E. Seashore, *Revision of the Seashore Measures of Musical Talents,* Univ. Ia. Stud. Aims Progr. Res., 1940, No. 65, pp. 1–62.

3. Abrupt transition between two comparison tones differing slightly in intensity is easier to detect than when the transition from one tone to another is gradual.[6]
4. As in pitch discrimination, we expect the differential sensitivity in loudness to be a function of the individual's life history of previous discriminations, and we believe that ability to discriminate fine differences in loudness can also be improved, although no experimental evidence seems to be available.
5. Any biological damage or disease in the ear will interfere with discrimination. This capacity is set by the structure of the ear.
6. Finally, loudness is a function of the duration of the stimulus. When a tone is turned on, its perceptible loudness passes through a period of growth before reaching its final value. In general, tones lasting less than one-half second appear less loud than tones of the same intensity whose duration is longer.[7] When the duration of a tone is made small enough, it reaches a point when we cease to call it a tone and report it as resembling a short noise.

How many different tones are perceptible throughout the entire auditory range? Once we know the values throughout the audible range of the DL's for both frequency and intensity, it is then possible to calculate the number of possible pure tones that the individual can perceive. When the intensity of a tone is varied in the middle range, there are about 325 different detectable degrees of loudness. We have already observed (in Chapter 2) that about 1,500 just perceptible frequencies in the middle intensity level could be distinguished by the average person. The multiplication of these two frequencies might, at first glance, seem to give us the answer. However, this is impossible because the area of auditory perception is not square. But when the

[6] S. S. Stevens and H. Davis, *Hearing: its psychology and physiology* (New York: John Wiley & Sons, Inc., 1938), p. 142.

[7] *Ibid.*, pp. 154–55.

auditory area is divided into cells or units, and each unit is computed, it is then possible to arrive at an estimate. When this is done we find about 340,000 distinguishable tones throughout the entire audible range of frequencies and intensities.[8]

Affective dimension of intensity.—While we will take up in detail the nature of feeling responses to music in a later chapter, let us consider momentarily what differences may exist with reference to the intensity of the stimulus. Ortmann [9] has investigated such feeling responses as pleasantness and unpleasantness as they were reported by subjects for various tonal intensities. He found that there was a range from mild unpleasantness for very low intensities through greater pleasantness for the middle range to marked unpleasantness for the extremely loud tones. We have already noted in our discussion of the auditory range that the upper threshold for sensitivity to loudness is limited by pain. That is, when the intensity of the sound is no longer tolerable because of the extreme pressure it exerts on our receptor organs, we report a painful response.

Other loudness phenomena: beating.—We learned in our discussion of pitch discrimination that no one can discriminate every single frequency change that may occur within the range of normal hearing. If we sound separately two tuning forks which are mistuned, that is, one cycle apart, a few of us will be able to distinguish a difference in pitch between the two of them. Let us sound the two forks simultaneously. Fork A has a frequency of 435 and fork B has a frequency of 436 cps. What we will respond to is one tone rather than two. However, this single tone tends to fluctuate in loudness. Such a regular fluctuation we call "beating." In this case the fluctuation will occur once every second. If we tune fork B to 437 cps. and again sound the two forks together, the number of fluctuations will increase to

[8] *Ibid.*, p. 152.
[9] O. Ortmann, Tonal intensity as an aesthetic factor, *Mus. Quart.*, 1928, **14**, 178–91.

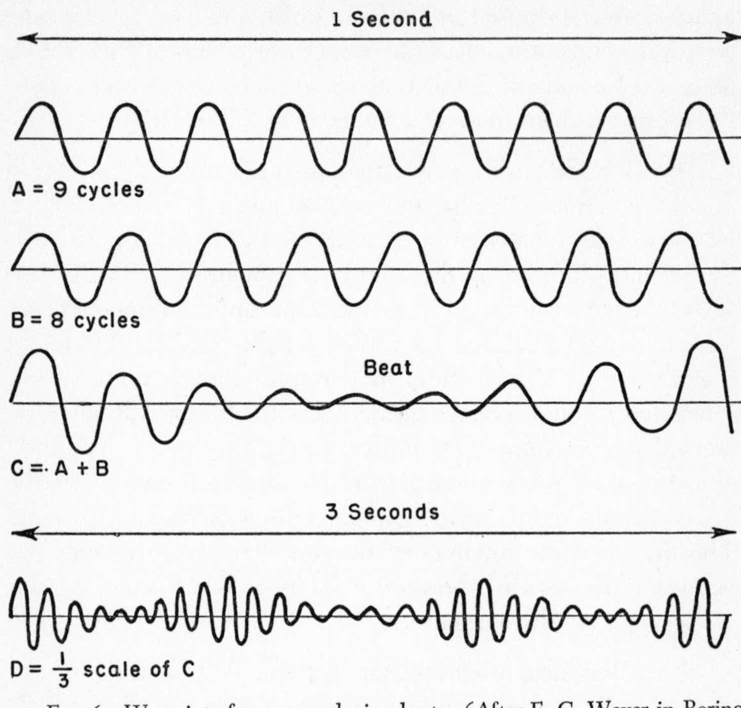

FIG. 6.—Wave interference producing beats. (After E. G. Wever in Boring *et al.*, *Introduction to psychology*, p. 583. Copyright, 1939, by John Wiley & Sons, Inc.)

two per second. As the difference in frequency between the two forks increases (providing they are sounded together), the number of fluctuations per second will increase. The number of fluctuations we hear, then, is equal to the difference in the frequency of the two forks. As we increase the frequency difference of these two tones, the number of fluctuations will continue to increase until we can no longer count them, and the tone will be perceived as a rattling, unpleasant sound. This roughness will continue until we finally begin to distinguish two tones instead of one. The physical basis for beating is due to a difference in phase of the two sound waves. If our two forks were tuned at the same frequency and played together, they would keep in phase, that is, the crests and troughs of the waves would coincide. The resulting sound would be louder than that of either fork played separately. This is because they reinforce each other. However, when our two tones differ only slightly in their frequency, say by one cycle, their wave crests coincide, causing reinforcement only once per second. The rest of the time they are out of phase (Figure 6). As a result, when the crests coincide, we hear an increase in loudness occurring once per second, giving the impression of beating. As the difference in frequency between the two tones increases, the crests coincide more often, giving more frequent fluctuations in loudness.

Masking.—Another interesting phenomenon of loudness is that of masking. It is a well-known fact that one tone may be blocked out by another tone which is sounding at the same time. This is known as "masking." The masking effect of a particular tone may be determined by finding out how much *louder* the masked tone must be made for it to be perceived in the presence of the masking tone. It has been observed that, in general, low

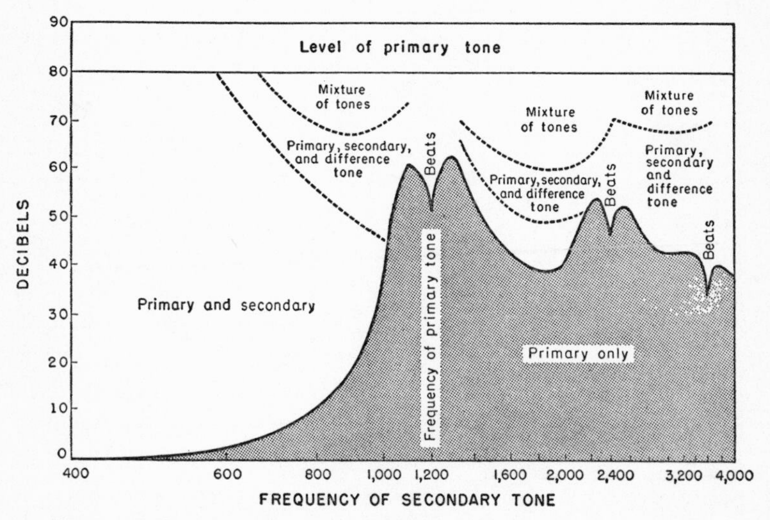

FIG. 7.—Auditory masking. (From Wegel and Lane—see footnote 10.)

tones have a greater masking effect than high ones. The phenomenon of masking can be understood by reference to Figure 7. The figure represents the masking effect of a tone of 1,200 cps. with a set intensity of 80 db. This is the primary tone. The frequencies of the secondary tones are distributed along the base line. The intensity necessary for the second tones to overcome the masking effect are represented on the side axis. The shaded portion represents the area of different frequency figures at which masking occurs. The masking will differ for different frequencies. The unshaded portion represents the area of hearing in which no masking appears, that is, both tones are audible. Note, for example, that at a frequency of 600 cycles a tone need only be raised above its normal threshold to be heard, whereas a frequency of 1,100 cycles must be raised to a threshold of 60 db. above its normal threshold for perception in order to be heard.[10]

[10] R. L. Wegel and C. E. Lane, The auditory masking of one pure tone by another and its probable relation to the dynamics of the inner ear, *Physiol. Rev.*, 1924, **23**, 266–85.

Chapter 4

THE DIMENSIONS OF TONE: TIMBRE, VOLUME, AND DENSITY

THE three tonal attributes of sound remaining to be discussed are timbre, volume, and density. As with pitch and loudness, we are considering the observable qualities of the stimulus object and the psychological responses to them.

Timbre

The tonal attribute of sound called "timbre" is also often referred to as "tonal quality" to distinguish it from the attributes of pitch and loudness. Timbre is that aspect of a tone that gives it its richness. We often speak of the rich tonal quality of a violin or cello in contrast to the rather thin quality of a tuning fork. Musical instruments differ in their qualities, and it is by means of quality that we can perceive differences when the same tone is played on the trumpet, piano, violin, oboe, or French horn. Each of these instruments has its own characteristic tonal quality or timbre.

Overtones.—As with our other dimensions, we will consider the vibrational aspect as well as the tonal. From a vibrational point of view, sound waves occur in all degrees of complexity, from the pure, even wave of the tuning fork or electric oscillator to the complicated mass of vibrations which we call "noise." Consider for a moment a vibrating violin string. When a bow is drawn across the string in open position, it vibrates as a whole. This basic rate of vibration or frequency we designate as the *fundamental* frequency. However, the string also vibrates in a series of parts, each part representing an overtone. The string may vibrate in halves, giving the first overtone or partial, or in thirds, giving the second overtone, or in quarters, giving the third overtone, and so on. The combination of these vibrations gives a much more complex series of vibrations than that produced by the simple tuning fork, which only vibrates as a whole and gives only a fundamental frequency. Although the quality of the sound is related to a number of factors which we will discuss, it is primarily correlated with the number of overtones or partials that the sound happens to have as a part of its vibrating frequencies. A simple sound such as that produced by a vibrating tuning fork is called a pure tone because it is lacking in overtones.

These overtones bear a frequency ratio to the fundamental of 1, 2, 3, 4, and so forth. If we play middle C (256 cps.) on the violin, the first overtone we hear will have a frequency of 512 cps., a frequency twice that of the fundamental. The second overtone will have a frequency of 768, the third 1,024, and so on. Some overtones are not readily perceived, and it often takes a good deal of training to be able to attend to them. Any single musical instrument when played will produce various overtones in addition to its fundamental. Figure 8 gives an analysis of the physical sound wave of an organ pipe, followed by its fundamental and overtones.

The same tone can be played on two musical instruments at the same frequency and intensity. Compare middle C played on a clarinet and a violin. Despite the fact that tonally their pitch and loudness may be perceived as the same, we hear a very different quality of tone. Each has characteristic overtones, so often the presence or absence of the overtones makes the difference in quality between the two instruments. (This may be the case in comparing a tuning fork and a violin, since the former is fairly free of overtones.) But quality differences which we observe between two instruments are also due to the different *number* of overtones produced by the two instruments, the *particular* overtones which happen to occur (first, third, or fourth) and the *distribution* of energy among the overtones. That is, some particular overtones are emphasized more by certain instruments, and they may vary with the instrument played. One musical instrument may emphasize the second overtone more than the first, while another simply has fewer overtones. The matter becomes a very complex problem, and is of greater interest to the physicist than to the psychologist.

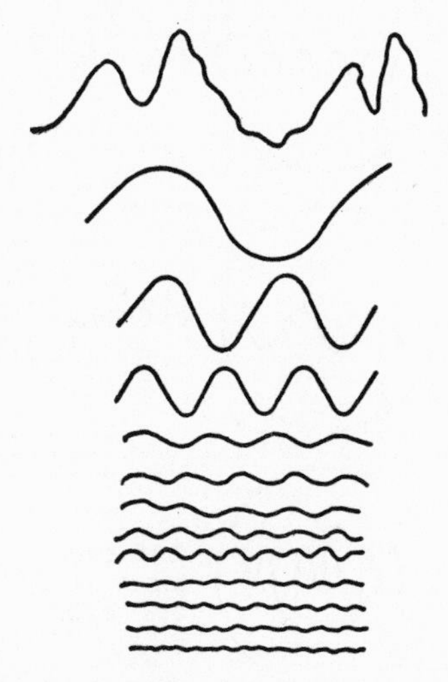

FIG. 8.—Analysis of an organ wave into its components. (From D. C. Miller, *The science of musical sounds,* New York: The Macmillan Co., 1926, p. 125.)

The harmonic structure of complex sound waves (fundamental and overtones) can be measured by accurate observations of the form of the wave, as demonstrated in Figure 8. This analysis is based on a mathematical formula called Fourier's theorem. In more recent years a device known as an *oscillograph* has been perfected which visually produces a wave form suitable for accurate analysis and measurement. A harmonic analysis in this manner is shown in Figure 8. The top wave is that of the original sound transformed by means of the oscillograph into visual form. This is, then, a picture of a sound wave in its original form produced by an organ. In the analysis, we see the total sound as being broken down into its fundamental and overtones. When these are sounded together as a series, what we actually hear is a series of individual pure sounds. See also Figure 9.

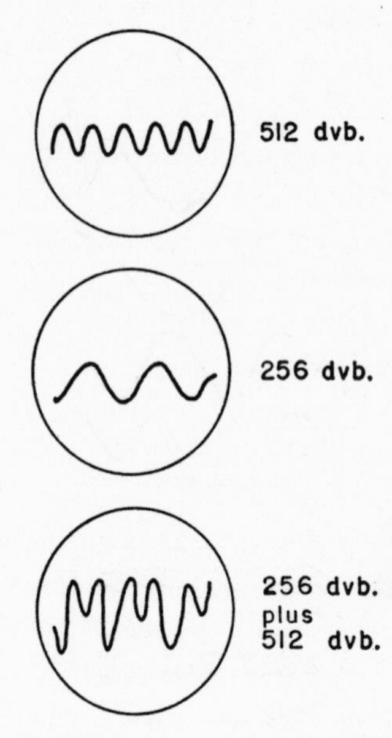

Fig. 9.—Single and combined waves produced by two tuning forks of different frequency.

All musical instruments, including the human voice, produce sounds composed of series of overtones, whether they originate from a reed, string, or vibrating column of air. Beside the harmonic structure which we have described, there will also be other accessory noises accompanying the tone, such as the click of a key or the rasping of a violin bow. All of these may be measured and contribute to the quality of the sound as we perceive it.

Such quality of the sound is then a function of the *number of partials* or overtones present. These may vary from a single fundamental (as in a tuning fork or oscillating tone) to one with as many as thirty or forty partials. The most important variable in determining the quality of the sound wave is, according to Seashore, the *distribution* of the partials. A sound may have its fundamental and several of the partials absent. Often difference tones (see below) may fill in the gaps left by the missing partials.[1]

The *intensity* of the fundamental and particular partials also affects the quality of the sound. When a musician varies the intensity of his produced tone, he varies its quality also, because the greater the intensity, the more partials will be present. This is illustrated in the different interpretations of two people each playing the same instrument. We often speak of some individuals having a superior quality in their "touch" or approach to an instrument. Consider the piano as an example, where the quality of the heard sound is partially determined by the force of the hammer on the string, that is the physical intensity.

The matter of the *distribution of energy* among the partials is another significant factor in determining the quality. The strong partials in terms of intensity may be located in the upper, lower, or middle regions of the partials, that is among the first, second, and third, the fourth, fifth, and sixth, or the seventh, eighth, and ninth overtones.

Resonance.—The different overtones which happen to be emphasized are often due to the resonating qualities of the instrument which produced them. Resonance, then, is another factor affecting the tone quality. One instrument may make high overtones predominant, another low. Strike a tuning fork away from the box on which it is mounted, and the result will be a very weak sound. Then strike it on the box, and the tone be-

[1] C. E. Seashore, *Psychology of music* (New York: McGraw-Hill Book Co., Inc., 1938), chap. viii.

comes much stronger. Musical instruments are so constructed that they accentuate certain overtones and not others. Famous instruments such as the Stradivarius violins have become costly because of the beautiful quality of tone they produce. Although this quality of tone may be a function of the performer, it is also related to the excellence of workmanship which went into the construction of the resonating box. The quality of the strings used might be exactly the same as that used on a beginner's model, but the tone is different, the difference being due to the resonating qualities of the instrument.

Finally, quality is related to the intensity and frequency of the sound wave. If you amplify a violin tone, for example, its timbre will change, although the relative strength of the overtones is the same. Fletcher[2] has also demonstrated that lowering or raising frequency alters the timbre.

Combination tones.—Another factor which will add to the sound quality is the generation of combination tones. If one sounds two pure tones, providing they are at least thirty cycles apart, they will produce, beside their own frequencies, others which are called "combination tones." These are of two types, *summation tones* and *difference tones*; a summation tone produces a sound whose frequency is the *sum* of the two fundamentals, and a difference tone produces a sound whose frequency is the *difference* between the two fundamentals.

If we should sound simultaneously two frequencies, 1,000 and 1,200 cps., a third tone, a difference tone, would be heard whose frequency would be low, namely 200 cps. This would take the form of a low hum, but if we listened carefully we could hear it. Difference tones can best be perceived when the primary tones are (*a*) of equal intensity, (*b*) of fairly strong intensity (quite loud), and (*c*) within a frequency range of 500 to 2,000 cps. More than one difference tone may be produced

[2] H. Fletcher, Loudness, pitch, and timbre of musical tones and their relation to the intensity, the frequency, and the overtone structure, *J. acoust. Soc. Amer.*, 1934, **6**, 59–69.

by a combination of the first difference tone and the primaries. Let us label our difference tones by D1, D2, D3, etc., and our primaries by the letters L and H (lower and higher). By so doing we would get a series of difference tones as follows:

$$
\begin{aligned}
L &= 1{,}000 \text{ and } H = 1{,}200 \\
D1 &= H - L\ (1{,}200 - 1{,}000 = 200) \\
D2 &= 2L - H\ (2{,}000 - 1{,}200 = 800) \\
D3 &= 3L - 2H\ (3{,}000 - 2{,}400 = 600) \\
D4 &= 4L - 3H\ (4{,}000 - 3{,}600 = 400), \text{ etc.}
\end{aligned}
$$

Summation tones are produced by the addition of the two primaries. In our example of 1,000 and 1,200, our first summation tone $(L + H) = 2{,}200$ cps. The summation tones are more difficult to hear. If one hears a frequency higher than either of the two primaries, it is the summation tone. More than one summation tone may be produced in a manner similar to that of the difference tone. Harmonics or overtones also produce summation and difference tones. Although they are difficult to differentiate from the total sound effect, let us suppose we hear two violin strings, one at 256 and the other at 435 cps. The first difference tone would be 179 $(H - L)$ and the first summation tone would be 691 $(L + H)$. Each of these fundamentals has a first overtone, 512 and 870 cps. respectively. These produce a difference tone of 358 and a summation tone of 1,382 with each other. It is clear by now that the matter of partials, difference tones, and summation tones becomes quite complicated when we consider all the possible combinations and differences which can be produced by simply playing two tones together. Imagine the increase in complexity when more tones are added.

Timbre discrimination.—In measuring responses to pitch and loudness, we noted individual differences existing in the ability of individuals to discriminate small changes in these qualities. This is also true for timbre. One of Seashore's *Measures of Mu-*

sical Talents, in its revised edition,[3] attempts to test ability to make such discriminations (see Chapter 13). In this particular test the tone F♯ is presented by a specially devised tone generator[4] which presents a fundamental tone and its first six partials. In the test the intensity of all partials except the third and fourth is held constant. A change in timbre can be brought about by alternating the intensity of the third and fourth partials. Acuity of discrimination is determined by the method of just noticeable differences similar to that described for the two measurements of pitch and loudness discussed previously. Those persons with fine "timbre acuity" can detect small differences in the intensity of the partials when such a variation occurs. In making such a measurement (as in pitch and loudness), the stimuli are presented in pairs of tones which are the same and different in timbre. The responder is asked to note whether the two tones are the same or different in timbre. This particular test is recorded on phonograph records and is available with other of the *Seashore Measures of Musical Talents*. A critical evaluation of these tests is reserved for a later chapter (Chapter 13).

Kwalwasser and Dykema[5] have attempted to measure timbre differences in their Tests of Music. Their measure is less controlled and has been reported to be less reliable than the Seashore method.[6] In the Kwalwasser Test of Quality Discrimination, actual musical instruments are played, and the subject is asked to tell whether the two instruments—for example, a violin and a clarinet—are the same or different. In this case, the subject would correctly judge the timbre as different. In other cases a violin is played twice and subject judges the timbre as the same.

[3] J. G. Saetveit, D. Lewis, and C. E. Seashore, *Revision of the Seashore Measures of Musical Talents,* Univ. Ia. Stud. Aims Progr. Res., 1940, No. 65, pp. 1–61.

[4] E. B. Kurtz and M. J. Larsen, An electrostatic audio generator, *Elec. Eng.,* Sept., 1935.

[5] J. Kwalwasser and P. W. Dykema, *Kwalwasser-Dykema music tests* (New York: Carl Fischer, Inc., 1930).

[6] See Chapter 13 for reports on reliability and validity of Kwalwasser-Dykema and Seashore tests.

In this test the intensity of the compared items is not always the same because of the human factor involved. This test was extremely costly to make and suffers from low reliability and validity (see Chapter 13).

The exact relationship between ability to discriminate small differences in timbre and general musical ability is yet in the speculative stage. The timbre test is the newest of the Seashore measures and its value as a measure of musical talent remains to be proved.

Volume [7]

Pitch, loudness, and timbre had been traditionally considered the primary tonal attributes of sound. But there is certainly no a priori presumption that other attributes may not exist which would help to describe our tonal stimulus. The only limitation as to the number of characteristics of our stimulus from a tonal point of view would be a practical one. Pitch and loudness have received the greatest attention and their relationships to the vibrational attributes have been fairly well established. Volume has received less extensive treatment, but its place as an attribute of tone is now being recognized. That the low tones of an organ tend to be described as "bigger" than the high tones of a cricket's chirp is not too difficult to observe even when the loudness of the two tones is equal.

In 1916, Rich made a preliminary examination of volume as a tonal attribute and its relation to the vibrational attributes of sound. He concluded that: "The larger (lower) tones seem to have a greater diffuseness. It seems as if the smaller (higher) fill space more compactly, what they fill." [8] In a later study [9] he pre-

[7] We are not referring here to volume as controlled on the ordinary radio dial. This really is a misnomer. The dial should really be labeled "loudness," since that is what it regulates.

[8] G. J. Rich, A preliminary study of tonal volume, *J. exp. Psychol.*, 1916, **1**, 15.

[9] G. J. Rich, A study of tonal attributes, *Amer. J. Psychol.*, 1919, **30**, 121–64.

sented two tones of different frequency and asked his subject to decide which tone appeared more voluminous. He did the same for brightness and for pitch. Results showed a small difference between the latter two, a difference too small to justify separate classifications. However, the subjects reported differences of volume easily. As frequency increased, volume decreased. Halverson[10] demonstrated the relation of volume to intensity and found a loud sound to be more voluminous than a weak one. Probably the most substantial demonstration of volume as an attribute of tone has been described by Stevens.[11] As with equal pitch contours and equal loudness contours, so also with volume, a subject is given alternately tones of different frequency and asked to vary the intensity of one, in this case until it equals the other with respect to volume. This is achieved by making the higher tone more intense than the lower one. This study has demonstrated the fact that volume is a function of both frequency and intensity. Greater volume goes with greater intensity and with less frequency. Therefore, the volume of a tone increases with intensity and decreases with frequency. At high intensities the relative effectiveness of intensity is greater than that of frequency as a determining factor. The reverse is true at low intensities.

Thomas' mapping of equal volume contours[12] appears in Figure 10. The question has been raised as to whether tonal volume is not merely a matter of associating low, loud tones with big instruments such as the tuba and high, soft tones with little instruments like the flute. Stevens[13] found that a congenitally blind person made judgments of tonal volume in a similar manner to the subject with normal eyesight who was used in his previous experiments.

[10] H. M. Halverson, Tonal volume as a function of intensity, *Amer. J. Psychol.*, 1924, **35**, 360–67.

[11] S. S. Stevens, The volume and intensity of tones, *Amer. J. Psychol.*, 1934, **46**, 397–408.

[12] G. J. Thomas, Equal-volume judgments of tones, *Amer. J. Psychol.*, 1949, **62**, 182–201.

[13] S. S. Stevens, Are tones spatial? *Amer. J. Psychol.*, 1934, **46**, 145–47.

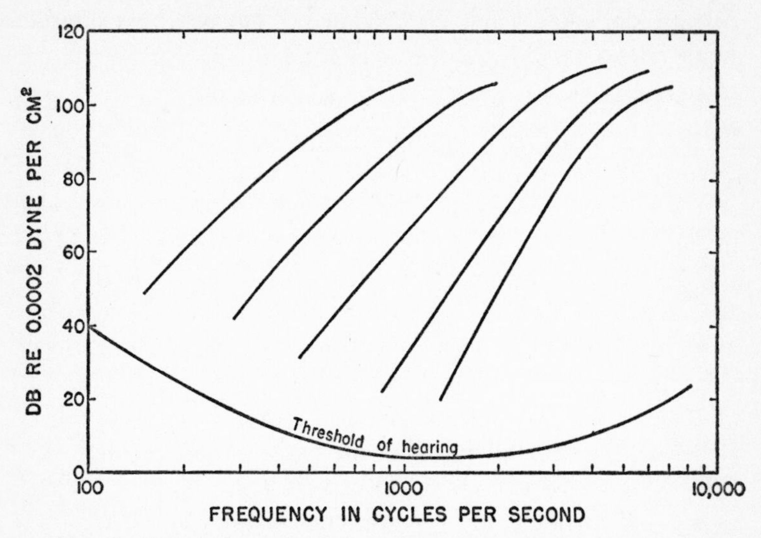

FIG. 10.—Smoothed equal volume contours determined by the method of frequency adjustment. The curves are plotted in decibels of sound pressure at the eardrum. Tones are judged equal in volume when their frequency and intensity coordinates fall along one of the curves. The upper left-hand curve is the largest volume and the lower right-hand curve is the smallest. (By permission of G. J. Thomas and the *American Journal of Psychology*—see footnote 12.)

Density

The descriptions of tones as "tight," "hard," "compact," or "dense" has led Stevens to investigate the attribute of density. In his study of volume, he used the equation method whereby two tones of different pitches are presented in rapid alternation. The subject adjusted the intensity of the two tones until they appeared to be equal in volume. Tonal density was tested in a similar way.[14] High tones were found to be more dense than low ones, and loud tones more dense than soft tones. Compared with volume, he found that with increasing *frequency*, volume decreased, density *increased.* As intensity increased, volume and

[14] S. S. Stevens, Tonal density, *J. exp. Psychol.*, 1934, **17**, 585–92.

density increased. High tones tended to be small and compact, while loud tones were large and dense.

Brightness.—Tones are often described as bright or dull. However, writers have questioned whether or not *brightness* is a separate attribute of tone. Boring and Stevens [15] have concluded that brightness varies with intensity and frequency in the same manner as density. Thus, the two attributes are probably identical. Of the two terms, they prefer density, since it has been definitely established by quantitative descriptive measurements.

Further evidence reported by Stevens and Davis [16] to support this observation is suggested by the fact that, when observers are asked to equate two pure tones for brightness and density, it becomes a difficult task when they are told that brightness is something different from density. Observers unfamiliar with density as a tonal attribute make consistent judgments of brightness, which turns out to increase with intensity and frequency according to the relation which has been previously established by other observers for density. They conclude that "brightness and density vary together to such an extent that the two attributes ought, at least for the present, to be considered identical." [17]

Interrelationship of pitch, loudness, volume, and density.—The relationship of attributes of pitch, loudness, volume, and density (brightness) to each other and to the vibrational attributes is illustrated in Figure 11, which is from Stevens.[18] The axes indicate the vibrational dimensions, frequency and intensity. The curves are lines of *equal* volume, pitch, loudness, and density. Any part on a single curve is equal to the next in the attribute represented.

To summarize, we note that loudness increases with intensity

[15] E. G. Boring and S. S. Stevens, The nature of tonal brightness, *Proc. nat. Acad. Sci.*, Wash., 1936, **22**, 514–21.

[16] S. S. Stevens and H. Davis, *Hearing: its psychology and physiology* (New York: John Wiley & Sons, Inc., 1938).

[17] *Ibid.*, p. 166.

[18] S. S. Stevens, The attributes of tone, *Proc. nat. Acad. Sci.*, Wash., 1934, **20**, 457–59.

but also varies with frequency. If loudness were a direct function of intensity, its curve would have to be parallel with the frequency axis, as all points on the loudness curve are equal in loudness.

Pitch increases with frequency, but it is also a function of intensity. If this were not the case, the pitch curve would have to parallel the intensity axis.

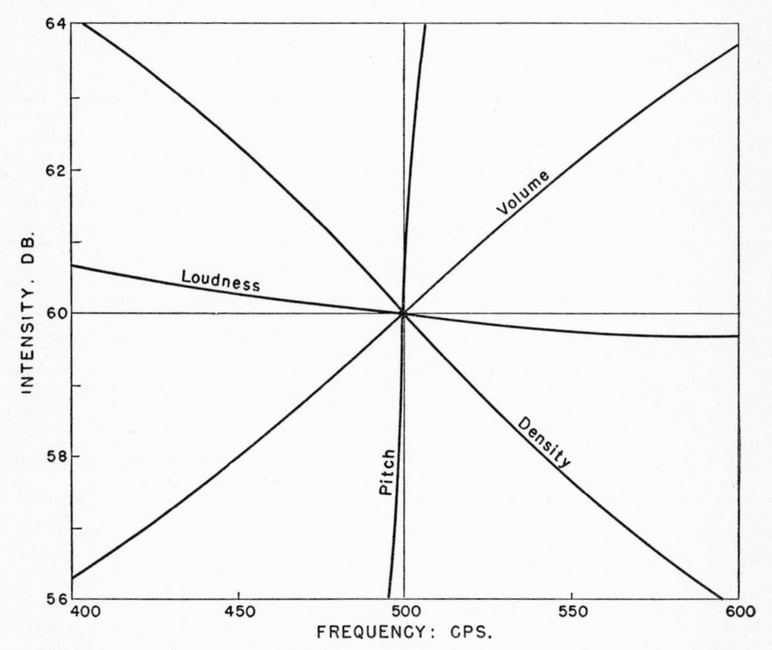

FIG. 11.—Pitch, loudness, volume, and density plotted in relation to intensity and frequency. (From Stevens—see footnote 18.)

Volume increases with intensity and decreases with frequency. High, soft tones are small in volume, and low, loud tones are large.

Density (brightness) increases with frequency and intensity. The densest tones are high and intense.

This concludes our discussion of the dimensions of tone. We

have attempted to characterize the various aspects of the tonal stimulus and have tried to clarify a basic confusion which has existed between the tonal and vibrational aspects of the sound stimulus. The tonal aspect refers to the attributes or characteristics of pitch, loudness, timbre, volume, and density of tone, whereas the vibrational aspects are the frequency, intensity, form, and duration of the sound wave. Psychologically, we respond to a stimulus object, sound, in both its tonal and its vibrational aspects. When we consider it as a stimulus, our responses to it become the legitimate object for psychological investigation.

Thus far, we have been considering only single tones or tones in isolation. As any musician knows, music does not consist of mere single isolated tones but a combination of these. Our next section is devoted to a study of the combination of tones as they occur in melody and harmony and as they bring forth the responses of consonance and dissonance when played together.

Chapter 5

THE COMBINATION OF TONES: MELODY AND HARMONY

In our discussion so far, we have been considering tones as single stimuli rather than in combination. Our analysis has been concerned with the characteristics of single tones and the organism's responses to them. However, we know that in music tones occur in combinations which may be successive or simultaneous. The successive combination of tones and tonal intervals constitutes the basis for melody, while the simultaneous combination of tones serves as the ground for what we call harmony. Yet a haphazard combination does not result in melody or harmony. The problem for the psychologist is to discover what attributes these combinations have which entitles them to be called melody or harmony and why other tonal combinations do not warrant these titles. The question of the nature of melody and its attributes will be considered in the first part of this chapter and the problem of harmony in the last part. Before considering melody and harmony from the psychological point of view, it is necessary to look at the basic structure from which melody and harmony are built. This is the *scale*.

Scales

In Chapter 2 on the attributes of pitch we mentioned the report of Stevens and Davis[1] regarding the greatest possible number of perceptible pitches which can be distinguished by the

[1] S. S. Stevens and H. Davis, *Hearing: its psychology and physiology* (New York: John Wiley & Sons, Inc., 1938), p. 152.

average human at a medium intensity level. There were found to be about 1,500 of these. However, our Western music actually utilizes only about 100 different pitches in all.[2] Nevertheless, within the range of frequencies most often applied in Western music, there are about 135–200 possible just noticeable pitch variations which we can distinguish in any single octave. The actual number depends on what particular octave range we are including. For example, a greater number of different pitches can be distinguished in the lower octaves than in the higher ones. This is, of course, within the limits of Weber's Law.[3] Despite this fact, we know that any single octave in our musical scale makes use of only twelve different pitches at the most.

The tuning of our pianos and organs follows this system, and vocal and instrumental music has tended to conform. The greatest range of musical tones is possible on the organ, with the pianoforte a close second. Table 1, which is from Ruckmick,[4] illustrates the relationship between audible frequency range and the musical scale. Most orchestral instruments have, of course, a narrower range of possible frequencies than the piano or organ. Orchestral instruments can produce tones with a range of about two or three octaves with the exception of the violin and cello, which have a greater range.[5]

An octave may be divided into any number of equal or unequal units within the range of perceptible differences. The

[2] A. R. Chandler, *Beauty and human nature* (New York: Appleton-Century-Crofts, Inc., 1934), p. 168.

[3] Weber's Law states that a stimulus change (in this case, a change in frequency) that will give a just noticeable difference in sensation will bear a constant ratio to the magnitude of the stimulus. Thus, if at a pitch level of 450 cps. the stimulus change necessary for the subject to report a just noticeable difference were three cycles, we would conclude from Weber's Law that at 900 cps. the necessary stimulus change would be six cycles and at 1,800 cps. it would be twelve cycles. The law is applied to various sense modalities, such as brightness, heaviness, etc. It was expounded in E. H. Weber, *De pulsu, resorptione, auditu, et tactu* (1834).

[4] C. A. Ruckmick, A new classification of tonal qualities, *Psychol. Rev.*, 1929, **36**, 172–80.

[5] Chandler, *op. cit.*, p. 169.

TABLE 1

RANGE OF PITCHES

Number of Vibrations	*Musical Notes*
20,000 to 25,000	E9 to G9 (highest audible notes)
16,384	C9
8,192	C8 (highest note on the organ)
4,096	C7 (highest note on the piano)
2,048	C6
1,024	C5
512	C4
256	C3 (middle C)
128	C2
64	C1
32	C0 (The A below this is the lowest tone on the piano.)
16	C (lowest tone on the organ and lowest audible tone.)

well-tempered scale which Western music employs today is bound by the limitations of the fixed pitches of musical instruments first used by the Greeks (namely, the lyre and the flute). Some people believe that the intervals employed in our music today are "natural," being either determined by the discriminative "power" of the human ear or by natural mathematical relationships. As an example of the latter, they take middle C, which is 256 cps., with an octave above of 512 cps., next 1,024, 2,048, etc. The frequencies double each other as we go up the scale octave by octave. This power-of-2 relation between octaves was considered to be the real cause of our octave division. However, the history of music does not seem to substantiate any "native" elements in the scale or in the human ear. Our octave was too large an interval for the early Greeks, who had a smaller scale. Furthermore, many different kinds of scales have been developed in both Eastern and Western cultures. In our own Western music, the scale which had its origin with the ancient Greeks has undergone a number of modifications.

The development of the well-tempered scale.—In describing the development of our modern scale Boring writes:

> The primitive base of Greek music was, then, the descending cadence of approximately a fourth, two notes elaborated by a third intermediate note to provide the rudimentary possibilities of melody. In modern notation we might represent such a cadence by A-G flat-E. This sequence, however, presently became complicated by the addition of a leading note just above the final note, and the adjustment of the position of the intermediate note to a place halfway between the initial and leading notes: thus, A-G-F-E, which is the diatonic tetrachord basic to early Greek music. . . . The Greeks also came to use two other forms of the tetrachord: the chromatic tetrachord, in which the middle note was moved down so that it was practically a leading note to the leading note (as A-G flat-F-E); and the enharmonic tetrachord, a descending fourth with two notes before the lower separated by quarter tones (like A-F-e-E, if e signifies a quarter tone above E). These three kinds of tetrachords were different genera and were used contemporaneously. To each genus different musical effects were ascribed; the diatonic was said to be manly and austere; the chromatic, sweet and pathetic; the enharmonic, animating and mild.[6]

In the acceptance of the tetrachord as the scale unit instead of the octave which we now use, as well as the placing of small intervals at the bottom of the series, we have the fundamental bases of Greek music. The early melodies for the Greeks were of necessity very confined in scope.

It is clear now that music was not based first on the "natural" octave, for this was introduced later when the range for melody was extended to more notes.

The lyre of the Greeks was typically of seven strings. When the Greek musicians tried to increase this number to eight or even more, they met with opposition. About 530 B.C., the great philosopher and mathematician Pythagoras brought music into his philosophy of numbers by establishing the octave by the limits

[6] E. G. Boring, *Sensation and perception in the history of experimental psychology* (New York: Appleton-Century-Crofts, Inc., 1942), p. 314.

of a vibration ratio of 2:1. The properties of number were of major importance in his consideration of music. Next, Pythagoras separated the two tetrachords of the lyre by extending them to fill out the octave and adding the hitherto objectionable eighth string. This scale approximated in our modern notation (E-D-C-B)–(A-G-F-E).

> It was in this way, by the necessity of establishing fixed pitches in musical instruments, that the system of tones became defined as discrete units, the notes of scales, and not as continua, like the colors of painting. The important thing to realize is that, although historically scales have been basic in the understanding of tone, the intervals of the scales are not "native" and inevitable, rather, they have been set up, one way and another, in a long history of experimentation. The first interval to be fixed was the fourth, the limits of the tetrachord. Its strings gave the *soni stabiles* which were not changed, and upon them all other intervals were based.[7]

The development of the equal-temperament scale (see page 64) that is now in use has been a complicated one. In summary we may say it has passed through the following stages:

1. *Just temperament* consisted of the Pythagorean octave, modified by Didymus and Ptolemy to give simple mathematical ratios. The great difficulty with this scale was that its eight notes would suffice for only a single key. All notes in the scale had a simple mathematical ratio to the keynote as follows, beginning with unison and going on to the octave:

C	D	E	F	G	A	B	C
1,	9/8,	5/4,	4/3,	3/2,	5/3,	15/8,	2/1

However, it cannot be adapted to our contemporary musical instruments if a change in key is required.

2. *Meantone temperament* tried to solve some of the problems created by the introduction of key modulations into music that could not be handled by the just-temperament scale.

[7] *Ibid.*, p. 315.

> Actually it [meantone] requires 27 notes in the octave, but the early organ builders because it was impracticable to interpolate more than five notes in their proper places kept the octave down to a total of 12 notes. C, C♯, D, E flat, E, F, F♯, G, G♯, A, B flat, B, [and C] making only six keys possible, viz., the keys of C, G, D, A, F, and B flat. If an organist got into the key of E flat, and wanted to sound the chord A flat, C, E flat, he had to strike G♯ instead of A flat, and G♯, being almost a quarter tone flatter than A flat, created a discord which came to be known as "the howling of the wolves." Until its displacement by equal temperament in 1841–46, meantone temperament, nevertheless, was used almost universally on organs, claviers and pianos.[8]

3. The *equal-temperament* or *well-tempered* scale was favored by Johann Sebastian Bach, who wrote *Das wohltemperirte Klavier* (finished 1744) for it. This work contained forty-eight preludes and fugues, each in one of the twelve major and twelve minor keys. Bach solved the problem of the meantone-temperament scale by introducing twelve equal semitones. This made every interval deviate slightly from the theoretical ratios, but it enabled one to play in all keys on the same instrument. We can readily see that the equal-temperament scale which is used today has had its practical foundations. It is neither "native" nor based on psychic properties inherent in nature or in the individual. Its evolution has been a gradual one arising out of certain social conditions. This scale has its basis in practical social purposes. Any proposal to alter it might run into serious economic difficulties. Consider for a moment the changes necessary in the manufacture of musical instruments and the methods of printing the score if this happened. Our scale is an attempt to make available a means whereby our musical expressions may be communicated.

Other kinds of scales.—We have already observed that scales are built upon one of two principles: (1) those which depend on an equal subdivision within the octave and (2) those which

[8] *Ibid.*, p. 318.

utilize an unequal set of divisions. Our eight-tone diatonic scale (C-D-E-F-G-A-B-C) is an example of this latter principle. The tempered scale consisting of twelve equal intervals within the octave illustrates the former. For all practical purposes the *equal-temperament scale* does this except for the fact that each one of the intervals is slightly distorted, as we have already observed. We do not actually hear thirds, fourths, seconds, sevenths, fourths, fifths tuned to the precise ratios. This matters little, however, since the mistuning is within the limits of tolerance. It is interesting to note that many compositions call for scales of both equal and unequal divisions.

There are other varieties of scales beside our own. The Siamese employ the heptatonic (seven-tone) and the Javanese a pentatonic (five-tone) scale. Both of these scales depend on an equality of intervals within the octave. Because of the peculiar relationships between these tones, we should expect considerable difficulty in tuning. This problem is largely overcome by having instruments which permanently hold their pitches, such as the xylophone and bells which are frequently used in Java and Siam.

Chinese music also shows a marked deviation from our own. Its characteristic form is said to date from about 2697 B.C., during the reign of the mythical emperor Huang Ti. Today a five-tone scale is the one in most common use, but this scale may be based on any number of accepted tones. The scale is considered a descending rather than an ascending one. The cultural value of the number five is of special interest, since five plays an important part in Chinese philosophy. Unlike Western melodies, Chinese melodies have a peculiar wandering character. Less emphasis is placed on the progression of the individual tones, again showing the cultural imposition on ways of writing music.

The music of India appears to be of a higher type than that of the Chinese. Brahmin musicians are of two classes. The first consists of high-caste maidens who are devoted to the service of the gods, and the second contains members of the lower castes. This type of music employs a large number of different scales, twenty of which are now in common use. These are based on twenty-two nearly equal divisions of the octave. Neither Chinese nor Indian music has had much effect on the development of our own system.

Melody

Divergent usage of the term "melody" has led to considerable dispute and misunderstanding among musicians and psychologists alike as to just what it is or how it should be defined. We know that it consists of a successive combination of tones, but we have already pointed out that any combination of tones is not necessarily a melody. In an attempt to explain why certain combinations constitute a melody while others do not, various theories have evolved. For example, Theodor Lipps, one of the earliest investigators, considered melody as a unity or whole. He formulated a theory to account for this configuration. For him melody consisted of separate tonal elements which were dominated by a single tone, the tonic.[9] In other words, the single elements were organized around and dominated by the tonic. Such an idea of *subordination* of tones or elements to a chief element was opposed by Max Meyer.[10] He believed that a melody was a unity in itself. This was interpreted as meaning that we simply experience the relationships between tones. To say that tones are related is to say that they form a melody. By "relationship" he understands the "organization" to be the combination of related tones that form a complete structure. Bingham [11] points out that in these two conceptions, three distinguishable characteristics are evident:

1. A relationship between constituent tones
2. Esthetic unity or wholeness
3. Tonality, the domination of the entire sequence by a single tone, the tonic

[9] Th. Lipps, Zur Theorie der Melodie, Z. *Psychol.*, 1902, **27**, 225–63.

[10] M. Meyer, Unscientific methods in musical esthetics, *J. Phil. Psychol. sci. Meth.*, 1904, **1**, 707–15.

[11] W. V. D. Bingham, Studies in melody, *Psychol. Monogr.*, 1910, **12**:3, 1–88.

Meyer's definition stresses the first of these points, and Lipps's stresses the third. Bingham prefers the second of these relationships. This second characteristic has been especially emphasized by the school of Gestalt psychologists. In their studies of perception, they consider the various elements to combine into a whole or configuration which is *not* the same as the sum of its parts. The perception is experienced as a whole, not as perception of separate units. The combination of the elements gives rise to a new perception which can only be attained as a whole experience. A change in any of the elements would alter the entire configuration. For the Gestalt psychologists, then, the elements of a melody seem to cohere, they "belong" together. The entire series is felt as a unity in itself. This is perceived as such and cannot be broken down. Any series of tones which can cohere or be perceived as a whole would constitute a melody because the various elements fit together.

These theories of melody have emphasized the stimulus as determining the melody. Bingham[12] has suggested that the characteristics of a melody can also be described by reference to the responding organism. A *motor theory* finds the beginning of a melody in the upsetting of established muscular tensions. As a tonal sequence proceeds, certain incipient responses become explicit and overt. Each tone heard requires a specific adjustment on the part of the organism, for which a preparation has already been made, and each contributes to a further more definite organization of the attitude of the individual. If a tone appears to be of such a pitch that an utterly new adjustment is necessary, the tone is unrelated, the unity is destroyed. The mere succession of tones is not a melody. The end comes at the time when the balanced tensions can merge into each other and harmoniously resolve their opposing strains. The reason why the close on the tonic has to be prepared for by a leading tone in music phraseology is explained by this theory as follows: the expectations, that

[12] *Ibid.*

is, muscular strains and tensions, are developed followed by a relaxation.

A motor theory, according to Bingham, makes possible a better understanding of the ambiguous statement of the nature of melodic relationships. Unrelated pitches fall apart because each demands its own separate alternative act of adjustment. In the case of related tones, the attitude which appears as a response to the first is a preparation for the response to the second and is completed by the response rather than being destroyed.

The unity which makes the difference between a mere succession of discrete tonal stimuli and a melody does not arise from the tones themselves but is constituted by an act of the listener. When the individual can react adequately to each of the successive tones, the response to the successive members of the series is not merely a group of separate, conflicting acts but the continuation or further elaboration of an act already going forward. The tones are "felt" as related to each other, not as discrete or independent. Finally, when the series of tones comes to a close, that which has been a continuous response is brought to a definite completion, which is the balanced muscular resolution.

The theories so far considered to account for melody class themselves into two sorts, those in which the melody is accounted for on the basis of a *characteristic property of the stimulus object* and those in which the *responding organism* serves as the basis for the melodic configuration. The final answer probably lies somewhere between these two types of theory. What constitutes a melody will be determined both by the responding organism and by the stimulus object. Now, let us consider some of the factors which influence the perception of tones as melody.

Attributes of melody as a stimulus object.—We learned in Chapters 2, 3, and 4 that single tones have certain attributes. This also holds true for melody. From the experimental evidence available to us we are able to discover what some of these are.

PROPINQUITY. Chandler[13] mentions propinquity as a first characteristic of melody. A tonal progression proceeding from one note to another by small intervals gives greater unity and coherence to a series of tones than large skips do. That is, the closeness of the tones gives them organization, so that we are able to call the result a melody. An analysis of melodies shows that skips of sevenths are rarer than skips of seconds and thirds. When large skips do occur, they are usually followed by smaller changes in the interval progression. We notice that the closer any two tones are, the greater is going to be their association by contiguity. The association of tones occurs both in space and time since the melody is a successive combination of tones. Ortmann[14] has experimentally demonstrated the principle of propinquity by analyzing musical scores. He counted the various intervals as they occurred in 160 songs by Schubert, Schumann, Brahms, and R. Strauss. This gave approximately 23,000 intervals. In 97.5 per cent of the songs, unisons and seconds were the first in frequency, with thirds being most common in the other 2.5 per cent. In 60 per cent of the songs, the order in frequency of occurrence was as follows: (1) unison, (2) seconds, (3) thirds, (4) fourths or (1) seconds, (2) unison, (3) thirds, (4) fourths. Taking the total occurrences of all the intervals examined, he found that the order of frequency closely resembled the order of intervals on the scale from smallest to largest with two exceptions. First, octaves, fourths, and fifths were more frequent than their relative order would imply, and second, whole steps were more frequent than half-step intervals.[15]

REPETITION. Another attribute of melody is the repetition of its elements. Ortmann believes this to be the most easily recogniz-

[13] Chandler, *op. cit.*, p. 180.

[14] O. Ortmann, Interval frequency as a determinant of melodic style, *Peabody Bull.*, Dec., 1937, pp. 3–10.

[15] O. Ortmann, On the melodic relativity of tones, *Psychol. Monogr.*, 1926, **35**, 1–47.

able attribute of melody.[16] In tests of tonal memory he found students missed the immediate repetitions of a tone in a five-tone series only six times in 724 cases. The point to be remembered is that melodies frequently involve the repetition of the same notes, and this attribute helps us characterize a particular tonal configuration as a melody.

FINALITY. A third attribute of melody is *finality* or what is often called *cadence*. The feeling of ending expressed by a falling movement of tones or a certain sequence of tones may give the feeling of conclusion, that it is a proper ending. If we consider the tonal progression F-G-E-D-, we expect C to follow and conclude this phrase. Other things being equal, a downward progression is more final than an upward one. However, the feeling of finality is also accounted for by the fact that the last note of the series is one which is often repeated in the phrase or emphasized in the body of the melody. This aspect might be called a subprinciple under that of finality and is known as the *principle of return.*[17] For example, finality is produced by ending on a member of a major triad (C-E-G) in the key of C. In this key the favored ending indicated by Farnsworth, who asked subjects their preferences, was C, with G and E next favored in that order. This does not, of course, tell us why we prefer this ending. To answer this question he trained different groups each to listen to the various endings (C, E, G) in one of the three ways.[18] Results indicated that the endings which had been made familiar to the group received the most votes. Familiarity seemed to be an important factor. Preferred endings are those most familiar, because they are most constantly repeated in music.

We have emphasized that the ending preference in a melody is a result of what we are used to hearing. Certain endings are

[16] O. Ortmann, Some tonal determinants of melodic memory, *J. educ. Psychol.*, 1933, **24**, 454–67.

[17] P. R. Farnsworth, Ending preferences among three positions of the tonic chord, *J. comp. Psychol.*, 1926, **6**, 95–102.

[18] P. R. Farnsworth, The effect of repetition on the ending preferences in melodies, *Amer. J. Psychol.*, 1926, **37**, 116–22.

preferred because they appear more often that way, thus showing the cultural evolution of our music. However, all musicians and psychologists do not follow this interpretation. Meyer has suggested the factor of strain as a possible explanation for our feelings of finality. Rising intervals result in a certain amount of strain, whereas falling intervals suggest relaxation. This type of explanation again attempts to account for melody as being determined by the physiological responses of the organism.

The Lipps-Meyer Law.—A further attempt to explain finality and preference for certain melodic endings has been made on the basis of certain mathematical ratios or relationships between the various tones of a melody. This type of explanation places the determination of melodic endings not necessarily in the response equipment of the organism but in some special feature of the stimulus object. One particular explanation of this type gives the stimulus object certain endowed properties and has been the subject of considerable investigation and speculation. The *Lipps-Meyer Law,* or the "law of the tonic," states that in any tonal sequence, the tone which bears the ratio symbol of 2 is preferred over all others as a melody ending. This was set down by Lipps[19] and has been experimentally demonstrated by Meyer.[20] The tonic effect is a well-known fact in musical aesthetics. Consider a melody consisting of only two tones, C and G (with the ratio 2:3). The majority of listeners will prefer the ending of C. Most classical composers have adhered to this principle of closing a composition on its keynote, which is generally the tonic. In the key of C, we end on C; in the key of G, on G, and so forth. Of course, there are exceptions, particularly in our modern atonal composers such as Alban Berg, or Arnold Schönberg. Meyer states the law as follows: "One of the tones being a pure power of 2, we wish to have this tone at the end of our succession of

[19] Th. Lipps, *Psychologische Studien* (Leipzig: Durr'sche Buchhandlung, 1905).

[20] M. Meyer, *Contributions to a psychological theory of music* (Columbia, Mo.: University of Missouri, 1901); Elements of a psychological theory of melody, *Psychol. Rev.*, 1900, **7**, 241–73.

related tones, our melody."[21] He found in his experimental investigations that the ratio symbol of 2 was preferred over 3 as an ending in a proportion of 77:23.

A few other examples as illustrations will help us see just how this principle might be applied. A minor second (C, C♯), for example, consists of two tones in a frequency ratio of 15:16. To transfer ratio numbers into symbols, we divide by 2 as often as possible so the symbol ratio is 15:2. This gives us a rising effect, supposed to be preferred in this interval. On the other hand take a major second (C, D) which has a frequency ratio of 8:9. Reduced to symbols, we get 2:9. This has a descending trend because the symbol 2 stands for the lower tone. Now consider a perfect fifth (C, G) with a ratio of 2:3. This does not need to be further divided or reduced. The preferred movement in this two-tone interval is from G to C because 2 represents the C. A final example will illustrate this fact. Consider the perfect fourth (C, F). If heard in isolation, we accept it as such, with F being the tone possessing finality. The ratio numbers are 3:4, which reduced to ratio symbols is 3:2. (In reducing the ratio numbers, we divide each number by 2; since 3 will not give a whole number when divided by 2, we leave it as it is.) Add to this interval a third tone G, so that our progression is now C, G, F. This gives an entirely different effect, as the value of F is changed. According to this principle, C now becomes the tonic in relation to G (2:3) and the F no longer is a fourth above C, but rather a natural seventh above the G below.

To recapitulate, according to the law any interval in which there is a "pull" upward or downward will be toward the tone whose ratio is 2 or a power of 2. When the ratio of 2 or its power does not occur, there is no noticeable tendency. Lipps has stated that this tendency for a second tone to return to the first tone, which it "seeks," is natural if a power of 2 exists. The first tone is like a natural gravitational center.

[21] M. Meyer, Experimental studies in the psychology of music, *Amer. J. Psychol.*, 1903, **14**, 456–78.

Bingham[22] also attempted to demonstrate this experimentally. He presented two tones in succession to his subjects and asked them to state whether the second tone gave a feeling of finality. He used tones whose ratios were 2:3, 5:6, 3:5, 15:16, 45:64, 4:5, 9:16, 32:45, 8:9, 8:15, 5:8, and 3:4. Intervals were presented in both ascending and descending sequences. Results showed subjects reported a major third (4:5) and a perfect fifth (2:3) descending gave the greatest effect of finality. The intervals reported to lack finality were ascending and descending diminished fifth (45:64), descending minor second (15:16), ascending minor seventh (9:16) and descending major seventh (8:5). However, they also conform to the law of the power of 2.

It is obvious that other factors effect the preference for endings. Bingham compared the effect of ascending and descending intervals. He found usually a decided preference for the lower tone, such as in an end tone. However, in general his studies do conform to the principle of the tonic.

Farnsworth[23] added further facts on atonic endings which served to extend the scope of the law. He found that when the tonic is absent, the ratio 3 is preferred most frequently as a point for ending a melody. The ratio symbol 5 is next most preferred, and 7 is the least preferred, in proportions of 41, 34, and 25 per cent respectively. By comparing the sequences of E, G, and B flat in the key of C, which do not contain the power of 2 but have ratios of 5:3:7, he asked subjects to give their preferences by telling which tone gave the most final, complete, or restful feeling. Results showed that when G is paired with E as an end tone, G is preferred (3). When E is paired with B flat as an end tone, the E (5) is slightly preferred. G, then, gives the greatest feeling of finality, with E and B flat next. As a result of his studies, he suggests a restatement of the Lipps-Meyer Law as

[22] Bingham, *op. cit.*

[23] P. R. Farnsworth, Atonic endings in melodies, *Amer. J. Psychol.*, 1925, **36**, 394–400.

follows: "The ratio symbols, 2, 3, 5, 7, when employed as endings, display repose effects in the inverse order of their size. Specific training can markedly change this order."[24]

Farnsworth[25] has also attempted to determine whether the preferences for endings can be changed. In doing this he used various tonal sequences and introduced drill periods which consisted of listening to prepared sequences of tonal combinations. The purpose of these periods was to see whether they affected the ending preferences which had already been made. He found that ending preferences can be permanently altered by training, so that increasing the familiarity with a certain ending results in an increasing preference for it.

Updegraff[26] attempted finally to answer the question of whether the finality feeling which is reportedly present in a tonic ending is determined by mathematical relationship (power of 2) of the vibrations or by tonal sequences to which the individual is accustomed. In other words, should the explanation for tonic be made on the basis of inherent characteristics in the stimulus object or in terms of the cultural conditioning? In her first experiment she presented twenty pairs of four-note melodies to subjects half of whom had more than three years of musical training in instrumental work and at least one year in theory. The other half had little or no instrumental training and no theory. The object of this experiment was to determine which was more influential in determining finality, the resolution of suggested harmony or the power-of-2 ending. The first three notes of each pair were the same (diminished seventh chord). The vibration ratio of the last (the fourth) note of one melody was in a power-of-2 ratio to the first note. In the second melody, the last note was the resolution of the chord. The subjects were asked to

[24] P. R. Farnsworth, A modification of the Lipps-Meyer law, *J. exp. Psychol.*, 1926, **9**, 253–58.

[25] P. R. Farnsworth, The effect of repetition on ending preferences in melodies, *Amer. J. Psychol.*, 1926, **37**, 116–22.

[26] R. Updegraff, A preliminary study of the nature of finality in melody, *Proc. Ia. Acad. Sci.*, 1926, **23**, 279–82.

indicate which melody left them with a more final feeling. Finality was explained as a feeling of rest. The resolution of the chord was judged to be most final (50 per cent) as against the power-of-2 ending (44 per cent), 6 per cent being uncertain. These melodies were presented on the piano in such a way that the last notes were approached from above and below an equal number of times. There was a decided preference for a falling inflection, 59 per cent as against 34 per cent for rising ones. A resolution ending was preferred to a power-of-2 ending, even when the rising inflection was given.

In another experiment in the same series, this investigator presented five melodies to American and Chinese students. Each was nine notes long and played in the tempered scale and in the Chinese scale. The rhythms in both series were the same, so this factor was held constant. Results showed the Chinese students judged 52 per cent of their own melodies final as opposed to 44 per cent of American melodies. The American students considered 64 per cent of their own melodies final as against 34 per cent of the Chinese melodies. On the basis of this evidence she concluded:

> Our results, so far, point against Meyer's conclusions that finality is based on a mathematical relationship. It is rather determined, in addition to the influence of the falling inflection, by the suggested tonality of the melody, and, therefore, by the experience of the observer.[27]

Summary: an interbehavioral interpretation of melody.—From our survey of the studies, we find that what constitutes a melody is a function of both the previous experience of the responding organism and certain characteristics of the stimulus. Farnsworth[28] has shown us that familiarity with certain endings in melody is an important factor in determining preferences. He found people preferred endings which they were used to hearing.

[27] *Ibid.*, p. 282.

[28] Farnsworth, *Amer. J. Psychol.*, 1926, **37**, 116–22.

Certain endings are preferred because they are the ones which constantly appear in music.

Music in our Western civilization has developed certain prescribed forms. Some intervals do not follow each other well, and other successions of tones are considered to be strange or trite. This attitude of what is correct has been imposed upon us by composers and adherents who have followed these principles. Of course, musicians are searching for new ways of expressing themselves in an attempt to replace the old methods which have become monotonous to some.

What we perceive as melody is not any haphazard combination of tones. It is the result of the many centuries of musical development along with the scale and harmonic evolution. The particular tones which we include in our melodies are dependent upon the kind of scale we employ. Scales are used to simplify and standardize notation so that the melodies derived from them can have some lasting communicative value. The octave can actually be divided into any number of equal or unequal parts provided that the divisions are not so numerous that the average person cannot detect the differences in pitch.

Once more we find that the origins of melody are cultural in nature, being functions of musical development from early times. The strange and dissonant quality which we note in Chinese, Javanese, or Siamese music bears witness to this fact. Thus, scales, particular progressions of tones followed, and endings used are all peculiar to each different civilization.

Harmony

When tones occur simultaneously rather than in succession, the listener perceives a stimulus of a different sort. This simultaneous combination of tones serves as the unit for harmonic writing, just as the single tone served as a unit for melodic composition. The term "harmony" in a musical context refers to the progression of these simultaneous sets of tones. This progression can be *homophonic,* of the sort where there is one main voice or melody and the remaining parts serve to enhance it and are subordinate to it. A melody is combined with other tones and the progression which takes place is usually dictated by the melodic pattern. The tones are usually lower with the melody in the top voice, where it is most easily heard. However, this need not always be the case, as sometimes the melody may be in one of the lower voices. At any rate, the other tones serve to enhance the melody and the perception becomes a more complex kind of response. Harmonic progression may also be of the *polyphonic* sort, where there are two or more equally significant voices (melodies) occurring simultaneously.

The development of harmonic writing.—The general characteristic of Western music from the Greeks until about the tenth century A.D. was that of *unison.* In early times music did not need harmonization nor did it progress in any measured time.[29] Biblical psalms were often taken as texts in the early Christian era, and the movement of the voices was like that of free recitation. Of the creators of such music little is known. The two names most often associated with this early Christian period were Ambrosius, Bishop of Milan about 390 A.D., and Pope Gregory the Great 200 years later. The latter legitimized music as an important part of the worship of the church. The Gregorian plain song was probably the greatest contribution to music in the first ten centuries A.D.[30] Music thus became a part of the celebration of the mass and was performed similarly in various places. This was a style of music in which the scales were named "Gregorian modes" and were modeled after the Greek modes. They consisted of a succession of whole and half tones corresponding to the intervals found in our major scale. Notation was originally by letters as in the Greek system, but in the eighth

[29] P. Bekker, *The story of music* (New York: W. W. Norton & Co., Inc., 1926), p. 10.
[30] *Ibid.*, p. 49.

century a system involving a number of graphic signs placed over the words evolved to suggest the trend of the melody.

The first attempts to combine sounds are unknown.[31] A form known as the *drone bass* in which one part sang a continuous bass note to another moving part may have been the earliest form. Also due to the various ranges of the human voice, octave singing has probably existed from earliest times. During the Middle Ages, singing in the lower voices appeared, at a distance of a fourth or a fifth below the upper. This custom has been recorded in the words of writers of the tenth and eleventh centuries. It was known as the *organum.* Eventually two and three parts were added to the original melody at distances of a fourth, fifth, and octave from each other, so that they usually moved in parallel courses.

In the eleventh and twelfth centuries, an attempt was made to relieve the monotony of this style. Other intervals were introduced, called *symphonics.* Thus, a composer could take a known melody as a basis or *cantus firmus* and add an additional part to be sung along with it. This might differ in rhythm and involve a few other intervals beside the fourth, fifth, and octave. The term *descant* or singing apart was applied to this type of writing, which came from secular influences. The melody was rather free-moving and was sung along with and usually above the main cantus. Without intending to do so, this style of writing allowed the use of thirds and sixths, which previously had been forbidden. The descant reached its culmination in the double descant or *faux bourdon,* which consisted of three parts but was essentially homophonic in nature, allowing consecutive fifths and octaves, which were later forbidden in harmonic writing.

Finally, the stage was set for *counterpoint.* It was soon discovered that a great many possibilities for the development of this principle were available. About 1200 A.D., counterpoint, as it came to be called (originally *punctum contra punctum*) was

[31] C. G. Hamilton, *Outlines of music history* (Bryn Mawr, Pa.: Oliver Ditson Co., Inc., 1924).

developed. Beginning by adding a simple melody to the given cantus, it later permitted adding three or four or sometimes more parts. Various schools of contrapuntal writing emerged in the next centuries. They developed in various parts of Europe, the Netherlands, northern France, Venice, and Rome, as well as elsewhere. Counterpoint continued in popularity and is considered to have had its greatest expression in the works of Johann Sebastian Bach (1685–1750).

Counterpoint is *polyphonic* writing, consisting of the combination of various melodies following accepted rules of agreement and contrast. These rules usually did not allow for consecutive fifths or octaves, and contrary motion of voices was emphasized. In polyphonic writing, chords are merely chance happenings determined solely by the progression of the separate melodies.

During the Renaissance, a new technique was invented in which a single melody had its accompanying parts subordinated. This was the harmony or *homophonic* writing which we now recognize. Chords were treated as entities and subject to the inversions which we use today. In homophonic writing the chords take a leading place. This style became extremely popular and probably had its first great expression in the works of Claudio Monteverdi (1567–1643). The sixteenth century was largely polyphonic in style, but as time progressed homophonic writing became increasingly more popular. Of course, the transition was gradual and such composers as Monteverdi used it only in part. Today, both forms still exist and most of the composers of the classical, romantic, and modern periods have employed both styles.

Consonance and dissonance in harmonic writing.—In the early compositions, octaves, fifths, and fourths were regarded as the most consonant intervals. This was interpreted as meaning that they sounded well together. As time progressed, the thirds and sixths were also allowed and considered as consonant. Seconds and sevenths were regarded as dissonant and were to be avoided as often as possible, to be used only when necessary as passing tones. As we shall see in the next chapter, there is no real sharp line which can be drawn between consonance and dissonance. Particular chords which are considered consonant or dissonant are usually referred to as *concords* and *discords*; for, strictly speaking, consonance and dissonance refer only to two-tone clangs.

The cultural nature of harmonic writing.—In both counterpoint and harmony, innumerable rules have been elaborated. Some of these are superfluous, but their justification lies mainly in a certain practical aid to the beginning student of musical composition. "One must learn the rules before he can break them" is a common adage in musical composition classes.

Like melody, harmony has its principles of progression, indicating which harmonies may follow one another and which may not. Many of the same melodic principles hold for harmony, particularly those of propinquity and finality. Textbooks in harmony lay down certain rules which the aspirant student must follow or risk failure in his course of study for continued violation. The rules set down follow in a general fashion the form of composers who are held in the highest regard. From time to time rules are broken and changed, even by the most fastidious composers.

Many of the harmonic progressions which we hear and enjoy today are the result of centuries of the same practice. Certain conventional forms have arisen. When a new composer comes into the public eye with different ideas about writing harmonic progressions, he may be criticized and scorned in his time as being radical, and his music may sound quite unpleasant, even to the sophisticated ear. With repetition, we become accustomed to the new harmonic progressions and may accept them. Contemporary modern music deviates quite radically from the standard practices of the classical and romantic periods, and today it is considered by some to be odd and unpleasant-sounding, but to others who have become accustomed to the new styles and progressions, it is interesting and enjoyable.

There does not seem to be anything inherent either in melodic or harmonic progressions which makes them correct or incorrect. Interesting examples of new forms of harmonic and melodic writing are coming into use, such as the *polytonal* music of Darius Milhaud, in which the voices or instruments each play in a different key, or the *atonal* writing of Arnold Schönberg, where no key signature is used at all. Whether or not these styles will survive remains to be seen, but they do illustrate the cultural evolution of musical styles.

Chapter 6

THE COMBINATION OF TONES: CONSONANCE AND DISSONANCE

We are now ready to consider some of the ways in which individuals respond to tones in combination. When tones are played together, we may judge them as consonant or dissonant. We ask ourselves, then, what does this mean? Why do some tonal combinations sound consonant and others dissonant? What aspects of the stimulus and response give rise to these judgments? Consonance and dissonance judgments in music are usually made as responses to simple two-tone clangs. When three or more notes are played, the terms "concord" and "discord" are often applied. However, this distinction between the two sets of terms is far from a universal one.

Reporting what constitutes a consonant or dissonant interval in music is one of the oldest problems confronting the psychologist interested in music. If we will remember that here, as in other discussions of musical behavior, we are dealing with a special sort of response to stimuli called musical, much of our confusion will immediately be eliminated.

In this chapter we will attempt to survey some of the better-known attempts to explain these responses and try to arrive at an answer which is in keeping with what are considered the data of psychology.

The controversy over the nature of consonance and dissonance has been a lively and speculative one. Not as much has been written about it recently as in previous years, but the problem still remains unsolved for some.

Helmholtz theory.—One of the earliest answers of a psychological nature came from H. L. F. von Helmholtz.[1] Consonance, he said, was continuous tonal sensation, while dissonance referred to an intermittent sensation. Thus, consonance occurred when tones sounded together possessed identical overtones. Tones sounded together which gave a rough sensory quality due to beating were judged as dissonant. When the primary tones were so far apart on the scale that the beating could not occur from sounding the fundamentals, dissonance was explained by reference to the beatings of the partials or overtones. The criterion for consonance, then, was the absence of beats which would be heard as roughness. And contrariwise, dissonance was due to the rough sensation caused by beating. This beating could be due either to fundamentals or to partials. In Chapter 3 we recognized the fact that tones which have frequencies fairly close together may beat rapidly, giving rise to a perception of roughness. However, the objection which immediately arises is: How can all dissonance be accounted for by beating? This explanation is based on judgments of the natural properties of the stimulus object.

Stumpf.—One of the first to voice an objection to Helmholtz's theory was Carl Stumpf, who set forth an alternate theory in his *Tonpsychologie.*[2] If dissonance is due to beating of fundamentals or their overtones, how does it happen that it may occur in the absence of any beating? Play two tones simultaneously (700 and 1,000 cps.), and many will report a dissonant interval which will be free from beats. Stumpf further observed that dissonance can be produced when one sounds two tuning forks at an intensity which is too weak to produce beating.

Stumpf called his explanation a theory of fusion. Two clangs were judged consonant to the degree that they could fuse into a single tone sensation. That is, the listener experienced two

[1] H. L. F. von Helmholtz, *On the sensations of tone,* trans. Ellis (4th ed.; London: Longmans, Green & Co., 1912).

[2] C. Stumpf, *Tonpsychologie* (Leipzig: S. Hirzel, 1883–90).

tonal elements as one. Since two tones sounded together gave the impression of a single tone in *different degrees,* the more they were heard as one, or fused, the greater the consonance. Fusion did not mean merely the perception of a single tone, but a unitary impression which defied further analysis. The blending or fusion of tones was characteristically inherent in themselves. It was again due to a natural property of the sound just as roughness or color may be natural properties of visual objects. Stumpf, then, said it would take no special act of the mind to establish consonance or dissonance in tonal sensations, for the greater the fusion the greater the consonance. He recognized various degrees of fusion, beginning with the octave as the most perfect or consonant interval, next the perfect fifth, then the fourth, third, and sixth in that order.

In establishing this order of consonance or fusion, he set forth certain laws of fusion:

1. Consonance is a function of the vibration ratio of the tones (octave, fifth, etc.) and is independent of the region of the musical scale in which the tones occur.
2. The degree of consonance is the same for the intervals beyond the octave as for those within it.
3. Consonance is independent of timbre, intensity of tones, or the relative location of source of the tone.

This theory is especially significant in that it followed Helmholtz, who had tried to find some physical basis for *consonance.* Stumpf, finding that Helmholtz was unsuccessful, decided that any physical analysis was impossible and so resorted to *fusion,* which he said could not be further analyzed, since it was inherent in the nature of the object.

Krueger.—A theory set forth by Felix Krueger[3] differs only slightly from that of Helmholtz. This explanation shifts the explanation of dissonance from the beating fundamentals or

[3] F. Krueger, Die Theorie der Konsonanz, *Psychol. Studien,* 1910, **5,** 294–409.

overtones to the beating difference tones. All dissonant intervals contain difference tones that beat. Consonant intervals are free from the difference tone beats and contain only pure unisons because the difference tones coincide or are at least in a 2:1 ratio. The psychic effect is consonance, as contrasted with the blurred quality of dissonance. The same objections apply here as in the case of the Helmholtz theory.

Ogden.—Specifically, Robert M. Ogden [4] objected to Krueger's theory as being no more satisfactory than that of Helmholtz. In the first place, difference tones are weak and inaudible in most cases. Helmholtz and Krueger developed theories which depend on the interaction (beating) of components within the sound mass. Helmholtz is in error because partials or overtones (which beat) may be completely absent and the interval is still dissonant, and Krueger because his derivation of difference tones is incorrect. As an alternative, Ogden fosters a theory stating that intervals are consonant because of a racial adaptation due to hearing them in the "chord of nature." Developed over innumerable generations, the "chord of nature" contains every partial in a harmonic series. Thus, the consonant intervals are the ones most conspicuous among the partials of a tone. "Consonance," says Ogden, "depends upon a dispositional readiness to perceive as a uniform impression any simultaneous combination of tones embracing intervals that have been frequently encountered as inherited and individual adaptation." [5]

Lipps.—For his explanation of consonance, Theodor Lipps resorted to what he called *micropsychic rhythms.*[6] In this arrangement, the mind became an unconscious calculator. Each physical vibration causes a separate unconscious vibration (psychophysical

[4] R. M. Ogden, A contribution to the theory of tonal consonance, *Psychol. Bull.*, 1909, **6**, 297–303.

[5] R. M. Ogden, *Hearing* (New York: Harcourt, Brace & Co., Inc., 1924), p. 144.

[6] Th. Lipps, *Psychologische Studien* (Leipzig: Durr'sche Buchhandlung, 1905).

parallelism). When the rhythms bear a simple ratio to each other, the experience is a consonant one; the more complicated the ratio, the greater the dissonance. The micropsychic rhythms correspond to the vibration frequency of a tone. The degree of consonance will depend on this vibration ratio. The system, as Lipps saw it, operated as follows. For example, let us sound together two tones, 100 and 200 cps. The micropsychic rhythms will be set up accordingly. Here we have every second beat of the 200 corresponding with one of the successive beats of the 100. The octave is the most consonant because its micropsychic rhythm coincides most often. As this coincidence decreases, the intervals become less consonant and more dissonant. Such an explanation in terms of the subconscious psychic rhythms accounts for nothing more than an acceptance of the problem as its own solution.

Moore.—More recently, Henry T. Moore[7] has brought forth what he calls a genetic theory of consonance. The degree of consonance of an interval increases as a result of the frequency with which that interval has been heard by the individual or his ancestors. Further, each interval in its development undergoes a characteristic affective (pleasing-displeasing) development corresponding to the different stages in its course. There is a rise in affective value of a consonant interval up to a certain point, with increasing repetition and consonance followed by an affective decline. The octave, which may be judged the most consonant of all intervals, is not the most pleasant.

For an explanation of this change in consonance, he says, we must look into man's history, individually as well as collectively. Looking back into the history of music, Moore reports that the fifth appears to have been the most pleasant interval for a ninth century listener. After repeated hearing, the fifth became a less interesting interval and the third came into vogue. For a tenth century listener, a minor seventh was, Moore believes, a discour-

[7] H. T. Moore, The genetic aspect of consonance and dissonance, *Psychol. Monogr.*, 1914, **17**:2 (Whole No. 73), 1–68.

aging complex, but more frequent hearing made it more attractive. At some future time, this will rank as a consonant interval. When this happens, according to Moore, it will be the most pleasurable of all intervals because it makes more demands on the mind than any other previous consonance. For any single individual, the degree of synthesis will depend on the number of times the interval has been heard by the person or by his ancestors.

> . . . If thirds are acquired as consonance in one generation, they will be heard so much the more by the next and therefore become more completely consonant. We may accordingly interpret the degree of synthesis of a given interval either in Lamarckian fashion as being part of congenital association resulting from race experience or, in accordance with Weismann, as resulting entirely from an individual experience which has had the benefit of the accumulations of the race.[8]

First, the degree of consonance of any interval will depend directly on the degree to which the mind is able to synthesize the two tonal elements into a unified whole.

Second, the degree of pleasure derived will depend on how successful the mind is in accomplishing the synthesis. If it is barely successful in fusing the two tones; if, that is, the fusion is accomplished with difficulty, one will derive the greatest amount of pleasure. If the synthesis is accomplished without effort, and one has little awareness of his accomplishment, there will be little pleasure. Finally, if in spite of his efforts, one is unable to synthesize the complex of tones, he will experience acute displeasure.

This theory makes an attempt to explain not only how consonance occurs, but also the reason for our liking and disliking certain intervals.

Evaluation of these theories.—In general, these theories suggest explanations of consonance in terms of (*a*) numerical relationships (Lipps's micropsychic rhythms), (*b*) absence of beats

[8] *Ibid.*

(Helmholtz, Krueger), (*c*) genetics (Ogden, Moore), and (*d*) fusion (Stumpf).

1. As far as numerical relations are concerned, a theory which appeals to unconscious calculations as an explanation gives a mentalistic solution. This type of explanation has been found inadequate by performing the simple experiment of taking a consonant interval (200:300 cps.) then mistuning it to 201:300 (Peterson and Smith).[9] This mistuning should upset the micro-psychic rhythms, according to the theory, and cause dissonance, but it does not. The human ear finds it difficult to perceive a difference between the interval with a ratio of 200:301 cps. and that with a ratio of 200:300 cps.

2. We have already reported that two tones may beat without causing dissonance and that intervals are reported dissonant in which no beating occurs. This is sufficient evidence to refute any theory (such as those of Helmholtz or Krueger) which seeks an absence of beats as an explanation of consonance.

3. Any theory which implies the inheritance of acquired characteristics (Moore, Ogden) need not be taken seriously today in the light of our present knowledge of genetics. Acquired characteristics are not inherited. Further, if Moore's "infinity of limit" explanation, which expects all musical intervals to reach an affective peak followed by a gradual decline, is correct, we may expect music eventually to die out as an art, because after we have been able to synthesize all prevailing intervals, their aesthetic value will decline, leaving only an attitude of indifference among the listeners.

4. A theory which attributes consonance to fusion as a natural property of the sound waves (Stumpf) seems unlikely, as our judgments of consonance do change. According to this theory, consonance would be the same for everyone and not subject to modification. This latter point will be elaborated in the following section.

[9] J. Peterson and F. W. Smith, The range and modifiability of consonance in certain musical intervals, *Amer. J. Psychol.*, 1930, **42**, 561–72.

Toward a solution: a cultural theory.[10]—One of the greatest difficulties encountered in attempting a solution of any problem in consonance theory is the disagreement in the use of terms. According to Seashore,[11] consonance judgments are made in terms of smoothness, blending, or fusion. However, if we are asked to apply all three in our judgment of any interval, we are really being asked to apply conflicting judgments. Seashore demonstrated this when he asked a group of psychologists and musicians to judge intervals as consonant or dissonant, using these criteria separately. Bugg[12] also found that more reliable results could be obtained in consonance judgments when the criteria (blending, smoothness, purity, etc.) were applied separately rather than together.

If we consider that responses of consonant or dissonant, like other musical responses, are influenced by our cultural background, the reason for such diversity of criteria becomes clear. Moore[13] has pointed out how the consonance value of intervals has changed throughout the history of music. However, he has found it necessary to appeal to some sort of genetics for the transmission of the cultural change, although he admits the possibility of a social transmission.

It is one of the fundamental aims of this book to show that musical responses are acquired through one's life history. We have already demonstrated this principle as applied to pitch discrimination. In considering a cultural theory of consonance, we realize that a large part of anyone's responses are culturally determined. Our musical discriminatory reactions are no exception. Whether we judge a particular interval as consonant or dissonant will depend on the conditions under which we build up our mu-

[10] R. W. Lundin, Toward a cultural theory of consonance, *J. Psychol.*, 1947, **28**, 45–49.

[11] C. E. Seashore, *Psychology of music* (New York: McGraw-Hill Book Co., Inc., 1938).

[12] E. G. Bugg, An experimental study of factors influencing consonance judgments, *Psychol. Monogr.*, 1933, **45**:2 (Whole No. 201).

[13] Moore, *op. cit.*

sical behavior. These conditions refer, not only to one's intimate musical surroundings, but in general to his whole musical culture. We, therefore, include not only the general Western musical culture but also our own family, school, and other intimate sources of musical stimulation.

Evidence for a cultural theory.—That the consonance or dissonance of a musical interval is merely an individual judgment which is culturally determined, rather than caused by some absolute property of the stimuli, is supported by the following evidence from the experimental literature.

1. Concerning the criteria for consonance, we mentioned the fact that different individuals will select different criteria for their judgments and that these will vary according to the culture selected. Bugg[14] has further demonstrated that musically untrained people were more influenced by affective factors (liking or disliking an interval) than were trained ones. That is, if the subjects liked an interval, they called it consonant, and if they disliked it, they called it dissonant. Valentine[15] has demonstrated that children's preferences also differ between different school groups. For example, his study indicated that children at six and seven years of age showed no constant preference for consonance over dissonance. As the children grew older, preferences for certain concords were shown. It is obvious, then, that what we call consonance depends on the particular criteria we select, and these will be a function of the particular musical culture we live in. Individual judgments will differ from group to group and individual to individual, since no two people are subjected to entirely the same sort of musical stimuli during their development.

2. Further evidence to support a cultural theory shows that judgments of consonance may be modified. In another study,

[14] E. G. Bugg, An analysis of conditions influencing consonance judgments, *J. exp. Psychol.*, 1939, **24**, 54–72.

[15] C. W. Valentine, The aesthetic appreciation of musical intervals among school children and adults, *Brit. J. Psychol.*, 1913, **6**, 190–216.

Valentine[16] found that consonance judgments may change according to the method used in presenting the intervals. Moore, in his extensive study[17] on consonance, found that the repetition of dissonant intervals made them more consonant. Finally, Meyer,[18] experimenting with quarter-tone music composed in an Asiatic style, found that the subjects reported it displeasing at first, but further repetition increased their liking for it.

3. Our judgments of consonance are comparative rather than absolute. We must remember that these judgments are made in a musical context. Those who believe the ability to judge consonance to be an elementary, unchangeable musical trait base their discussion on intervals which are heard in isolation.[19] Gardner and Pickford[20] have investigated judgments of certain dissonant intervals played in a musical context. Passages from musical literature, each of which contained a dissonant chord, were presented to thirty observers. Analysis of the results indicated that the dissonance level of each test chord was not even approximately constant but varied with its musical setting, so that the dissonance as reported depended more on the relation in which it stood than on the nature of the intervals themselves.

The support for a cultural theory has shown that consonance is not an absolute judgment based on mere natural properties of the stimulus object, as was supposed by previous theorists and investigators. The particular stimulus function, consonant or dissonant, that a stimulus interval will have is culturally acquired. There is no reason to believe that any intervals are absolutely consonant or dissonant. The judgment which we make will be

[16] C. W. Valentine, The method of comparison in experiments with musical intervals and the effect of practice on the appreciation of discord, *Brit. J. Psychol.*, 1914–15, **7**, 118–35.

[17] Moore, *op. cit.*

[18] M. Meyer, Experimental studies in the psychology of music: III. Quartertone Music, *Amer. J. Psychol.*, 1903, **14**, 207–14.

[19] D. L. Larson, An experimental critique of the Seashore consonance test, *Psychol. Monogr.*, 1928, **38**, 49–81. (See also note 11 above.)

[20] P. A. D. Gardner and R. W. Pickford, Relation between dissonance and context, *Nature*, 1943, **152**, 356.

a function of many conditions. Some of these we have mentioned: the particular criterion which one selects as a standard for his judgment, previous experience with the interval, the context in which the interval appears, and general and specific cultural background so far as music is concerned, and more particularly so far as consonance and dissonance are concerned.

Chapter 7

RHYTHM AS STIMULUS AND RESPONSE

ALONG with musical tones, melody, and harmony, rhythm constitutes another important factor in the musical event. In this context, rhythm refers to the temporal pattern that the tonal stimuli follow. In this analysis it will be necessary to limit our discussion to rhythms as they occur in music, leaving the problems of rhythm in other forms for some future study.

Rhythm must be considered both as a stimulus object and as a response of the organism. On the stimulus side, it includes such things as markings on a printed page of music, a series of auditory beats or the particular temporal pattern some tonal stimuli follow. On the response side, rhythm is both perceptual and motor. It is often very difficult to separate the two kinds of reaction, since in any rhythmic response the entire organism is usually involved. The perceptual side is emphasized when we simply listen to a rhythmic pattern or analyze some composition for its rhythmic content. The motor aspects of the responses are evident in actual performance, such as playing a series of tones on a musical instrument in a particular rhythm or simply tapping a beat with our hands or fingers. In performing a musical composition, rhythm is one of the variables in the event. Actually, the perceptual and motor activities are interdependent. The mere listening to a composition involves motor responses which can be either quite overt or implicit, and in the actual performance of rhythm a perception of the pattern must also occur. In performance, of course, the motor reactions are more obvious.

Rhythm as a Stimulus

The characterization of the rhythmic stimulus is best understood by considering a hierarchy of groupings which can be analyzed for purposes of study. At the bottom of this hierarchy we would find the simplest and least divisible rhythmic unit or what is often called the *unit group*. Examples are the iamb, trochee, dactyl, etc. When the simple unit groups are combined, a sequence of simple unit groups is referred to as a *rhythmic line*. Finally, when two or more rhythmic lines occur simultaneously, as in most compositions involving more than one voice, the result is a *rhythmic pattern*.

The unit groups.–The seven basic rhythmic units listed by Mursell,[1] who has combined the analyses of Raymond B. Stetson[2] and George H. Wedge,[3] are:

Iamb	– /	Anapaest	– – /
Trochee	/ –	Amphibrach	– / –
Dactyl	/ – –	Tremolo	– – –
		Single beat	/ /

In this scheme the / represents the accented beat. One of the first characteristics of a unit group is that it contains only one strong beat (except for single beat and tremolo). Secondly, a unit is distinguished by its *form* as seen in the diagram, and finally these are *musical* rhythms and not poetic ones, although some similarities do occur. However, the tremolo and single beats seldom if ever appear in poetry.

The *iamb* is a simple unit in which one unaccented beat is followed by an accented one. This may be visually understood by observing an orchestral conductor who wishes to indicate an attack by means of a preliminary movement which then leads in

[1] J. Mursell, *The psychology of music* (New York: W. W. Norton & Co., Inc., 1937).

[2] R. B. Stetson, A motor theory of rhythm and discrete sensation, *Psychol. Rev.*, 1905, **12**, 250–70, 293–350.

[3] G. H. Wedge, *Rhythm in music: a textbook* (New York: G. Schirmer, Inc., 1927).

to the downbeat. The iamb is common in all forms of music, both simple and complex. Mursell[4] gives a good example of this rhythm in the first bars of Schumann's "Träumerei."

The *trochee* is just the reverse of the iamb. A strong element is followed by a weak one. This is very common in most march rhythms either in $\frac{2}{2}$ or $\frac{2}{4}$ time. Consider various pieces of music in which the accents fall on the first and third beats, and we have examples of the double trochee.

The *dactyl* is a slightly more complex form in that it involves three beats, the first accented, followed by two unaccented ones. This is popular in waltz rhythms, where a strong beat is succeeded by two weak ones. Perhaps an even more obvious example, although not particularly aesthetic, occurs in the accompaniment rhythm of the old German band tunes, where the tuba or some other bass instrument keeps the time moving by playing in the familiar oom-pah-pah fashion.

The *anapaest* is just the reverse of the dactyl, being made up of two weak beats followed by a strong one. Some authorities question the validity of such a rhythm, insisting that it can be analyzed into other forms. However, when we consider rhythms found in many Latin American dances such as the rumba, this form is obvious.

The *amphibrach* contains three beats: a strong one preceded and followed by weak ones.

Thus far our discussion has considered rhythms which can be found in poetry also. The next two rarely, if ever, occur in that art form. The *single beat* is just what the term implies, a series of equally strong beats where the accent falls on each beat. This most obviously occurs in music played in a slow tempo. Parts of the "Transformation Scene" from *Parsifal* by Wagner or the "Dead March" from *Saul* by Handel would exemplify this rhythmic unit. The *tremolo* has been described by Stetson[5] as a rapid series of even, light beats. It appears in all sorts of music

[4] Mursell, *op. cit.*, p. 179.
[5] Stetson, *op. cit.*

such as the tympani roll, the trill, or the unshaded scale run. Just as the single beat becomes more obvious in a slow tempo, the tremolo occurs most frequently in fast passages where a series of notes is played without accent.

The rhythmic line.—Rhythmic units in music almost always occur in combinations, and our analysis so far has only considered the simplest units, those which presumably cannot be further divided. As soon as two or more of these simple units combine, the result is a *rhythmic line.* The particular kind of rhythmic line we hear is frequently going to be partially determined by the nature of the melody as well as the harmony. Often, rules of harmony and melody serve to determine the extent and form of the particular rhythmic line. We know of no hard and fast rules for subdividing the rhythmic line into its component units. Mursell [6] points out that such divisions are dependent upon one's own aesthetic perception of what seems appropriate and any possible muscular reactions which seem comfortable in terms of tensions and relaxation.

The rhythmic pattern.—It is quite possible and frequently common to have two different rhythmic lines occurring at the same time. We have spoken in Chapter 5 of *polytonality* in which two or more melodic lines occur, each in a different key. *Polyrhythms* also occur. However, unlike polytonality, which is limited mainly to modern music, polyrhythms or rhythmic patterns are the usual form in most compositions, classical as well as modern. In modern music the polyrhythms are probably the most obvious. Various unique and rather complicated rhythmic lines occur simultaneously and are often given greater emphasis by the composer than the tonal patterns. These latter often become of secondary importance so far as perception is concerned. It is the rhythms which command the greatest interest, and without them the tonal elements often give to many listeners the impression of being dull, monotonous, and senseless.

[6] Mursell, *op. cit.*, p. 188.

However, *rhythmic patterns* are not limited to modern music. They may be found in this style in obvious and exaggerated forms. Nevertheless, polyrhythms or rhythmic patterns occur in the music of all our great composers. The fact that more than one rhythm occurs at once gives interest and aesthetic value to the composition. Compare a Gregorian chant, which is monorhythmic (one rhythmic line), and almost any orchestral composition, where several rhythmic lines occur simultaneously. The latter is far more musical. Of course, many chorales and hymns are monorhythmic and musically very desirable, but in the main these compositions are fairly short in length, and the melodic and harmonic progressions hold the musical value.

Rhythm as a Response

Having considered the characteristics of rhythm as a stimulus object, let us now turn to the rhythmic response.

The rhythmic response is a perceptual-motor one.—The perceptual side is evident when one *observes* or listens to the various groupings of the rhythmic stimuli. This need not be entirely implicit. Consider for a moment the behavior of an audience listening to a symphony concert. Some people may be tapping their fingers ever so slightly in time to the music, others may be moving their programs in rhythm, while still others may be swaying the entire upper half of the body. Of course, some may appear relaxed so that we are able to observe very little. This does not mean, however, that no muscular responses are being made. Perhaps these slight muscular movements are concealed by articles of clothing. If the proper apparatus were available, action currents could be measured, as demonstrated by the studies of Max[7] and Jacobson.[8]

[7] L. W. Max, Action-current responses in the deaf during awakening, kinaesthetic imagery, and abstract thinking, *J. comp. Psychol.*, 1937, **24**, 301–44.

[8] E. Jacobson, Electrophysiology of mental activities, *Amer. J. Psychol.*, 1932, **44**, 677–94.

In musical performance the overt motor rhythmic responses are most obvious, but a perceptual reaction to the notation of the printed score is necessary too. Observe the complex behavior of a drummer or player of some other percussion instrument. These rhythmic responses involve the entire organism. The fatigue reported by musicians after a concert or a period of practice is partly the result of these motor rhythmic reactions. It is obvious that the rhythmic response is not an isolated one. When listening to music we react to the *tonal* aspects of the stimulus as well as the *rhythmic* aspects. We have treated these two characteristics separately for convenience in discussion, but the musical reaction involves both.

The rhythmic response is an organizational one.—The perceptual *organization* of separate rhythmic stimuli involves also a *differentiation* of stimuli. The organizational nature of rhythm may be demonstrated when we listen to a series of uniform clicks spaced at equal intervals in time. We often tend to perceive these regular stimuli in groups or phrases, often placing greater emphasis on one aspect than another. Instead of hearing a series as click-click-click, etc., we may group them as CLICK-click-click or CLICK-click CLICK-click, etc. The Gestalt psychologists [9] considered this tendency to group the stimuli as an example of the "primitive organization of behavior," stating that this tendency to perceive single units as groups is an inherent characteristic of the organism and is uninfluenced by learning. Seashore [10] has called this organization of single, unaccented beats "subjective rhythm" to distinguish it from "objective rhythm," where the organization of the stimuli is already made for the listener by accents and inheres as a property of the stimulus object. He also claims that the capacity for "subjective rhythm" is inherent in the organism and occurs without training. How-

[9] K. Koffka, Experimental-Untersuchungen zur Lehre von Rhythmus, Z. *Psychol.*, 1909, **52**, 1–109.

[10] C. E. Seashore, *In search of beauty in music* (New York: The Ronald Press Co., 1947).

ever, there does not appear to be any substantial evidence in support of such a view. It is our contention that such an ability to organize equal-appearing auditory stimuli into groups is just as much dependent on learning as are other kinds of musical behavior. At any rate, the organizational quality of rhythm is an important characteristic of the response, whether it is implied in the printed score or initiated by the organism itself.

To facilitate the organization of stimuli or make what we have referred to as "objective rhythm" more apparent, a device called *accentuation* is employed. This is possible through manipulating the stimuli in different ways, for example increasing the *intensity* of one of the members of the rhythmic group, *prolonging* one of the beats, or changing the *quality* of one of the tones. The aim of accenting is to facilitate the particular organization of the stimuli in whatever groupings one desires.

Accents are generally produced by an increase in the intensity or length of the stimulus. If the first one of a group of beats is more intense than the others, this serves to organize them into a group. An increase in the length of a *pause* between beats or a *prolonging* of a beat at the end of a group also helps organization. The organist makes use of the prolongation of certain tones in order to give the impression of accent, because on that instrument, intensity cannot be regulated so quickly as to serve effectively in accentuation. Finally, we have mentioned *quality* as a means of accentuation. Herbert Woodrow[11] experimented on changes in pitch as aids to rhythmic grouping by using a series of stimuli in which every second or third beat was changed in pitch. His results indicated that the rhythmic groupings produced with the changes in pitch were the same as if all tones had the same pitch. In other words, the pitch factor did not serve as an effective means of organizing the stimuli. However, more recently Papinski[12] gives us evidence to the contrary. He

[11] H. Woodrow, The role of pitch in rhythm, *Psychol. Rev.*, 1911, **18**, 54–77.

[12] A. Papinski, The nature of rhythm response, *Proc. Mus. Teach. nat. Ass.*, 1946, pp. 321–29.

has found that periodic pitch variations do have a rhythm-producing influence. Finally, changes in the *timbre* of the tones will serve to organize the units. This can be done by adding chords or changing instrumentation on the beats to be stressed. This technique has been found to be effective even if the intensity factor is kept constant for all the stimuli.

The rhythmic response is regular in occurrence.—The characteristic of regularity applies to poetry as well as to music, as does the characteristic of organization. To indicate the speed or rate at which a rhythm progresses, we make use of a *time* description or *tempo* mark. We must realize that rhythm implies regularity or periodic groupings. Of course, a rhythmic line need not be completely periodic or regular throughout. Changes do occur in time. These may be frequent, particularly in many modern compositions. We have our accelerations as well as our retards to give greater interest to the expression, but, for a rhythm to be perceived as such, a degree of regularity in the grouping is necessary, even though it may change from phrase to phrase.

Tempo and rhythm.—So far, our discussion has been largely about rhythm, with only incidental reference to time. Of course time refers to the rate at which our rhythmic groupings occur. *Tempo* is an Italian term for time and is used in music to describe the rate or speed at which tones follow one another. Because of the Italian influence, the terms used on a printed score, the time markings, are usually printed in that language. Some of these are *largo, adagio, lento* for the slow rates, *andante* or *moderato* for the more moderate rates, and *vivace* and *presto* for the most rapid speeds. Often more precise markings are given by figures telling how many notes are to be played in a minute; ♩ = 90 would indicate that the composition should be performed at a rate of ninety quarter notes per minute, with other notes in proportion. A metronome is often used by the student for this purpose. In this mechanism the time markings are indicated and the beats correspond. It can be set at various desired speeds and will help the student play complex rhythmic relations in correct time. However, because the time relations in composition are seldom constant for any very long time (the music is full of accelerations and decelerations), the metronome cannot always be used, unless one wishes to play in a completely mechanical fashion. *Rhythm*, then, in contrast to *time*, is the *organization of the time relationships.*[13]

To facilitate the temporal organization of our beats in music, we divide the flow into measures, indicated on the printed page by vertical bars. Usually, the first note of the measure bears the accent, but we have already indicated in the iamb-rhythm unit that this need not be the case. The measures are simply arbitrary devices to facilitate the musical notation. Such rhythmic notations at the beginning of a composition serve to indicate the nature of the groupings as $\frac{3}{4}$, $\frac{4}{4}$, $\frac{6}{8}$, etc. This indicates the number of beats or units per measure. However, all rhythms with the same markings are not necessarily alike. For example, consider the $\frac{3}{4}$ rhythms. Both the waltz and the polonaise are marked $\frac{3}{4}$ but their rhythms are quite different.

The measurement of rhythmic discrimination.—In Chapters 2, 3, and 4 we considered briefly the problems of the measurement of pitch, loudness, and timbre discrimination. We now must consider this problem in regard to rhythm. The pioneer in this field of measurement again was Seashore.[14] He believed in a "sense of rhythm," which is the capacity for hearing and recalling rhythmic patterns with precision in time. In his *Measures of Musical Talents,*[15] a test is included for such a capacity. The revised version contains thirty pairs of rhythmic comparisons, each containing a series of rhythmic clicks. The number of

[13] A. R. Chandler, *Beauty and human nature* (New York: Appleton-Century-Crofts, Inc., 1934).

[14] C. E. Seashore, *The psychology of musical talent* (New York: Silver Burdett Co., 1919).

[15] C. E. Seashore, D. Lewis, and J. G. Saetveit, *Seashore Measures of Musical Talents* (rev. ed.; Camden, N.J.: Education Department, R.C.A. Manufacturing Co., 1939).

notes, the time signatures, and the tempos in any pair of phrases are always constant. The factor varied is the time value of the individual notes. The rhythm of the two phrases presented is sometimes the same and sometimes different. The subject is to make the appropriate discriminations. This test uses unmusical clicks instead of tonal stimuli, as the author believes that such an isolation of the rhythm enables us to measure the pure sense of rhythm without reference to past training or experience. The Kwalwasser-Dykema Test[16] also has a measure of rhythmic discrimination similar to that of Seashore, but it has been found to be less valid and reliable (pages 203–15). The Lundin Test[17] also makes use of a measurement of rhythmic discrimination. In this test, rhythmic sequences are presented to subjects on phonograph records or by means of a piano. Tonal and rhythmic stimuli are combined. The first three sequences are correct in rhythm, while the fourth may be the same or different. The subject is asked to indicate his judgment. The advantage of this type of test is that it does not isolate the tonal from the rhythmic aspects of the stimuli, but tests rhythm discrimination in a tonal setting. However, Seashore would consider this a disadvantage, since pure rhythm capacity is not being measured.

Rhythmic discrimination and training.—As with other forms of musical behavior, the problem of improvement with training arises with reference to rhythm. Seashore, of course, states that "sense of rhythm" is inherent like pitch, loudness, timbre, etc. However, there is some experimental evidence to the contrary, although it is not as substantial as that found in the field of pitch discrimination. Recently Coffman[18] presented series A and B of the Seashore Rhythm Test to eighth-graders and college music majors. The twenty-four eighth-graders and ten college students

[16] J. Kwalwasser and P. Dykema, *Kwalwasser-Dykema tests of music* (New York: Carl Fischer, Inc., 1930).

[17] R. W. Lundin, The development and validation of a set of musical ability tests, *Psychol. Monogr.*, 1949, **63**:305, 1–20.

[18] A. R. Coffman, Is rhythm subject to training? *Sch. Musician*, 1949, **21**:14, 45.

who scored *lowest* were selected, and each group was divided into experimental and control panels. The eighth-graders were given sixteen hours of various types of rhythmic training, including eurhythmics, and the college students were given ten hours of training each. Upon retesting, Coffman reports that both trained groups (experimental) made "remarkable improvement," while the untrained (controls) showed little or no change in their discrimination. However, since the author does not present his data, we are unable to ascertain the amount of improvement, or whether or not this improvement is statistically significant. These findings do corroborate those in other fields of music testing and substantiate our thesis that musical ability can improve with training.

Henderson [19] studied the problem of training in rhythmic performance. He set up a specific rhythmic pattern on the Seashore rhythm meter.[20] This meter, developed by the late Robert Seashore, consists of a metal disk with attachments on a turntable in which contacts can be made at any point on the circumference. In this way a rhythm within the period of revolution of the disk can be set up. The performer is then asked to reproduce or follow the rhythm by tapping on a telegraph key so as to make the telegraph click coincide with the stimulus. Henderson selected nine students of piano as his subjects. His results show that although the subjects started at different levels of achievement, since there were individual differences in ability at the onset, as a group they made distinct progress over the five days of practice. He presents graphic data to substantiate this claim. C. E. Seashore explains this improvement on the students' part as a development of ear-hand coordination, not as the actual "sense of rhythm," because a discrimination capacity cannot be improved. This breakdown of kinds of rhythm seems somewhat arbitrary, for, as we have already shown, rhythm is both a perceptual and a motor

[19] M. T. Henderson, Remedial measures in motor rhythm as applied to piano performance (thesis), University of Iowa, 1931.

[20] R. H. Seashore, Studies in motor rhythm, *Univ. Ia. Stud. Psychol. Music,* 1926, No. 9, pp. 149–99.

response, the whole organism being involved. It is difficult to isolate the discriminative (perceptual) from the motor aspects of the response.

Are there any racial differences in rhythmic responses?—In Chapter 13 we will take up the problem of racial differences in musical talent. However, it might be useful to introduce this topic now with a few studies which deal specifically with rhythm. Streep[21] gave the Seashore rhythm test to 637 white and 678 Negro children from the third to the sixth grade. Results showed a consistent though very slight superiority for the Negro children. However, the difference is not large enough to be considered absolutely reliable. More positive evidence for Negro superiority in rhythmic discrimination comes from Van Alstyne and Osborne.[22] They gave to 483 two and one-half to six and one-half-year-old Negro and white children an adaptation of the Seashore rhythm test and a motor rhythm test of their own devising. The Negro children were found to be 50 per cent better than the white on the "fast" and "slow" rhythms in both tests. The racial differences decreased with the complexity of the rhythmic patterns and with the increasing age of the subjects.

It has been generally thought that Negroes are superior to whites in rhythmic responses. Many have attributed this difference to inherent racial capacities as evidenced by the strong rhythmic emphasis in Negro music. From our data we cannot be absolutely sure that a difference does exist, but should that be the case, which is quite possible, the explanation may just as easily lie in culturalization as in inherent tendencies.

Theories of Rhythm

Earlier in this chapter we presented the thesis that rhythm is both a perceptual and a motor response involving the whole or-

[21] R. L. Streep, A comparison of white and Negro children in rhythm and consonance, *J. appl. Psychol.*, 1931, **15**, 53–71.

[22] D. Van Alstyne and E. Osborne, Rhythm responses of Negro and white children two to six, *Monogr. Soc. Res. Child Devel.*, 1937, **2**:4.

ganism. Our account of rhythm has been in terms of a learned response of the organism. However, there are alternate explanations for the nature of the rhythmic response which must not be overlooked. These have received a great deal of attention in the psychological literature and are still held to be true by many. These theories fall into three main types: (*a*) instinctive theories (*b*) physiological theories, and (*c*) a motor theory. Let us consider each separately.

Capacity to respond rhythmically as an instinctive tendency of the organism.—A major proponent of this theory is Seashore, who believes that rhythmic responses are inherited. This idea is not new in the field of music. He presents a clear statement of this attitude not only in the literature but in his Measures of Musical Talents. We must consider the rhythm response, he states,

> . . . as an instinctive disposition to group recurrent sense impressions vividly and with precision, by time or intensity, or both, in such a way as to derive pleasure and efficiency through the grouping.[23]

Seashore thinks subjective rhythm is deeply ingrained in us, since we have an irresistible tendency to group uniform successions of sound. A series of sounds uniform in time and stress inevitably becomes divided. Such subjective rhythm is a projection of the personality. For those who are not endowed with this capacity for subjective grouping, says Seashore, any objective groupings in nature and art are largely wasted. If one does not have the capacity to perceive these groupings, he cannot learn an ultimate appreciation for these forms.

The instinctive tendency to act in rhythmic groupings is a biological principle of preservative value.

> If a person does not know where to put his hand or foot in the next movement, he is ill at ease and will be inefficient in the

[23] C. E. Seashore, *In search of beauty in music*, p. 128. Copyright, 1947, by The Ronald Press Co.

movement. But, if movements may be foreseen and even fore-felt, and an accompanying signal sets off the movement without conscious effort, a more effective action, a feeling of satisfaction prevails. Anything that accomplishes these ends in the life of a species will tend to become instinctive, to develop a natural tendency always to move in rhythmic measure. . . . The bearing of this instinctive motor tendency on the perception of rhythm lies in the fact that with the motor instinct goes an instinct to be in a receptive attitude for the perception of such rhythms, both subjective and objective.[24]

There are, of course, individual differences in the capacity to respond to rhythm, according to Seashore. These inherent differences he has attempted to test in his Measures of Musical Talents. From the point of view of measurement, two factors must be kept in mind. First, these capacities determine the development of the rhythmic aspect of the musical mind, and second, absence or presence of such capacities in childhood may be regarded as a fair index of one's ability to profit from training. The theory serves as a basis for what Seashore calls the "sense of rhythm," which is the capacity for hearing and recalling rhythmic patterns.

Aside from any criticism of this type of theory as being mentalistic, which is obvious, the fact remains that such a theory is contrary to the facts at hand. Heinlein[25] studied rhythmic responses in children of kindergarten age by asking them to walk in time to music. The children were told to walk on a runway which had electric contacts designed to record their steps. At the same time, the beat of the music was also recorded. Only one of his eight subjects showed any degree of coordination between the walking movements and the musical beat. Heinlein believes adults are apt to project their own musical attitudes on to children. They are likely to think the children are keeping time with the rhythm when actually this is not happening.

[24] *Ibid.*, pp. 132–33.

[25] C. P. Heinlein, A new method of studying the rhythmic responses of children together with an evaluation of the method of simple observation, *Ped. Sem. and J. genet. Psychol.*, 1929, **36**, 205–28.

Despite this kind of evidence, Seashore maintains:

> The natural capacity for this (motor rhythm) may be measured before musical education has been undertaken. It consists of determining, under experimental conditions, what degree of precision the individual can show in tapping out rhythmic patterns, either by imitating standard patterns or by setting up his own patterns in metronomic time.[26]

Rhythmic responses as dependent upon physiological processes.—During the 1920's the school of eurhythmics became fashionable. The main proponent of this movement was Jacques-Dalcroze.[27] Rhythmic education for children emphasized the learning of correct rhythmic movements for two reasons. The first was purely physical, for training the muscles and improving bodily health. The second involved the aesthetic value of teaching self-expression in one of its most beautiful forms.

The bodily processes are the essential elements of rhythm, which in the last analysis is the sense of time. Most important of these processes is the heartbeat, for by its regularity we can attain a clear idea of time. This activity is, according to this theory, unconscious and of greater value in the perception than in the execution of rhythm. The action of breathing also provides a regular division of time and is the model for a measure. Since breathing is more subject to voluntary control than the heart beat, we can sense more in this motor response. Finally, a regular gait serves as a model for the division of time into equal proportions. Consciousness of rhythm can only be acquired by reiterated experience of the whole body.

What evidence is there in support of this theory? The school of eurhythmics has pointed out that music at a tempo greater than the normal heart rate is considered fast, while that considerably below it is taken as slow. The possibility that our judgment of the passage of time is made by reference to bodily processes is

[26] By permission from *Psychology of music,* by C. E. Seashore, p. 146. Copyright by McGraw-Hill Book Co., Inc., New York, 1938.

[27] E. Jaques-Dalcroze, *Rhythm, music, and education,* trans. Rubinstein (New York: G. P. Putnam's Sons, Inc., 1921).

given as further evidence. We must not, however, neglect the observation that our judgments of time are also made by references to acts and intervening circumstances. For example, time judgment during sleep is often very poor and certainly less accurate than during waking because of the exclusion during sleep of stimuli which have occurred. Ordinarily, during our waking lives time judgments are relatively more accurate, since we have learned the length of time it takes for various happenings to occur.

Another theory which tries to account for rhythm in terms of bodily processes is that of Robert McDougall.[28] He believed that rhythmic responses are based on the primitive rate of nervous discharge. The fundamental conditions of a rhythmic experience are to be found in the laws of periodicity of functioning in the nervous system. An objective stimulation (rhythm) must be correlated with some internal mechanism in order for the impression of rhythm to arise. There is, presumably, a periodic facilitation and inhibition of nervous activity which arises out of the relation between the periodicity of the neural rhythmic discharge and certain intervals in the objective series of stimulations. Thus, a physiological rhythm appears in the functioning of the central nervous system which gives a periodic increase and decrease in the intensity of the sensations coordinated with a series of unchanging objective stimulations. These objective elements are correlated with the positive and negative phases of expectation and its fulfilment which characterize the experience of rhythm. They will be resolved into psychological attitudes which are physiologically conditioned by the strains and releases due to the rhythmical operation of these phases of motor innervation which the reaction accompaniment involves.

The obvious criticism of this idea is that it involves a type of mind-body interaction which is not at all clear, even if one were to accept the mind as a conscious correlate of the nervous system.

[28] R. McDougall, The relation of auditory rhythm to nervous discharge, *Psychol. Rev.*, 1902, **9**, 460–80.

The fact that the nervous system shows periodic phases of discharge has little to do with the perception of rhythmic stimuli. Any attempt to correlate the two is somewhat of an imposition on the observable data.

Mursell[29] has further pointed out that an explanation of rhythm in terms of regular bodily processes overemphasizes the regularity of rhythmic occurrence, for the regularity of rhythm is extremely flexible. Changes in rhythm may be marked within a given work without the feeling response being interfered with or lost.

Rhythmic responses as dependent on the action of the voluntary muscles (motor theory).—According to this theory we perceive rhythms as such because we have a bodily machinery which can be trained to react. We are able to grasp and respond to complex rhythms, not on the basis of instincts or nebulous physiological mechanisms, but because we have a neuromuscular system which is complex and capable of being trained to make these responses. The perception of rhythm, or what Mursell calls a "feeling for rhythm,"[30] is possible because we respond to our own sequential voluntary muscular activity. What is the evidence in support of this theory?

1. The fact that we make muscular responses to music is already obvious. All of us have a tendency to tap our feet or hands in time to a definite rhythmic beat. One proponent of this motor theory was Stetson,[31] who has stated that even when the larger muscle groups are not observed responding to rhythmic stimuli, there are smaller muscles still operating, often in a more implicit way. This fact we have mentioned earlier in the chapter.

Consider dancing for a moment. It is obviously easier to respond with skeletal movements in time with the rhythm than to act contrary to it. Your author has frequently observed the behavior of high school and college students at jazz concerts which

[29] Mursell, *op. cit.*
[30] *Ibid.*, pp. 157–58.
[31] Stetson, *op. cit.*

periodically become the rage on our campuses. In these instances not only the legs and feet are responding to the rhythmic beat, but every other possible part of the body, including the arms, fingers, neck, and head, as well as facial muscles. At times the assembled students are responding so overtly to the rhythmic stimuli that should a naïve outsider inadvertently walk in, he might think that he was witnessing some primitive ritual.

2. Ruckmick[32] has given experimental evidence in support of this theory in the following study. He used a variety of auditory rhythmic stimuli of equally and unequally spaced patterns which also varied in intensity, duration, and pitch. There were also light flashes which varied in intensity, giving a visual rhythmic stimulus. His subjects were asked to attend to these stimuli and report verbally their reactions. He found the subjects' muscular movements to be an essential part of the rhythmic response. However, these responses were not confined to any particular set of muscles but were reported as occurring in various parts of the body, indicating that a rhythmic response like other kinds of psychological activity involves the activity of the whole body. Ruckmick reports:

> Kinaesthesis is prominent; but it may be kinaesthesis of the limbs or head, of gross bodily movements, of respiration, of vague organic disturbances in chest and abdomen, or of articulation. . . . In almost every case of reported head, limb, or respiratory movement made by O, E was able to verify the report by actual observation of movement.[33]

In summary he writes:

> These points are certainly clear: (1) the kinaesthetic complex changes for accent and non-accent, (2) kinaesthesis on the accent is more intensive and felt as strain or tension, while kinaesthesis on the non-accent is less intensive and is felt as relaxation, and (3) kinaesthesis, prominent as it is, may be

[32] C. A. Ruckmick, The role of kinaesthesis in the perception of rhythm, *Amer. J. Psychol.*, 1913, **24**, 303–59.

[33] *Ibid.*, pp. 334–35.

temporarily or entirely replaced by visual or auditory complexes . . .[34]

Of the three theories, the motor theory seems the most plausible, and it is closest to the available data. We have presented in an earlier part of this chapter what we might call a modified motor theory which does not need repetition at this point. The rhythmic response is clearly an observable one involving various parts of the responding organism. Since the kinds of situations under which a rhythmic response may occur will vary—dance floor, concert hall, or music room—it is obvious that different parts of the organism are going to be involved. One cannot isolate the rhythmic response in any particular musculature or body parts. During listening to music, the response pattern will include more perceptual behavior with the motor aspects of secondary importance, whereas in dancing, the perceptual responses are minimized and the motor reactions are predominant.

[34] *Ibid.*, p. 336.

Chapter 8

LEARNING AND REMEMBERING MUSIC

EVER SINCE Franz Liszt in the middle of the nineteenth century created a new vogue when, in a moment of interpretive fervor, he cast his musical score from its rack and continued his recital from memory, it has become the custom of musical soloists to perform their works without the use of the printed notation. Today audiences might look askance upon any player who found it necessary to resort to musical notation as a prop. Their immediate conclusion probably would be that the performer simply was not very well acquainted with the work he was playing and a lot more preparation might be helpful before he displayed his talents publicly. More recently this matter of performing from memory has been taken up by orchestral conductors. Perhaps some day in the future whole groups of musicians will be obliged to perform large works from memory.

Since learning music is a kind of behavior pattern practiced by many individuals from childhood, it is unfortunate that this application of psychology to music has been largely neglected. This is particularly unfortunate in view of the amount of material available on other forms of human learning. Both professional performers and teachers of music have written on this subject from their own personal experience, but the number of experimental studies available on the learning and remembering of music is comparatively small. Mursell,[1] in a bibliography of 256 titles relating to the psychology of music, lists only seven related to learning in music. Before approaching our discussion

[1] J. L. Mursell, Psychology of music, *Psychol. Bull.*, 1932, **29**, 218–41.

of learning and remembering in music, let us examine momentarily the nature of these psychological processes in the light of an objective approach to psychology. Remembering, or memory, refers to behavior once acquired which is repeated in some fashion following the passage of a period of time. A memory response, then, necessitates a period of delay. This, of course, may be extremely brief, as exemplified in tests of tonal memory. Remembering is, then, a forward-looking kind of action which is started at one time but may not be completed until some future time (definite or indefinite). "I play a piece from memory" means partly "I have learned a complex set of movements and can repeat the series of movements when called upon." Because such a behavior is a complex one, many other different stimulus-response connections will be involved beside the motor (playing); these will include visual, intellectual, emotional, etc.

In musical language, when we say a person has a good "tonal memory," we refer to this type of behavior. We mean that he is able easily and effectively to repeat a sort of musical response after a period of delay following a previous contact with the musical stimulus.

Learning, on the other hand, is defined as a contrived stimulus-response coordination.[2] It involves certain conditions which are regarded as controls. Among such controls we would mention goals or ends toward which one directs his actions. The adequate performance of a piece might serve as an illustration of this goal. The specific techniques of learning constitute other controls. Some of these techniques will be considered later in this chapter. One example might be the spacing of practice periods. Is it more efficient to learn a piece of music by distributing the practice or massing it all at one time? Another technique might have to do with the distribution of the material itself. Again, is it more efficient to learn a piece by practicing the piece as a whole, or is it better to break it up into parts and learn each part separately?

[2] J. R. Kantor, *A survey of the science of psychology* (Bloomington, Ind.: The Principia Press, Inc., 1933), p. 242.

The experimental material available to us on this topic seems to divide roughly into two areas of investigation, (*a*) tonal memory and (*b*) efficiency in learning music.

Tonal Memory

Tonal memory has been considered by many an important attribute of musical talent. Its relation to the general problem of musical ability and its development will be reserved for a later section. The importance laid on good tonal memory as a constituent of musical talent is exemplified by the fact that all the leading music tests (Seashore,[3] Kwalwasser-Dykema,[4] and Drake [5]) contain, at least as one part, some measure of it. Drake [6] believes it to be the one factor on which general musical ability may be most accurately predicted. While music tests are notoriously invalid, the Seashore Measure of Tonal Memory and the Kwalwasser-Dykema Test of Tonal Memory correlate highest with various criteria of musical success as reported by Mursell.[7] In this report, Mursell lists in chart form various investigations in which the Seashore test has been validated.[8] Some of the criteria which he mentions include performance in sight singing, grades in music theory, ratings of teachers on a student's performance, and grades in sight singing and dictation. Whether one agrees with Seashore that musical ability is a series of specific talents or with Mursell, who believes in an "omnibus theory," it

[3] C. E. Seashore, D. Lewis, and J. G. Saetveit, *Seashore measures of musical talents* (rev. ed.; Camden, N.J.: Education Department, R.C.A. Manufacturing Co., 1939).

[4] J. Kwalwasser and P. W. Dykema, *Kwalwasser-Dykema Music Tests* (New York: Carl Fischer, Inc., 1930).

[5] R. M. Drake, Four new tests of musical talent, *J. appl. Psychol.*, 1933, **17**, 136–47. See also Drake Test of Musical Talent (Fredericksburg, Va.: The Author, 1942).

[6] *Ibid.*

[7] J. L. Mursell, *The psychology of music* (New York: W. W. Norton & Co., Inc., 1937), p. 12.

[8] For further reports see Chapter 14 of this volume.

would appear that tonal memory has been considered by some as an important aspect of musical ability. It might well be, as Mursell[9] points out, that ability to perform a composition from memory is quite an arbitrary matter and may have no psychological or artistic justification. Despite the importance placed on tonal memory by the music-testers, one should not conclude that just because he has a good tonal memory he will necessarily be a successful musician or that without it he is doomed to failure. Hughes[10] points out that there are several pianists who might be considered excellent musicians in their technical performance of a work and who possess most remarkable tonal memories, but whose playing will seem painful to anyone with a pianistically educated ear. We say their playing is purely mechanical. Further, he believes that, although memory may be one of the technical requisites of the pianist, it may have as little to do with the art as have fleet fingers or supple wrists in themselves. We should, then, recognize the importance of tonal memory but not rate it so high as to exclude those whose ability is poor, nor should we rate too highly those people who happen to have developed tonal memory to a marked degree without a consideration of other aspects of their musical personality. Hughes[11] gives us an interesting example of one of the ablest vocal artists of the nineteenth century, Mme. Schröder-Devrient, who had the greatest difficulty in learning a role from memory. He also mentions the elder Rubinstein, a pianist, who abandoned the concert stage merely because he could no longer depend on his memory in public performances.

If tonal memory as measured is such an important aspect in musical ability, why does it not correlate with actual success? Of course, the general low reliability of music tests[12] helps to ac-

[9] J. L. Mursell, *The psychology of music* (New York: W. W. Norton & Co., Inc., 1937), p. 256.

[10] E. Hughes, Musical memory in piano playing and piano study, *Mus. Quart.*, Oct., 1915.

[11] Hughes, *op. cit.*

[12] See Chapter 13.

count for this, but Heinlein's criticism also seems most pertinent. He suggests that when we alter one tone of a melodic sequence, the "whole" is changed and musical persons in particular apprehend a sequence of tones as a totality with a characteristic constitutive contour, rather than a mere number of separate tones.[13] In this matter he has reference to the Seashore Measure of Tonal Memory, which presents a series of unrelated tones twice in succession, the position of one of the notes being changed in the second playing. The subject is asked to identify the changed note by writing down the number of the note which has changed.

Current tonal memory tests are measuring only the immediate memory span. Writers have assumed that a person with a large span of tonal memory will be able to learn music easily. Whether or not this assumption is true for music as yet remains to be adequately demonstrated. On observing the Seashore and Kwalwasser-Dykema tests, we find that the amount of material in terms of the number of notes to be repeated is related to the character of the material. The Seashore test uses a series of unrelated notes. In this case the average memory span is five or six notes. Seashore's reason for selecting unrelated notes in the test goes back to his fundamental assumption that since musical talent is an inherited trait, it must as such be measured without the influence of training. By using a presentation of unrelated notes, he believes he eliminates any effect of previous training. In so doing he is forgetting the fact that music is not merely a series of unrelated tones but a configuration of interrelated tonal patterns.

The Kwalwasser-Dykema and Drake tests use simple melodies. When the notes are combined into a configuration, the immediate memory span is increased to twelve or more notes for the average individual. The analogy of sense and nonsense verbal material seems appropriate. We also think of studies on the span of appre-

[13] C. P. Heinlein, A brief discussion of the nature and function of melodic configuration in tonal memory with critical reference to the Seashore Tonal Memory Test, *J. genet. Psychol.*, 1928, **35**, 45–61.

hension of visual material where unrelated letters, words, and sentences are flashed on a screen for a split second and the subject is asked to report how much he can remember seeing. The span is greatest, as measured by the number of letters, when the material is presented as meaningful sentences, next as disjointed words, and finally poorest for simple unrelated letters.

Realizing the essential difference in memory span for unrelated notes and melodies, Van Neuys and Weaver[14] have gone a step further in studying the memory span for various kinds of meaningful melodies. Among other things they found that the memory span for the group tested decreased as the complexity of the note relations increased, both for rhythm and melody. In other words, the more complicated the rhythms and melodies became, the smaller the memory span for them.

In this decrease, an order of difficulty was observed as follows:

1. Easiest phrases: rhythms composed of a simple repeated figure involving only three different note values
2. Next most difficult phrases: melodies progressing scalewise or symmetrically arranged in thirds
3. More difficult than the simplest melodies: rhythms having four or more notes in varied patterns
4. Most difficult phrases: melodies having pitch intervals of a fifth or larger arranged in irregular progression

The memory span for a combination of rhythms was found to be only slightly greater than for each alone. An increase in memory span was found to depend largely upon improvement in ability to apprehend pitch patterns as stable melodic segments of composition.

On the basis of the evidence so far given, we must keep in mind the following:

1. Although a good tonal memory as measured by the Seashore, Kwalwasser-Dykema, and Drake tests seems to be one aid

[14] K. Van Neuys and H. E. Weaver, Memory span and visual pauses in reading rhythms and melodies, *Psychol. Monogr.*, 1943, **55**, 33–50.

to successful musicianship, it is not the only necessary attribute of musical talent. One may have an excellent tonal memory and lack the other necessary musical abilities, so as an accomplished musician he may be quite mediocre.

2. It is apparent that there are good musicians who possess very poor tonal memories. If they play from a written score, this poor tonal memory need not interfere with their success providing they have the other necessary requisites for good musicianship.

3. Memory span for music which is meaningful is greater than for purely unrelated tones, and this memory span for tones decreases as the complexity of the tonal relationships increases for both rhythm and melody.

Efficiency in Learning Music

Because of our tradition of solo performance without reference to a printed score, a second problem confronts us. What is the most efficient way to learn music?

Before attempting a consideration of some of the studies in this area, one semantic distinction often made by musicians should be noted. For many, *learning* in music refers to the practicing of a piece using a written score, whereas *memorizing* refers to the process of learning the material with the final goal of reproduction without reference to the printed score. Whereas our attention will be centered on both behaviors, most studies refer to the latter.

Whole and part learning.—Which is the most economical way to memorize a piece of music? Should one practice the material as a whole—that is, play it all the way through each trial—or should he practice it in parts, learning each part by itself and then combining all parts? Eberly first considered the problem in an unpublished master's thesis reported by Rubin-Rabson.[15] He asked five subjects to learn several classical, roman-

[15] G. Rubin-Rabson, The influence of analytical prestudy in memorizing piano music, *Arch. Psychol.*, 1937, **31**:220, 1–53.

tic, and modern compositions, using both the whole and part methods. In spite of the prejudice on the part of the subjects in favor of the part method, an economy of from 27 to 87 per cent in learning time was found to the advantage of the *whole method.*

Brown [16] did a similar study using whole, part, and combination methods. Her results agree by and large with those of Eberly. In the whole method, the score was played by the subject from beginning to end without stopping to correct or repeat any measures. In the part method, the score was divided into units and each unit was practiced an equal number of times. In the combination method, the score was played from beginning to end, but all measures in which errors occurred were repeated an equal number of times. Of the three methods, she found the whole method most effective. The part method was least efficient, and the combination method was most efficient on the single occasion when an easy score was assigned.

Rubin-Rabson [17] studied the problem of whole vs. part with reference to the length of time required to learn the music and the amount retained after two weeks. After each memorized relearning the subject was asked to transcribe the learned score on paper. Results showed (*a*) that neither the whole nor the part method of learning or relearning showed any advantage in the number of trials necessary and (*b*) no superiority could be found in either of these approaches. Retention was in no way affected by first having learned by either the whole or the part method. Since keyboard fluency occasionally obscures differences in clarity of details in recall, it was thought that the transposition might have been expected to show weaknesses at the point of juncture of smaller parts, but it did not. More recently O'Brien [18]

[16] R. W. Brown, A comparative study of "whole" and "part," and "combination," methods of learning piano music, *J. exp. Psychol.*, 1928, **11**, 235–47.

[17] G. Rubin-Rabson, Studies in the psychology of memorizing piano music: III. A comparison of whole and part approach, *J. educ. Psychol.*, 1940, **31**, 460–76.

[18] C. E. O'Brien, Part and whole methods in memorization of piano music, *J. educ. Psychol.*, 1943, **34**, 552–60.

has found results favoring the part method. Four graduate students in music served as subjects in learning various piano selections of equal difficulty under different conditions. The saving of time for the *part method* ranged from 25 to 65 per cent. This discrepancy in results is not surprising, as differences in whole versus part learning are found in other studies of learning, both in verbal and in motor tasks. A number of factors can account for this disagreement. In both studies mentioned here, advanced piano students were used. In the Rubin-Rabson study, however, a relatively small amount of material was given, only eight measures to be memorized; whereas in the O'Brien study, thirty-two measures were memorized. Under normal conditions of memorizing a score, the number of measures may be quite large, running into the hundreds, unless, of course, it happens to be a simple song. Further, it is obvious that different subjects and kinds of music were involved in each study.

On the basis of this evidence, we conclude that the whole method may be an effective one so long as the amount of material being learned is small. It is quite possible, as in other learning studies, that a larger score of music will be most effectively learned by the part method. Here the results agree fairly well with those in other studies of learning. The method used will depend on the size, difficulty, and meaning of the material to be memorized as well as the performance level of the subjects involved.

Massed and distributed practice.—A second problem in efficient learning concerns the distribution of the practice periods, whether the material is acquired more efficiently by continuous practice until learned or by splitting up the period of practice. The former method is referred to as massed practice, the latter as distributed. Rubin-Rabson[19] divided subjects into three groups: (*a*) massed practice, (*b*) distributed practice with an interval of

[19] G. Rubin-Rabson, Studies in the psychology of memorizing piano music: II. A comparison of massed and distributed practice, *J. educ. Psychol.*, 1940, **31**, 270–84.

one hour between trials, and (*c*) distributed practice with an interval of twenty-four hours between trials. As in her study on part and whole learning, the results showed no difference between methods with regard to time spent in learning. However, when relearning was used as a test for the amount retained, a real economy for the two distributed methods was demonstrated. In this study the advantage of distributed practice was in inverse relation to the proficiency of the subject in playing the piano. Thus, by distributing the practice periods, she showed that the subjects remembered more than by the massed method. This report agrees with most work done in other fields of learning, where the method of distributed practice is usually most effective.

Unilateral and coordinated approaches.—Any student of piano will remember his early days of study when he first learned to play his pieces by practicing each hand separately before they were combined. "Unilateral" refers to the "hands alone" technique and coordinated to the "hands together." This is, in a way, a variation of the whole and part methods. In Brown's study,[20] pairs of musical scores were equated for difficulty. Each score was learned by the unilateral and by the coordinated approach. She found that the coordinated approach (hands together) was more efficient both in speed and in number of trials. Further, the unilateral (hands alone) method was progressively more inefficient with more practice as the music for each hand became partially memorized, thus making the combination of the two hands more difficult.

Rubin-Rabson [21] found similar results. Four separate-hand trials were required in a unilateral method to effect a saving of one coordinated trial. She assumes that transfer exists but believes it to be both positive and negative. Both studies agree as

[20] R. W. Brown, The relation between two methods of learning piano music, *J. exp. Psychol.*, 1933, **16**, 435–41.

[21] G. Rubin-Rabson, Studies in the psychology of memorizing piano music: I. A comparison of unilateral and coordinated approaches, *J. educ. Psychol.*, 1939, **30**, 321–45.

to the superiority of the coordinated method so far as time is concerned. The obvious explanation is found in the fact that each hand's part must be learned separately. Then further time must be taken to combine the two.

Effect of prestudy.—What effect does an examination of the musical score before practice have on efficiency in learning? Kovacs[22] first attempted this problem in an unscientific manner. He tested the efficiency of learning small fragments away from the piano. Only the subject's announcement that he was ready was used to indicate the rate of learning. No time limit was set. Despite the lack of controls, he reports a superiority of the prestudy away from the keyboard in learning music.

Rubin-Rabson followed this up in two studies.[23] In the first, four methods were employed. Methods I and II involved study and analysis of the score before practice. In Method I the studying was done with the aid of a previously prepared analysis, and in Method II the analysis was prepared by the subject. Method III used no study previous to learning at the keyboard, and Method IV was designed to test the nature of familiarity with the musical material from hearing it before learning. A marked superiority of the methods (I and II) which employed analytical study periods before keyboard practice was noted. Since the differences were large, the author believes that the superiority of analytic methods over haphazard keyboard practice applies not only to the group tested but to other groups of piano students. Preliminary hearing of musical material before learning showed no advantage in relearning over doing without this preliminary hearing.

To test the value of various amounts of prestudy, this same author used nine examples of unfamiliar music which were

[22] S. Kovacs, Untersuchungen über das musikalische Gedächtnis, Z. *angew. Psychol.*, 1916, **11**, 113–35.

[23] G. Rubin-Rabson, The influence of analytical prestudy in memorizing piano music, *Arch. Psychol.*, 1937, **31**:220, 1–53; Studies in the psychology of memorizing piano music: V. A comparison of prestudy periods of varied lengths, *J. educ. Psychol.*, 1941, **32**, 101–12.

studied for three, six, and nine minutes before the subjects continued memorizing to a criterion of one perfect trial at the keyboard. All subjects performed the experiment three times, so that twenty-seven learnings were complete from each method. At the end of the prestudy period, the material was transcribed (written) from memory as a test of the degree of learning. Results showed that the amount of material transcribed in the case of the six-minute period of prestudy was reliably greater than that at the end of three, but because the music was well within the capacity of the subjects, the written transpositions at the end of nine minutes were not significantly better than at the end of six. In the case of the three-minute period of prestudy, roughly one-half of the total number of measures was written correctly. No difference in retention of the music exists when prestudy and no prestudy periods are compared. The author recommends that students study the whole composition for details of structure and form and then study some unit of comfortable length sufficiently to attempt it from memory at the keyboard.

Having shown that preliminary analytical study is advantageous to learning piano music, this series of studies of the problem was continued by attempting to measure the effect of mental rehearsal situated at points in the learning process after some keyboard learning had already been accomplished. This study used mental rehearsal before, during, and after complete learning of the material. Mental rehearsal is defined as implicit recall of the material already learned. Results showed that the mid-way period of rehearsal was superior to the other forms of distributed rehearsal. In all groups a period of prestudy was used. Four minutes of mental rehearsal placed after learning was completed appeared to be an inferior procedure. In a second relearning after seven months, all former differences disappeared. Several hypotheses are suggested to account for the superiority of the mid-way study method. First, this is a type of distributed practice which provides a period when the cessation of hand movements relieves the necessity of maintaining an unbroken sequence. Second, it allows further analysis and reorganization at points of confusion and presents a "reseeing" of small musical figures against the general background. For practical purposes piano students might well first prepare thorough analyses, then continue their learning at the keyboard until hand and tonal patterns have been established. Finally, they should pause for a period of mental rehearsal before completing the learned work.[24]

Overlearning.—By overlearning in music we refer to a continuation of practice beyond the point at which any particular piece has been memorized. Fifty per cent overlearning means practice one-half again as many times as was necessary to learn the piece for the first time. One hundred per cent overlearning would mean to practice again the same number of trials that was necessary before complete learning had taken place. The previous study gave indirect evidence that once a piano piece is memorized to a criterion of one successful performance, overlearning is of little effect. To substantiate this, various degrees of overlearning were considered. In this study, 50, 100 and 200 per cent overlearning periods were used. Although these three degrees of overlearning achieved large proportions of retention when compared with the first learning trials, none was more effective than the others. In other words, to practice once again as much is no better than practicing twice as much after a piece has been learned. Degrees of overlearning beyond 50 per cent are apparently ineffective so far as retention is concerned. In this experiment no comparison was made between 50 per cent overlearning and zero overlearning (no overlearning),[25] but in another experiment[26] it was found that 100 per cent proved no

[24] G. Rubin-Rabson, Studies in the psychology of memorizing piano music: VI. A comparison of two forms of mental rehearsal and keyboard overlearning, *J. educ. Psychol.*, 1941, **32**, 593–602.

[25] G. Rubin-Rabson, Studies in the psychology of memorizing piano music: VII. A comparison of three degrees of overlearning, *J. educ. Psychol.*, 1941, **32**, 688–98.

[26] G. Rubin-Rabson, Studies in the psychology of memorizing piano music: VI. A comparison of two forms of mental rehearsal and keyboard overlearning, *J. educ. Psychol.*, 1941, **32**, 593–602.

more effective than no overlearning at all. As a result of these studies, the most economical procedure seems to be one which employed an intensive learning to the criterion of smoothed memorized performance. Then the extra trials may be saved for subsequent periods when it is necessary to restore the learning to the same level as before.

Incentives.—What effects do incentives have on learning of music? Believing that plateaus (indicating lack of improvement) in plotted learning curves have been caused by the lack of incentive or will to do, Rubin-Rabson[27] designed an experiment to remove these plateaus and so show the effect of incentive. Three situations were used. Subjects were asked to learn unfamiliar piano music (*a*) under free unmotivated conditions except for factors already existing in the situation, (*b*) by being spurred on with verbal exhortation to work with maximum speed and intensity, and (*c*) using an incentive of cash reward in proportion to speed. Neither learning nor relearning showed any reliable differences in any of the methods used. On this basis, she concludes that for each individual, a minimum number of trials is required to bring the learning of a complicated skill such as piano-playing to a given point of perfection, and this number cannot be reduced by added incentives. The plateaus are "an intrinsic part of the learning curve and cannot be eliminated."

However, this experiment is open to criticism on a number of grounds. First of all, the motivating conditions used were rather superficial. Instead of concluding that motivation does not improve learning, it might be better to indicate that there was no real difference in the motivating conditions so far as their adequacy was concerned. The mere conditions of the experiment may be motivation enough. Secondly, the author assumes that plateaus in the learning curve are due to lack of incentive. Apparently, she does not recognize the possibility that plateaus can

[27] G. Rubin-Rabson, Studies in the psychology of memorizing piano music: IV. The effect of incentive, *J. educ. Psychol.*, 1941, **32**, 45–54.

be due to other factors. Since incentives do not eliminate the plateaus, the conclusions are that they are ". . . an intrinsic part of the learning curve and cannot be eliminated." [28] Even if her hypothesis were correct, this does not mean that her incentives were adequate. To say plateaus are intrinsic in the learning curve does not appear to explain much of anything except that the results were negative.

The beta hypothesis.—Although McGeoch,[29] in his *Psychology of Human Learning,* claimed that the beta hypothesis may be applied to the learning of piano music, he cites no reference to any experimental literature. It has already been demonstrated that practicing errors in learning certain materials, particularly when muscular movement is involved, will help eliminate the errors, providing one realizes that he is practicing a mistake. This has been known as the *beta hypothesis.* For example, in learning typewriting one may form the habit of writing *teh* instead of *the.* Practicing of this mistake helps eliminate it, providing, of course, one attends to the fact that it *is* an error he is practicing and that it should be eliminated. The only study reported on this subject, to the writer's knowledge, is a brief note by Wakeham [30] concerning a personal experience. The piece which he practiced on the organ contained several "perilous points," chords each of which contained an error that was likely to recur. This passage was practiced carefully ten times each day for two weeks. All the time during practice, he tried to impress on himself that this performance was wrong and should not be allowed in the regular rendition. On the fifteenth day, the whole piece was attempted at a suitable tempo and played without error. However, a few days later, he demonstrated the "perilous passage" and the result was disastrous: every one of the

[28] *Ibid.*

[29] J. A. McGeoch, *The psychology of human learning* (New York: Longmans, Green & Co., Inc., 1942).

[30] G. Wakeham, Query on a revision of the fundamental law of habit formation, *Science,* 1928, **68**, 135–36.

carefully practiced mistakes turned up again. As a result he suggests that this type of performance is not analogous to the practicing of errors in typewriting for the purpose of elimination and should not be used in piano practice.

Effect of music on learning other material.—One often hears about the soothing effect that music has on various types of activity. Does hearing music while learning other material have a facilitating or detrimental effect on the learning process? Whitley[31] found that when music served as a prior condition of learning "joy" and "sorrow" words, the results were slightly detrimental to learning as compared with learning under normal conditions. And learning under normal conditions of quiet is superior to learning while music is being played.[32] Different kinds of music had different effects upon the learning process. For example, music of a tempestuous sort is more distracting than smoother music, such as Dvorak's *Largo.*

In these studies on efficiency in learning music, we are aware of the artificiality of the laboratory situation. Material here learned is not always comparable to that studied in actual practice. Because of the time factor, these investigations have often used scores which are both short and simple to perform. Any artist knows that instrumental and vocal pieces will vary in difficulty *within the opus* so that some parts will have to be practiced more than others. Seashore[33] has caught sight of this fact and gives some advice which, although not based on experimentation, seems worth considering. He condemns the old method of rote learning of music, i.e., mere repetition of a piece time after time, because there is not much object in learning what you *already know.* Much time may be saved and proficiency gained by first discovering what *you don't know* and then tackling each of these

[31] P. L. Whitley, The influence of music on memory, *J. gen. Psychol.,* 1940, **10,** 137–51.

[32] However, see Chapter 15 on the use of music in industry.

[33] C. E. Seashore, Critical training by specific practice, *Educ. Mus. Mag.,* Sept.-Oct., 1941, pp. 4–5.

situations intensively in turn. The main fact to be considered is the analysis and identification of the difficulties. Many of them can be easily solved if attention is clearly drawn to them.

Summary.—On the basis of the evidence given, what answer to our question on the most efficient ways of learning music can be given?

1. Learning by the whole method is recommended for short pieces. For larger works, it seems advisable to break one's study into parts.

2. Practice which is distributed over a period of time rather than performed all at once is likely to be more economical, particularly when relearning is involved.

3. Practicing "hands together" is more efficient from the beginning of study so long as it is within the range of the performer's ability.

4. An analytical study of the score before practicing is begun serves as an aid to the most efficient learning of the piece.

5. Rather than spend time overlearning a piece, the extra trials should be saved for subsequent periods of practice to restore a piece to the level of performance attained when learning was first completed, as overlearning has not been demonstrated to be helpful in retaining piano music.

6. A period of mental rehearsal placed mid-way in any practice period is an effective aid to learning a score.

7. The playing of mistakes for elimination purposes (beta hypothesis) is a questionable method so far as the most efficient learning of music is concerned and is not recommended.

Chapter 9

THE AFFECTIVE RESPONSE TO MUSIC

AFFECTIVE or feeling responses to music have been recorded since earliest times. Poetic references to the sweet influence of the lyre or to Saul's favorable reactions to David's harp simply illustrate this fact. Poets have written of the "power" of music to stir or soothe the emotions and to inspire or suppress "desire." Literature and drama are full of stories of the influence of music on what they call the passions of man. That we respond affectively to music is no new observation, but just how and what aspects of the stimulus give rise to these responses are questions more difficult to answer. Our psychological literature is replete with attempts on the part of investigators to understand the nature of the affective response to music. Since the problem is a large and complex one, there still remains much to be understood. In this chapter we shall attempt to report some of the evidence demonstrating these affective reactions and find at least some partial answers to the questions of how we respond affectively to musical stimuli and why these stimuli arouse affective reactions in most of us.

The nature of the affective response.—In order to gain some insight into the problems proposed, it is necessary to understand the general nature of this particular kind of psychological reaction. Many terms such as "affective," "feeling," and "emotional" have been used to characterize this kind of behavior. For us, the terms "affective" and "feeling" are synonymous, while "emotional" is reserved for a more special kind of reaction which has little relationship to music.[1] Many writers include under "emotion" what this book refers to as "feeling."

An affective response is one in which the stimulus has made some definite change *in the organism.* It may be active and energy-consuming, but *it has no effect on the stimulus object.*[2] *Instead, the stimulus object acts on the organism.* In this way we distinguish an affective or feeling response from other kinds of psychological activity known as affective, that is, those in which the *organism does something to the stimulus.* In the feeling reaction, the result occurs in the responding organism rather than in the stimulus object. These are often internal reactions, intraorganic or visceral. We shall report later in this chapter some studies to illustrate responses to music which are primarily intraorganic. In many cases these can be measured as changes in blood pressure, heart rate or galvanic skin resistance. In other cases the observable feeling reactions are so subtle and difficult to measure directly that we must simply depend on the introspective reports of the subject. *He reports by telling how he feels* —excited, relaxed, pleasant, or depressed. These verbal responses have been associated with the internal reactions, and, although they often are inadequate expressions, we have to depend on them until more adequate measurements are available. However, we must be constantly on our guard against the mentalistic concepts of feeling as being some aspect of "conscious experience" or some "psychic state." During the mentalistic domination of psychology in the nineteenth century and before, feelings were regarded as psychic qualities or atoms of experience. For example, Titchener allowed for only one dimension of feeling, expe-

[1] The term "emotion" is reserved for the special kind of action in which the organism is temporarily "psychologically frozen" following some intense stimulus. Emotional activities are often disorganized and temporarily disrupting kinds of behavior.

[2] J. R. Kantor, *A survey of the science of psychology*, Bloomington, Ind.: The Principia Press, Inc., 1933. See also N. H. Pronko and J. W. Bowles, Jr., *Empirical foundations of psychology* (New York: Rinehart & Co., Inc., 1951).

rience which was pleasant-unpleasant,[3] while his earlier teacher, Wundt, allowed for a tridimensional spread, pleasant-unpleasant, excitement-depression, and tension-release.[4] For both these men, these atoms of experience could be combined with sensations to make up consciousness.

Kinds of affective reactions.—If we consider feelings to be psychological acts which are definite interactions between persons and stimuli, it is quite arbitrary to limit the list to any set number. They are limited only by our capacity to measure them directly or our ability to describe them. Certainly if we are to use descriptive terms such as "happy," "sad," "calm," "excited," "pleasant," and "unpleasant," we include only a few common characteristic terms frequently employed to describe the behaviors we are studying. Our inadequate measures of feeling reactions, plus the inadequate referents for these terms in actual behavior, have served to place this area of psychology often in the realm of the mystic. However, if we remember that what we are considering are actual behavioral events, subtle though they may be, we can continue to regard the psychology of music as an objective investigation. Thus, the kinds of affective reactions are almost limitless, but our understanding of them is sometimes limited by the methods of investigation available to us.

The field of affective response to music has been only recently explored by psychologists who have approached music as a proper stimulus for behavioral analysis using the same methods which have characterized other branches of objective psychology. In previous decades studies have been of the ultra-introspective sort. Investigations would classify persons as to "affective types" by asking them to set down their "stream of consciousness," associations and feelings evoked by the stimuli. However, today we have a sample of useful studies which serve to describe the kind of action we are investigating. In this chapter we have omitted

[3] E. B. Titchener, *A textbook of psychology* (New York: The Macmillan Co., 1909–10).

[4] W. Wundt, *Grundriss der Psychologie* (Leipzig: Engelmann, 1896).

some reports because their approach is of the sort described above. We feel that this former kind of analysis of affective reactions to music tells very little.

The Affective Response to Music as a Physiological Response

According to our definition of feeling reaction, the most basic function of the stimulus is to elicit an internal reaction which we can measure. We know that when music such as a march is played by a military band, it usually elicits some skeletal activity such as tapping the foot or hand and thus may also be accompanied by some visceral changes.

Respiratory, cardiac and blood pressure changes to music.— If one examines some of the studies demonstrating various physiological reactions to music in order to determine what they are, he finds agreement on one point, namely that music *does give rise to changes in the rate of these reactions.* One of the earliest studies, reported by Foster and Gamble, showed that music caused breathing to become faster and shallower regardless of whether it was loud or soft or played in the major or minor mode.[5] Although no *specific marked* differences appeared, loud music tended to have more effect on accelerating breathing rate and decreasing regularity, while soft music tended to increase regularity. Major passages had more of an effect in accelerating breathing than did minor ones. They found the breathing pattern during music tended to resemble that during certain implicit reactions as far as rate and amplitude were concerned, but it tended to be less regular.

Weld[6] played a variety of musical compositions and recorded changes in pneumographic (breathing) and plethysmographic (blood supply) response. He found that when musical compo-

[5] E. A. M. Gamble and J. C. Foster, The effect of music on thoracic breathing, *Amer. J. Psychol.*, 1906, **17**, 406–14.

[6] H. P. Weld, An experimental study of musical enjoyment, *Amer. J. Psychol.*, 1912, **23**, 245–308.

sitions were played, there was a tendency for cardiac activity to increase, and changes in the distribution of blood supply were noted. There was also a pronounced irregularity in the rate and amplitude of respiration. These changes tended to vary directly with the intensity of the feeling responses as reported verbally by the subjects.

Washco[7] attempted to discover what changes in blood pressure and heart rate occurred when music was played. His musical stimuli consisted of eight recorded instrumental compositions including both jazz and classical numbers. He found that pulse rate and blood pressure changes occurred when certain compositions were played. In order to determine how these changes were related to the type of music played, he divided his compositions into four classes: melodic, rhythmic, harmonic, and "mixed dominance." (This last type contained the preceding three elements in balance.) Each of the kinds of compositions elicited a particular pattern of physiological reaction. Marches such as those composed by John Philip Sousa were principally rhythmic and tended to create the greatest rise in pulse and blood pressure. The more definite the melodic and rhythmic elements in the musical compositions, the more certain the physiological reactions were to occur. Selections which were popular or semiclassical in nature tended to raise both pulse rate and blood pressure, indicating an exhilarating effect on the listener responses.

Hyde[8] also investigated cardiac and blood pressure responses to music. Her investigation had as its aim a discovery of such changes as might be a function of (*a*) the kinds of musical selections, (*b*) media of stimuli presentation (vocal, instrumental), (*c*) attitudes of listeners, or (*d*) kinds of listeners (nationality, training, etc.). The physiological reactions measured were pulse

[7] A. Washco, *The effects of music upon pulse rate, blood pressure, and mental imagery* (Philadelphia: Temple University, 1933).

[8] I. M. Hyde, Effects of music upon electrocardiograms and blood pressure, in M. Schoen (ed.), *The effects of music* (New York: Harcourt, Brace & Co., Inc., 1927).

rate, systolic and diastolic blood pressure, and relative velocity of blood flow. The musical selections used in her experiment included the following selections:

Tchaikovsky: *Symphony No. 6 (Pathétique)*
Bizet: "Toreador's Song" from *Carmen*
Sousa: "National Emblem March"

She found that persons who show an appreciation for classical music as a rule also showed a lowering of the physiological functions measured. Secondly, the "Toreador's Song" tended to increase the physiological functions, but this song exerted no influence on those listeners not sensitive to music and those that were familiar with the song but did not care for it. Finally, as a rule, the "National Emblem March" caused an increase in cardiovascular activity, especially in velocity of blood flow and increase in blood pressure. However, for those who "lacked a fondness for music, the records remained unchanged."

> We may conclude from the results of this investigation that most people are unfavorably affected psychologically and physiologically by music that is characterized by tragic, mournful tones, and favorably affected by gay, rhythmical, rich-toned harmonic melodies. . . . The indications are that these selections of music rendered either vocally or instrumentally exert a favorable reflex action on the cardiovascular system, have also a favorable influence upon the muscle tone, working power, digestion, secretions, and other functions of the body.[9]

In summarizing the studies discussed so far on physiological reactions to music, we find that:

1. Music tends to cause changes in breathing, cardiac blood pressure, and blood supply. The tendency is more to increase the rate of these activities than to decrease it.
2. Music which is strongly vigorous and rhythmic has a greater tendency to increase these physiological processes than other kinds of compositions.

[9] *Ibid.*, p. 197.

Galvanic skin responses to music.—In 1888 Féré found that passing a weak electrical current through electrodes attached to an individual in a circuit with a galvanometer varied under different kinds of stimulation. The galvanic skin response, or psychogalvanic reflex as it is sometimes called, is due to the depolarization of the cell membranes of the skin through the action of the sweat glands, which are mediated by the sympathetic division of the autonomic nervous system. Although the galvanic skin response (g.s.r.) can be elicited by a large variety of stimuli, many of which are not affective in nature, it still holds that under certain conditions, the reaction is very definitely a part of the affective response pattern. For example, indifferent verbal responses as to the pleasantness or unpleasantness of a stimulus are related to minimal galvanic responses, while stimuli characterized verbally as pleasant or unpleasant are related to a greater g.s.r., the greatest changes being in the direction of unpleasantness.[10]

Wechsler[11] played a military march, an operatic aria, and a "ragtime" selection to a group of students. In some cases subjects reacted with g.s.r. curve changes while the music was played, particularly for the "ragtime" selection. The g.s.r. curves showed frequent excursions, as if to specific excitations. However, he noted that the g.s.r. for those musical selections was smaller than that provoked by such direct sensory stimulation as the prick of a pin or the sound of a gong.

Using the g.s.r., Phares[12] presented and re-presented musical selections to subjects over several months' time. She reports that this response was of little value in her analysis of their musical appreciation. However, it is quite possible that the stimulus function of the music could have been largely eliminated because of

[10] C. Landis and W. A. Hunt, The conscious correlates of galvanic skin response, *J. exp. Psychol.*, 1935, **18**, 505–29.

[11] D. Wechsler, The measurement of emotional reaction: researches on the psychogalvanic reflex, *Arch. Psychol.*, 1925, No. 76.

[12] M. L. Phares, Analysis of music appreciation by means of p.g.r. technique, *J. exp. Psychol.*, 1934, **17**, 119–40.

the complexity of the tasks which the subjects were instructed to perform while listening to the music. For example, they were asked to answer questions and press keys when the music appeared pleasant or unpleasant. She did note that the amount of skin resistance change did hold a positive relationship to the strength of the affective reaction (pleasant) reported verbally. Those musical selections which gave a greater than average change in skin resistance were also those where the corresponding verbal reports indicated a stronger affective reaction.

A recent study on the g.s.r. to music is reported by Dreher.[13] The purpose of his investigation was to discover any relationship between subjects' verbal reports and galvanic skin responses as they were affected by different types of music. (In the next section we will note that subjects' verbal reports on how they feel when music is played show a striking agreement.) Dreher used eight piano selections for musically trained and untrained groups of subjects. The g.s.r. responses were measured with a standard galvanometer to indicate the amount of sympathetic participation while listening to music on the phonograph records. The verbal reports were obtained by use of the Hevner Adjective Circle (see Figure 12). Dreher substantiated the findings of previous investigators on verbal reports of affective reactions. Responses of musically trained and untrained subjects are similar, although the trained subjects seem to show a greater variety of *reported* affective responses, as evidenced by the fact that they checked more adjectives on the "circle" and showed less variability in their checking. Accordingly, in the g.s.r. the trained subjects showed a greater rise in the level of skin resistance before, during, and after the playing of the music. The trained subjects also showed a significantly greater momentary decrease in resistance during the playing of the music. Musically trained subjects showed a relationship between affective mood as expressed by checked words on the adjective circle and the g.s.r.

[13] R. E. Dreher, The relationship between verbal reports and galvanic skin responses to music (unpublished Doctor's thesis), Indiana University, 1947.

This did not hold true for the untrained subjects. He interprets this differential responsiveness to modes of the musical stimuli as being built up in the course of a person's musical training. The lack of differential responsiveness in the untrained group is equally significant, since this group was selected for its poverty of training and lack of interest in music. By their own admission, these subjects found music not to be an important stimulus in their lives. However, that they do exhibit changes in g.s.r. during music is an objective indication that they are responding affectively to music. This response is less differentiated and far less intense than that for the trained group. Because their responses were less intense, they showed no consistent responsiveness pattern.

These findings support our belief that affective reactions to music, like other musical reactions, are learned behaviors acquired throughout an individual's life history of interaction with the stimuli. This is significant because the trained subjects showed a wider variety of responses as checked on the adjective circle and in g.s.r.

Misbach[14] considered the effect of variations in the pitch of tonal stimuli on galvanic and cardiovascular responses. He used a Hathaway galvanometer for measuring g.s.r. and a polygraph for the blood pressure and pulse changes. Stimuli consisted of tones ranging in frequency by octaves from 64 cps. to 4,096 cps. at two different levels of loudness. He found that tonal stimuli of relative purity did not elicit significant changes in pulse rate or blood pressure. Shock expectation and pain were eliminated in the presentation of the stimuli by gradually increasing the loudness. However, tonal stimuli which were loud enough to be unpleasant but not to give pain and which did not surprise or frighten the subject usually elicited a lowering of bodily resistance (g.s.r.). Galvanic responses occurred more frequently for tones of higher pitches (512 cps. and up) and increased in

[14] L. E. Misbach, Effect of pitch of tone-stimuli upon body resistance and cardiovascular phenomena, *J. exp. Psychol.*, 1932, **16**, 167–83.

magnitude as frequency became higher. Although Misbach's study deals only with isolated tones rather than music in context, his findings are worth reporting at this point.

Our evidence shows, then, that a galvanic response considered to be affective in nature is elicited by musical stimuli. The nature of this response is related to verbal reports of the subject as to how he feels. There is a relationship between this response and training in music, indicating that an affective reaction is one which is built up during the life history of the individual. It is more prominent in musically trained subjects than in those who are musically indifferent.

The Affective Response to Music as a Verbal Report

Mood effects.—Our experimental reports so far give us substantial evidence that physiological responses occur in both musical and unmusical subjects when music is presented as a stimulus. These physiological changes are measurable affective responses. Often the affective response is a very subtle one which can best be described by the subject himself. That these responses are affective is not doubtful because of the obvious observable effect that the stimuli have on the subject. Evidence comes from the subject's report on how he feels and from the fact that he remains fairly inactive with regard to the stimulus object.

Two early studies were conducted by Schoen and Gatewood,[15] based on the data obtained from 20,000 persons on their responses to a variety of vocal and instrumental phonograph records. The data were collected all over the United States from a wide variety of individuals of various training, experience, age, and interests. An analysis of this mass of data indicated some interesting findings. Musical compositions produce changes in mood (affective reactions) reported by the subjects, and the changes

[15] M. Schoen and E. L. Gatewood, Problems related to the mood effects of music (chap. viii); The mood effects of music (chap. vii), in M. Schoen (ed.), *The effects of music* (New York: Harcourt, Brace & Co., Inc., 1927).

induced by a selection or the same class of selections *are strikingly similar* for the large majority of listeners regardless of their training, age, or experience.

A more restricted follow-up study was undertaken by the same investigators to check the reliability of these subjects' affective reactions on two separate occasions. Using a check list of descriptive adjectives for verbal reports, they found a high degree of response agreement in the two different presentations of the same music.

Hevner[16] has developed a check list of adjectives characterizing various feeling responses. Any subject after listening to a particular musical composition may be asked to check every word on a list which seems to describe the music. The subject may check as few or as many of the adjectives as he likes. These adjectives are grouped together and arranged on an "adjective circle" (see Figure 12). Some examples from her studies of hundreds of musical compositions will illustrate the nature of her findings. The scherzo from Mendelssohn's *Midsummer Night's Dream,* her college students described as exciting and impetuous above all (group 7), also as playful and graceful (group 5) and happy and gay (group 6). It was not at all sad, plaintive, or serious. The subjects reported no difficulty in describing the mood which the composition supposedly intends to convey to the listeners.

Different mood responses were reported to the second part of the first movement of Tchaikovsky's *Symphony No. 6 in B Minor (Pathétique).* Reports characterize it as dignified (group 1), plaintive (group 3), and to a lesser degree, sad (group 2) and lyrical (group 4). There were no checks in the playful and gay groups.

However, all compositions cannot be so clearly characterized as eliciting affective responses or so clearly described and quan-

[16] K. Hevner, Expression in music: a discussion of experimental studies and theories, *Psychol. Rev.*, 1935, **47,** 186–204; Experimental studies of the elements of expression in music, *Amer. J. Psychol.*, 1936, **48,** 246–68.

titatively measured. An illustration of this is Debussy's *Reflections on the Water.* The respondents checked adjectives which were fairly well scattered among the eight groups on the adjective circle. The greatest number of checks occurred in two groups

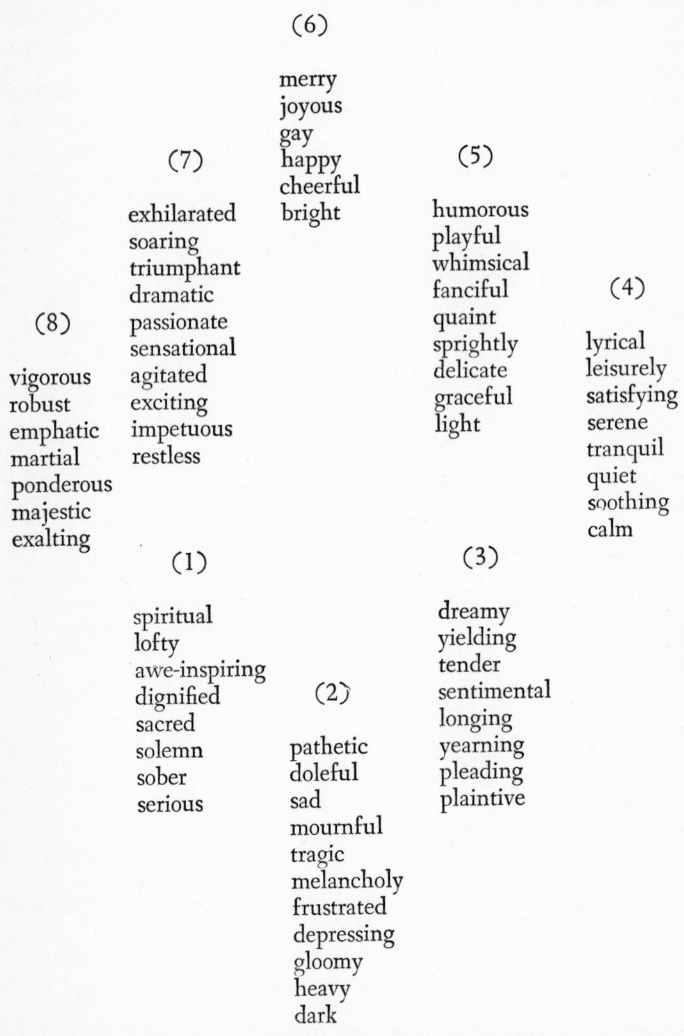

FIG. 12.—Hevner's Adjective Circle.

which are diametrically opposite each other, dreamy and sentimental (group 3) and exciting and impetuous (group 7). It is quite obvious that such a composition can elicit a variety of different responses because of its changes in structural content. This also holds true for many other compositions. Debussy has included several well-defined sections in musical structure. It may have been intentional on his part in his attempt to describe musically the nature of his subject, reflections on the water. They may be clear and still at one time and at another restless, changing, and distorted. If these several impressions are intentional on the part of the composer (who is to know?), then Hevner has experimentally demonstrated this very well.

To see if it is possible to separate out the various affective responses to different parts of a composition as in the above, Hevner selected another group of subjects and instructed them to check their adjective as soon as they felt some reaction to the Debussy selection. Tabulations were made for different sections of the composition. Results indicated remarkable agreement among subjects. Part I was described as serene (group 4) and dreamy-sentimental (group 3), also as somewhat playful (group 5). The middle section of the composition was in sharp contrast to the first, being described as restless, exciting, agitated (group 7) and playful (group 5). Hevner found that training, intelligence, or aptitude for music had very little effect on the students' ability to describe the selections played. The well-trained individual may be able to differentiate the moods more sharply, but the difference in the records of the trained and untrained students was not appreciable.

When subjects were asked to identify affective responses aroused by a composition from a list of "defined emotions," Hampton[17] found the degree of agreement was related to the nature of the composition. The more a selection could be characterized as program music, the easier it was for the subjects to

[17] P. J. Hampton, The emotional element in music, *J. gen. Psychol.*, 1945, **33**, 237–50.

describe their affective reactions to it. He also found unpleasant reactions like despair, agony, and grief more easily identified than such pleasant feelings as joy, amusement, and love. Rigg[18] found that students could tell whether music was intended to be sad or joyful, but when progressively finer discriminations had to be made, they were not so successful. He believes that when subtle feelings do occur, they are the result of previous associations and are more or less individual in nature.

From his survey of studies on mood effects of music, Dreher makes the following conclusions:

> 1. Subjects' descriptions of the moods of musical stimuli (excerpts or whole compositions), selected on a basis of certain clear-cut musical characteristics, are remarkably uniform. As these musical elements are altered systematically, changes in the subjects' responses occur in a generally predictable manner.
>
> 2. The close agreement among subjects in describing the mood effects of music does not appear to be closely related to intelligence, tested musical aptitude, musical training, or age level above the sixth grade.
>
> 3. Adjective check lists have proved an adequate and reliable procedure for obtaining subjects' responses in this type of study. Adjective lists using fewer than 15 choices have not generally been satisfactory, while longer lists with individual adjectives arranged into general mood groups have shown their experimental worth.[19]

Effects of major and minor modes.—What aspects of the musical stimulus object are especially important in eliciting certain kinds of affective responses? We are now ready to consider some characteristics of the stimuli which may influence our responses to them. The first of these is the matter of mode, major or minor. Listeners have been prone to describe two very definite affective reactions as being intrinsically related to the

[18] M. Rigg, An experiment to determine how accurately college students can interpret intended meanings of musical compositions, *J. exp. Psychol.*, 1937, **21**, 223–29.

[19] Dreher, *op. cit.*, pp. 8–9.

major and minor modes. Hemholtz,[20] Edmund Gurney,[21] and Halbert H. Britain,[22] have emphasized in considerable detail the inseparable relationship between the minor mode and feelings of grief and melancholy. To the minor triad has been attributed the "power" to initiate a nervous system reaction which terminates in organic depression, whereas the major mode has the "power" to elicit feelings of joy and happiness. Gurney assumed that these characteristics are natural properties of the musical stimulus in the same way he believed consonance and dissonance to be. This capacity of the stimulus to elicit a response is supposed to be an inherent quality of the object due to certain characteristics which can be called forth without the influence of experience or training.

An interbehavioral approach to this problem would not accept such a notion, namely that the mood of certain modes inherently calls forth affective responses any more than that certain combinations of sound are naturally consonant or dissonant. We have already seen in Chapter 6 that consonance and dissonance are responses subject to the same cultural conditioning as any other kind of psychological activity. Gurney's attitude resembles that of Helmholtz on consonance; consonance or dissonance were believed to be functions of natural properties of vibrating objects, in this case, beating. Gurney believed that affective differences which exist are due to the "characteristic notes of the minor scale as compared with the corresponding ones of the major." [23]

The significant experimental evidence for the function of the major and minor modes in affective reactions comes essentially from two sources, Heinlein [24] and Hevner.[25] Heinlein presented

[20] H. L. F. von Helmholtz, *On the sensations of tone*, trans. Ellis (4th ed.; London: Longmans, Green & Co., 1912).

[21] E. Gurney, *The power of sound* (London: Smith, Elder, 1880).

[22] H. H. Britain, *The philosophy of music* (New York: Longmans, Green & Co., Inc., 1911).

[23] Gurney, *op. cit.*, p. 272.

[24] C. Heinlein, The affective characters of major and minor modes in music, *J. comp. Psychol.*, 1928, **8**, 101–42.

[25] K. Hevner, The affective character of major and minor modes in music, *Amer. J. Psychol.*, 1935, **47**, 103–18.

forty-eight major and minor chords to thirty subjects who were classified as trained and untrained, musically speaking. All chords were in the tonic position and were presented under different conditions of loudness. His subjects were asked to give their verbal reports as to how they felt when these stimuli were presented. They were asked to select a word from a printed list such as "bright, cheerful, hard, clear, doleful, dull, gloomy, happy, joyful, melancholy, sad, soothing, yearning . . ."[26]

The list consisted of terms conventionally associated with major and minor chords. The musically trained subjects gave 35.7 per cent of "typical" minor responses to major and 11.5 per cent of "typical" major responses to minor chords. He found the intensity of the chord had the most marked effect on the responses. Soft chords, for example, were predominantly soothing, whether major or not. Heinlein concludes that the affective response was *not so much* a function of the nature of the chord, since subjects gave "typically" major responses to minor chords and vice versa. A loud chord is rarely judged soothing. Both major and minor chords were judged soothing when presented softly. However, loud major chords evoked major responses more often than soft major chords, and soft major chords evoked minor responses more often than loud minor chords. Finally, loud minor chords evoked major responses more often than soft minor chords. He concludes that feeling-tone responses (such as joyful or melancholic) commonly attributed to major and minor chords are due to training to respond in this specific manner rather than any intrinsic character of the chord. The theory long held by authorities in the field, that there are intrinsic properties in chords, should be abandoned. The mode in which a composition is written has little relation to the affective reaction aroused. Compositions written in minor keys may be reacted to by both trained and untrained subjects as bright, happy, cheerful, joyful, or exuberant, just as major key compositions can stimulate affective reactions of gloomy, plaintive, melancholic, and mournful.

[26] Heinlein, *op. cit.*

Hevner[27] has criticized this study on the basis that it used only single chords. Such stimuli, she says, cannot be considered "music" because they are presented out of the context of any composition. The composers who characterize a minor mode as dull and melancholic have in mind its effect when used in a musical composition. Secondly, the affective reaction to a minor mode, for example, may be a gradual reaction resulting from the accumulation of the auditory stimuli. To counteract this difficulty she presented ten short musical compositions with one version of each in the major and minor modes. These were presented to subjects who were asked to check words from her adjective list which seemed to them to best describe the composition being played. She found the adjectives checked did conform to the traditional attitudes regarding the effects of the two modes. For the minor mode, the melancholic, gloomy, depressing group of adjectives seemed most important to the subjects. Minor mode compositions were also characterized as plaintive, yearning, and longing. It is interesting to note that minor compositions were often described as being mysterious, mystical, and weird. For the major mode the most characteristic affective responses were happy, sprightly, cheerful, joyous, gay, and bright, followed by playful, graceful, quaint, and fanciful. A lack of training or musical ability (measured by the Seashore tests) did not obliterate the subjects' ability to discriminate the accepted meanings of the two modes.

However, just because the historically affirmed effects of the two modes have been upheld by Hevner's study does not *necessarily* mean that these responses *are due* to any inherent properties of the objects. Hevner has admitted training to be an important factor in facilitating affective responses to music in general. However, she states further that a lack of training or musical status or level of intelligence need not obliterate the ability to discriminate the generally accepted effects of the two modes.

[27] Hevner, *Amer. J. Psychol.*, **47**, 103–18.

These two studies are not necessarily contradictory, since each was considering the stimuli of music in a different way; one as separate chords, the other as chords in a musical context. Heinlein has demonstrated that there is nothing inherent in the chords which need elicit the historically accepted affective reactions to them. On the other hand, Hevner has shown that, when compositions are played, we do react to them with characteristic feelings of melancholy for the minor and happy feelings for the major. These responses are part of our cultural attitudes, and even though one does not have specific musical training, this does not mean that he has not acquired the typically cultural reactions.

Pitch and tempo.—In studying the affective reaction to differences in pitch and tempo of musical compositions, Hevner [28] used the same method which she employed in her studies on the major and minor modes. For each element (pitch or tempo), two versions of a composition were prepared in which every factor was held constant but the one to be investigated. She points out the difficulty in these investigations in the preparation of two versions of music for experimental use. In the pitch experiment, thirteen compositions were used which sounded pleasant and musical when transposed one octave either above or below their original positions. In the tempo variable, two contrasting rates of speed were chosen which would sound pleasing at both rates.

The effects of two speeds indicate that slow tempos are most effective in eliciting responses in the dignified, calm, and serene groups of adjectives. They also elicited sentimental-tender and sad responses, whereas the fast tempos aroused reactions in the happy-gay, exciting-restless groups and to some slighter degree in the graceful and vigorous groups. Tempos with markings of 102, 104, 112, 152 were considered fast; slow tempos were those marked 63, 72, and 80. These findings have been essentially

[28] K. Hevner, The affective value of pitch and tempo in music, *Amer. J. Psychol.*, 1937, **49**, 621–30.

substantiated by Rigg,[29] who has found that the fast tempo tends to make music happy, while slow tempo has the opposite effect.

Hevner found that high pitch affected the subjects' reactions in the direction of sprightly-humorous, while low pitch reactions centered more in the sad qualities as well as the vigorous-majestic and dignified-serious groups. In another experiment, Rigg[30] presented to his subjects musical phrases each played in different registers. He found that when phrases are shifted up in register as much as an octave, the responses are those of happier, or at least, less sad character. He presented five phrases in their original form and in four transformations such as shifts up or down an octave, shifts up a fifth or down a fourth, shifts to the key of the dominant, shifts down one step and up one half-step. The subjects were presented with check lists of words of two sorts, serious-sad and pleasant-happy. Shifts of as much as an octave upward always made the phrase happier or less sorrowful. Shifts of approximately half an octave "up or down" tended to show the higher register as happier. Lesser shifts showed inconsequential changes.

Effects of melody, harmony and rhythm.—In considering the variables of melody, harmony, and rhythm, the experiment proposed by Hevner[31] had to be limited to one of the many aspects of each. In rhythm two patterns were compared, one with a full chord on every beat, as in a chorale or hymn tune, the other a free-flowing rhythm. The particular aspect of melody chosen for study was the rise and fall in melodic line. In each of the compositions studied, the original melody was presented, and an alternate form which was an inversion was given. Many com-

[29] M. G. Rigg, Speed as a determiner of musical mood, *J. exp. Psychol.*, 1940, **27**, 566–71.

[30] M. G. Rigg, The effect of register and tonality upon musical mood, *J. Musicology*, 1940, **2**, 49–61.

[31] K. Hevner, Experimental studies of the elements of expression in music, *Amer. J. Psychol.*, 1936, **48**, 246–68.

positions had to be discarded as useless, either because the inversion was unsuitable or because the harmony of the new melody could not be made to follow that of the original. In studying harmonic structure, the changes made were from simple consonant harmonies resolved in a smooth manner to complex and dissonant harmonies which did not always reach a satisfactory resolution.

Results indicated a firm rhythm where a strong beat occurs is judged most often dignified, spiritual, and lofty, no doubt because of previous associations with hymns, chorales, and other church music. The factor of rhythm showed its greatest response function in two sections of the adjective circle; the firm strong-beat rhythms were responded to as being vigorous, dignified, and solemn, and the smooth-flowing rhythms were light, happy, and playful.

From the viewpoint of affective mood, Hevner has noted that excitement takes its rise from swift tempo. Complex harmonies also contribute to this feeling. Dignity was expressed in slow tempos, firm rhythms, and lower pitches, with some aid from major mode, simple melodies, and ascending melodies. Dreamy-sentimental reactions are called forth by minor modes, slow tempos, and flowing rhythms, with some contribution from simple harmonies and high pitches.

Happiness requires fast tempos, simple harmonies, and flowing rhythms. Melody played a very small role in arousing any particular affective reactions. Tempo, on the other hand, seems of greatest importance. Major modes give rise to happiness and brightness and minor modes to sadness, but both are quite useless in arousing responses of vigor, excitement, calm, or dignity.

Hevner summarizes her studies on the various aspects of the stimulus and the affective reaction in the following way:

> (*a*) The major mode is happy, merry, graceful, and playful. The minor mode is sad, dreamy, and sentimental; and such qualities as excitement, vigor, dignity, serenity, etc., are not determined by either mode.

(*b*) Firm rhythms are vigorous and dignified; flowing rhythms are happy, graceful, dreamy, and tender; and neither is particularly useful in determining such characteristics as excitement, satisfaction, and serenity.

(*c*) Complex, dissonant harmonies are exciting, agitating, vigorous, and inclined toward sadness; simple consonant harmonies are happy, graceful, serene, and lyrical.

(*d*) Differences in expressiveness caused by rising and falling of the melodic line are not clear-cut, distinct, or constant. There are tendencies toward the expression of both exhilaration and serenity by the descending melodies, and toward dignity and solemnity by the ascending.[32]

The Affective Response as a Function of Repetition and Familiarity

Gilliland and Moore[33] have investigated the effects of the repetition of classical and jazz compositions. The responses were recorded as introspective estimates of the subjects' enjoyment of the music. The phonograph selections played were:

Beethoven's *Fifth Symphony* (First Movement)
Tchaikovsky's *Sixth Symphony* (First Movement)
"That's It" (fox trot)
"Umbrellas to Mend" (onestep)

Their results indicate that with repetition the two classical selections gained more in enjoyment than did the popular selections. However, the greatest increase was noted for the Tchaikovsky selection. Very little change occurred for the popular selections. Another early study by Washburn, Child, and Abel[34] aimed at finding the effect of immediate repetition of a musical

[32] *Ibid.*, p. 268.

[33] A. R. Gilliland and H. T. Moore, The immediate and long-time effects of classical and popular phonograph selections, in M. Schoen, (ed.), *The effects of music* (New York: Harcourt, Brace & Co., Inc., 1927).

[34] M. F. Washburn, M. A. Child, and T. M. Abel, The effects of immediate repetition on the pleasantness or unpleasantness of music, in M. Schoen, (ed.), *The effects of music* (New York: Harcourt, Brace & Co., Inc., 1927).

selection on the responses of pleasantness and unpleasantness. Groups of listeners heard a section of a composition five times in succession. This procedure was followed for eight compositions. The selections chosen were taken from various types of orchestral works which were considered (*a*) severely classical, (*b*) serious-popular-classical, (*c*) easy-popular-classical, and (*d*) popular. Severely classical selections included Schubert's *Unfinished Symphony* (First Movement), Mozart's *Quartet in D Major* (Andante), and Beethoven's *Quartet in C Major* (Fugue). The serious-popular-classical group included Haydn's *Military Symphony* (Allegro), Haydn's *Surprise Symphony* (Andante Cantabile e Vivace), and Schubert's *Minuet in A Minor*. Easy-popular-classical selections included Tchaikovsky's *Andante Cantabile*, Nicolai's Overture to *The Merry Wives of Windsor*, and Mendelssohn's *On Wings of Song*, played by Heifetz. Popular selections were "On Miami's Shore" (waltz), "Rosalie" (waltz), and "Kismet" (fox trot). Subjects were asked to record the pleasantness of each selection on a scale of 1 to 5.

In the case of popular music, Washburn found that repetition tended to lower more than to raise the pleasant response. For more serious music, repetition tends to raise rather than lower the pleasant reaction. Repetition of very popular music reaches a maximal peak of pleasantness at an early performance in contrast to the serious-classical composition in which the greatest amount of pleasure is derived from a later performance. Musical individuals have a tendency to lose their pleasurable responses after repetition of the stimulus sooner than unmusical ones except for the seriously classical works. When subjects were asked their opinions as to why the pleasant reactions declined with repetition of the stimulus, their introspective reports indicated fatigue to be the cause of the diminished pleasantness.

In cases where pleasantness increased with repetition, subjects reported their reasons as being agreeable imagery, increased comprehension, and greater attention to the rhythm, melody, and instrumentation. These sources of increased pleasantness of the reaction the authors believe explain why popular music tends to decrease in pleasantness more rapidly than classical with repetition. Most classical music requires greater attention and has a greater variety of stimulus functions, so one can turn from one feature to another of the composition as he listens.

Downey and Knapp[35] investigated the effects of familiarity and sequence of selections on the affective response of pleasantness and unpleasantness. College students listened to a musical program of nine compositions of various sorts, including program music, national music, poetic thought, and formal construction. The students listened to these programs at weekly intervals for five weeks. They reported that repetition increased the pleasantness of the musical compositions. The reported gain was greatest for those compositions considered by experts to be more subtle and of greater aesthetic value, indicating that those of more artistic nature would come to be most strongly preferred. Those compositions which tended to increase affective reactivity and were considered greatest in artistic value were Mendelssohn's Overture to *A Midsummer Night's Dream*, Elgar's *Pomp and Circumstance*, Massenet's "Meditation" from *Thais*, Lumbye's *Dream Pictures,* and Crouch's *Kathleen Mavourneen.* Less artistic selections were "Columbia, the Gem of the Ocean," *In a Clock Store* by Orth, *Invercarill March* by Lithgow and *March Slav* by Tchaikovsky.

Verveer[36] played two jazz compositions to undergraduate students who were asked to rate these compositions on a scale of affective preference from unpleasantness to pleasantness. He found the reports following repetition of the selection conformed to Fechner's observations on affective change,[37] that with the repetition of a composition the affective value increases

[35] J. E. Downey and G. E. Knapp, The effect on a musical programme of familiarity and of sequence of selections, in M. Schoen, (ed.), *The effects of music* (New York: Harcourt, Brace & Co., Inc., 1927).

[36] E. M. Verveer, H. Barry, Jr., and W. A. Bousefield, Changes in affectivity with repetition, *Amer. J. Psychol.*, 1933, **45**, 130–34.

[37] G. F. Fechner, *Vorschule der Aesthetik* (1st ed.; Leipzig: Breitkopf und Haertal, 1876), II, 240–43.

up to a certain limit. If the stimulus is continued past the point of optimum affectivity, its value is lessened unless there is an intervening time interval. This held for both of the jazz selections played.

Krugman[38] played selections of classical and "swing" music to three types of subjects, some of whom were chosen for their extreme preference for "swing" music and disdain for classical music, others for their preferences for classical music, and the rest for their indifference to all types of music. The recordings of classical and "swing" music were so chosen as to have an initial very slightly pleasant value as judged by the subjects. They were played on a phonograph once a week for eight weeks. He found that with repetition subjects showed a shift in the direction of pleasantness. This was true for both classical and "swing" music. He concludes that "the positive affective shift can be produced by sheer repetition of the musical experience regardless of the classical or nonclassical character of the music."[39]

Although our studies do not show complete agreement, certain trends are evident in regard to the pleasant-unpleasant function of the stimulus with repetition and familiarity of the stimulus.

1. Classical selections tend to gain more in pleasant affective value with repetition than do popular ones.
2. Popular music tends to reach the maximum of pleasantness at an early repetition, whereas classical selections reach their affective height with later performances.
3. With repetition, compositions considered by experts to be of greatest musical aesthetic value show the greatest gain in affective reaction with repetition.
4. Popular music reaches a rapid peak in affective value followed by a rapid decline in pleasantness with continued repetition.

[38] H. E. Krugman, Affective responses to music as a function of familiarity *J. abnorm. soc. Psychol.*, 1943, **38**, 388–93.

[39] *Ibid.*, p. 392.

Why do our affective responses to music change as a result of repetition of the stimulus and increased familiarity with the composition? In Washburn's study, subjects were asked to account for decreasing and increasing pleasantness with repetition. In the case of decreased pleasantness, they reported fatigue to be a main reason. For increased pleasantness the reasons given included (*a*) better comprehension of the composition, (*b*) greater attention to the individual aspects of the stimulus (instrumentation, harmony, melody, form, etc.), (*c*) agreeable imagery, and (*d*) associations. These authors comment as follows: "These sources of increased pleasantness explain why simple popular music tended to decrease rather than increase in pleasantness with repetition. Nearly all of them are influences which require complexity, in order that attention may turn from one feature to another of the composition." [40]

Popular music often has a rapid rise followed by a rapid decline in pleasantness with repetition. Even untrained listeners, the individuals with little musical behavior equipment to draw upon, such as understanding musical form, harmony, melody, etc., are able to attend to and perceive the simple relationships in the stimulus object with repetitions, after which they report boredom and fatigue, both of which are correlated with an unpleasant reaction. Although a person responds affectively to the situation, he may also react intellectually to it in his analysis of the composition. The trained listener, with his increased knowledge of musical construction, perceives the simple relationships in popular music even sooner than the untrained and finds this music uninteresting at an early stage in the sequence of musical repetitions. The fact that the later performances of seriously classical music in the Washburn study were more favored by the listeners is further evidence that there is a great deal to be found and responded to in these compositions. Both musical and unmusical persons are continually learning something new. In classical music, subjects who are trained often tire more quickly than un-

[40] Washburn *et al., op. cit.*

trained subjects (except on some very serious compositions). This is because they reach the maximum of comprehension sooner and further repetitions of the musical stimuli fail to call forth additional interest, understanding, or feeling reactions.

Musical Taste

The nature of musical taste.—We have already recognized that an affective reaction to music is a function of many characteristics of the stimulus object (tempo, pitch, harmony, rhythm) as well as of the organism's life history of contacts with the stimuli (familiarity and repetition) and the kind of music it happens to be (classical, semiclassical, popular). However, as yet we have not accounted for why one person prefers jazz to classical music or why another prefers the compositions of Brahms to those of Beethoven. Our preferences (liking-disliking) for compositions, composers, or schools of music is what we refer to when we speak of musical taste. This is a *preferential response.* On the basis of some characteristic of the stimulus and functions of the responding organism, choices are made of liking to listen to some works more than others, or to music as compared to no music. Psychologists have attempted to analyze the nature of musical taste and the reasons for these preferences.

According to Farnsworth, "We agree on the composers we call eminent."[41] As evidence for this statement he cites a study in which he asked members of the American Musicological Society to consider a list of composers and check the names of those whose contributions to music were of the greatest importance. Dividing his responses in two subgroups alternately as the replies to his questionnaire were received, he found the first nine choices were identical for both groups as follows:

[41] P. R. Farnsworth, *Musical taste: its measurement and cultural nature* (Stanford, Calif.: Stanford University Press, 1950), p. 7. The reader is encouraged to read Dr. Farnsworth's monograph, as much of its contents give experimental evidence for the viewpoints expressed in this book.

Rank	*Group 1*	*Group 2*
1	Bach	Bach
2	Beethoven	Beethoven
3	Mozart	Wagner
4	Wagner	Mozart
5	Brahms	Haydn
6	Haydn	Palestrina
7	Schubert	Brahms
8	Palestrina	Handel
9	Handel	Schubert

Farnsworth[42] conducted a similar examination of students taken from psychology classes at Stanford University and of high-school and fifth- and sixth-grade students. Here again he found marked agreement: "While the high school choices do not agree as closely as those of the musicologists, the similarity between the two columns is marked."[43] Finally, he found names of popular composers to be similar in eminence as judged by two groups of college students. The nine names which headed the lists of both groups were Gershwin, Berlin, Kern, Carmichael, Porter, David Rose, Duke Ellington, Ferde Grofé, and Johnny Mercer.

"We agree on what we enjoy."[44] Farnsworth found a close correlation (.86) between rankings of rated eminence of composers and professed enjoyment of the composers' music. In other words, similar groups show similar likes for composers and music. "Conductors and disk jockeys arrange similar programs."[45] The evidence which Farnsworth presents for this statement comes partially from extensive studies done by Mueller and Hevner[46] of Indiana University showing that the programs arranged by the major symphony orchestral conductors in the United States resemble each other to a marked degree. In their analyses of the programs of seven leading American symphony or-

[42] *Ibid.*
[43] *Ibid.*, p. 9.
[44] *Ibid.*, p. 10.
[45] *Ibid.*, p. 14.
[46] J. H. Mueller and K. Hevner, *Trends in musical taste* (Ind. Univ. Publ., Humanity Series, 1942, No. 8, p. 59).

chestras from 1936 to 1941, they found agreement in frequency of composers appearing on the separate programs as follows:

1. Beethoven
2. Brahms
3. Mozart
4. Wagner
5. Tchaikovsky
6. Sibelius
7. R. Strauss
8. Bach
9. Ravel
10. Schumann

Thus, there tends to be great similarity in musical taste which is due to cultural conditioning. There is no evidence that taste is an inherent function of the organism or due to any necessary natural property of the musical stimuli. Musical taste tends to be a fairly stable kind of response; we tend to agree as a group on what composers and music we like, but our taste also may often be an individual matter and subject to change from time to time. We have spoken so far only of similarity in the United States. Farnsworth and Meyer have both studied musical behavior in other cultures and have found tremendous individual differences in kinds of and preferences for music and in capacity to respond to different aspects of music, indicating that musical preferences are not universal but are subject to many conditions of the particular culture involved.

> It has been shown that Occidental love for simple rhythms, careful tuning, fixed tonal steps, harmonies, the tonic effect, and the diatonic scale is not shared the world over. The African predilection for complicated rhythmic patterns was so far out of line with the taste and perceptual abilities of many of the early missionaries that they commonly reported the Africans to be arhythmical. The Chinese often appear to be oblivious to mistunings: they love music which has no harmony in the Occidental sense of the word. Yet Orientals can learn to love

Western music and, indeed, with continued residence in America come to appreciate our musical principles and gradually to develop facility in the perception of small auditory differences. Conversely, the people of the Western world often learn to love alien music forms and to master more complicated rhythmic patterns. When constantly subjected to poor tuning, the American slowly loses his need for any sensitivity to pitch exactitude.[47]

Some factors of which musical taste is a function.—In considering the responses of particular groups of musicians and college or high-school students, we noted considerable agreement *within these groups* as to musical tastes, and we noted that although these preferences tend to be stable, they are subject to change over a period of time. Mueller and Hevner have found that orchestral programs do change over a *long period of years.*[48] Finally, Farnsworth's studies with Oriental and Occidental students show the individual differences in cultures in responsiveness to various aspects of the musical stimulus, particularly rhythm and pitch.[49]

Recognizing that preferences for music are complexly determined, we nevertheless are interested in discovering some of the factors which influence our musical tastes.

C. E. Seashore in his book *Why We Love Music*[50] says that our taste for music creates a feeling of physiological well-being; it carries us through the realm of creative imagination; it is the language of emotion; it is self-propelling through natural impulses such as rhythm; it satisfies our intellectual cravings and lets us live with the ideal. An objective analysis of these statements leaves us with little more than mere words, with little bearing on actual events in space and time. From the viewpoint of descriptive psychology, an understanding of why we like music

[47] Farnsworth, *op. cit.*, pp. 22–23.
[48] Mueller and Hevner, *op. cit.*
[49] Farnsworth, *op. cit.*
[50] C. E. Seashore, *Why we love music* (Bryn Mawr, Pa.: Oliver Ditson Co., Inc., 1941).

can only be had by an analysis of some of the observable variables in the situation, and life histories of the individuals involved.

In Howes's book *Borderland of Music and Psychology*,[51] we find even less insight into why we enjoy music. He tells us that we love music which is sincere, not shallow, sentimental, or cliché, not marred by base motives and emotions. As in Seashore's criteria, we find vague and mentalistic statements. How do we judge music as sincere? By its melody, rhythm, or tempo? If so, how? What, indeed, is shallow music? Is cliché music that which is played often? If so, then Bach and Beethoven are good examples! How can we possibly know the motivation of the composer unless he introspectively tells us that either in his autobiography or on the printed score. This is not always done, and when it is, the results are often very mysterious. Again we find that such subjective mentalistic attempts at musical analysis are completely useless.

Training. As Farnsworth points out,[52] one of the most important factors influencing musical taste is our training. We are taught the importance of Beethoven and Mozart early in our careers. These names have great prestige value, and we learn to respect them in the same sense that we learn to respect other great artists and national heroes. This is not intended to mean, of course, that any composer or composition is great only because we are told so. Greatness has survived through the centuries for other reasons beside the simple passing-on of attitudes from one generation to another. The fact that the mediocre in most instances eventually dies out is obvious. Nevertheless, we are tremendously influenced by the early attitudes and opinions of our teachers and parents. The whole field of clinical psychology gives us evidence for the importance of early training and conditioning for proper adjustment to later life. Some of us prefer opera to the symphony because of the greater part that kind of

[51] F. Howes, *The borderland of music and psychology* (London: Kegan Paul, Trench, Trubner & Co., Ltd., 1926).
[52] Farnsworth, *op. cit.*, p. 63.

music played in our early musical lives. Those who have not had musical training often prefer the less serious music, since they are handicapped in their understanding of serious music because of their lack of ability to comprehend it. Those who have learned to analyze and understand the complexities of serious music show great preference for it, while individuals with little musical training do not have the behavior equipment necessary to understand and respond to the music of our great composers.

Repetition and familiarity. We have already considered the function of repetition and familiarity on affective reactions. Wiebe[53] has shown that although extensive playing of popular songs over the radio does not necessarily increase subject's preferences for these songs, a lack of "plugging" seemed to result in a decrease of their preferences. Our preferences for more complex music tends to increase with repetition, while simple music such as the popular reaches a maximum of preference early and then declines rapidly in popularity.

Conditioning. If we stopped to analyze our likes and dislikes, we would note that in many cases they are due to particular associations with pleasant and unpleasant stimuli we have had. Perhaps we like the name of Mary because this symbol serves as a substitute for another stimulus which arouses in us a pleasant reaction, or we dislike the name Fanny because we have once known a person by that name for whom we cared little. The same can hold true for music, particularly popular songs, since they often have little other reason to be valued. They have less intrinsic worth than much serious music. We might enjoy a jazz composition because we have undergone some pleasant experience while listening to that song. The song now serves as a substitute for the pleasant experience associated with it. The song takes on a new stimulus function because of its association with the previous pleasant reaction.

[53] G. Wiebe, The effect of radio plugging on students' opinions of popular songs, *J. appl. Psychol.*, 1940, **24**, 721–27.

Age and intelligence. Rubin-Rabson [54] has found musical tastes to be related to age and intelligence. She found that indifference to both modern and classical music is positively related to age. (Her subjects ranged from twenty to seventy years.) Further, enthusiasm for such music increases as age drops. Both of these trends are marked for classical music and emphatic with modern music. Finally, a higher average intelligence was evidenced in those persons who liked modern music. Intelligence is also high among those indifferent to classical music. While she does not go into the possible reasons for these findings, we might propose a few hypotheses. Possibly more intelligent people prefer modern music because of its greater intellectual demands, or perhaps because in some parts of our culture it is considered fashionable for intelligent people to "like" modern music. Why indifference to modern and classical music is related to age is not so clear. Perhaps with aging we have heard these selections more and more until they have reached their affective peak and further repetition has caused a decline in preference.

The development of musical taste.—We have tried to account for some of the factors operating in the formation of musical taste. It is obvious that such a preferential response is a complex one resulting from the interaction of the organism with many stimuli both individual and cultural in nature.

To say that there are any absolutes in musical taste is to deny its cultural origin. Indeed, judgments do exist as to what is good or bad in music, but such opinions need not be either/or propositions nor need they be eternal. We have seen that norms for our musical taste do tend to be relatively stable over a period of time, but as the years go by changes occur in our attitudes toward music in the same way as they do in the general folkways of our society.

Mueller has summed up the development of our musical tastes in the following manner:

[54] G. Rubin-Rabson, The influence of age, intelligence, and training on reactions to classic and modern music, *J. gen. Psychol.*, 1940, **22**, 413–29.

One can only conclude that musical opinions and tastes, like political and economic preferences, are forged in a matrix of social and psychological forces and, at any given time, represent a blend of both traditional factors and current experiences. One cannot come away from a study of a century of musical tastes without being struck by the perennial revision of human judgments, and the conviction that, under different circumstances, our tastes would have taken other channels with which we today would have been equally contented. . . .[55]

We therefore cannot resist the conclusion that musical taste is a system of very specific tonal habits, conditioned by an incessant flow of experiences of the individual person as a participating member of a complex culture group. A great range of experiences might conceivably contribute to the end result of finding pleasure in many given types of music, much as some trivial incident might influence the degree of affection for or aversion toward another person. In order to understand more fully how the aesthetic quality of a musical composition is acquired, it will be necessary to ascertain its psychological components, and to explore how the standards of beauty have been established.[56]

[55] J. H. Mueller, *The American symphony orchestra: a social history of musical taste* (Bloomington, Ind.: Indiana University Press, 1951), p. 384.
[56] *Ibid.*, p. 388.

Chapter 10

THE AESTHETIC RESPONSE TO MUSIC

SURELY without any art objects or aesthetic responses to them, life would be a rather drab existence. Consider for a moment a landscape devoid of grass or trees, or a world where the sky was always a cloudy gray, where all people were the same and all buildings were a muddy brown, or where all sounds were mere noise. Certainly there are some people who value the aesthetic above all other things in life. Numerous studies using the techniques of the Allport-Vernon-Lindzey *Study of Values*[1] illustrate this point. In this survey of an individual's value judgments, subjects are given pairs of comparative statements involving preferential responses about things, people, occupations, events, etc. These preferences are then scored in terms of their theoretical, aesthetic, social, political, economic, and religious significance. Thus, a person who constantly prefers statements regarding aesthetic things, instead of political, economic or religious, for example, would score high in the aesthetic trait. There are many people whose aesthetic values in life far outnumber all others, and again there are many others whose economic or political values are of utmost importance to them. At any rate, for a person to score highest in aesthetic values means that for him the attainment and appreciation of beauty is the most important goal in his life's activity. The test illustrates well the fact that individual differences exist in the population for aesthetic values as well as others.

[1] G. W. Allport, P. E. Vernon, and G. Lindzey, *Study of values* (rev. ed.; Boston: Houghton Mifflin Co., 1951).

We have no doubt that aesthetic responses exist. The history of art and music gives evidence enough of that. But to describe objectively the nature of such a response is a far more difficult task. This difficulty is the result of a variety of circumstances, such as numerous standards of aesthetic judgment, many of which are conflicting. The so-called subjective nature of the response itself is another condition which also causes trouble in an evaluation of the aesthetic event.

Until recently, the field of aesthetics had been restricted to the philosopher, and an understanding of the aesthetic object and response was largely dependent on his supposed clairvoyant sensitivity. It is only recently, since psychology has made use of the methods of science and become experimental, that any objective investigation or analysis of the aesthetic response has been undertaken. How can the aesthetic response be investigated? Essentially, in the same way and by using the same methods which psychologists employ to investigate other forms of human behavior.

Introspective reports.—As in the analysis of the affective response (Chapter 9), an introspective report is often necessary. Because the aesthetic reaction is frequently implicit and often involves immovable parts of the organism, we frequently have to rely on a verbal report. Of course, in using this method one immediately encounters a variety of problems relating to the nature of the response. There are individual semantic difficulties in describing one's own aesthetic reactions as well as the number of possible reactions reported. Just what the aesthetic response involves has become, for many, a muddle of verbalizations.

Paired comparisons.—A subject may be given a pair of aesthetic stimuli and asked to indicate which one he prefers. One thing is certain, aesthetic responses are frequently preferential. One likes some art object more than one likes another. He may be presented with a pair of pictures or musical phrases and asked to choose which he likes better. Hevner's test of musical appreciation [2] (Chapter 14) is an example of the application of this method to measurement of musical appreciation. The Allport-Vernon Study of Values also involves this technique. The subjects are presented with pairs of statements and asked to indicate which they prefer. As an example, they might be asked, which would you rather be, a lawyer or a painter? The more aesthetic, economic, political, social, or other preferences the subject indicates, the higher will be his scores in that value.

Autonomic recordings.—The aesthetic response also involves affective reactions, as we shall demonstrate later in this chapter. Therefore, records of one's pulse rate, breathing, or other physiological processes may be made. The reader may wonder what difference exists between the aesthetic and affective responses. This also we will attempt to explain in this chapter. For the moment, let us accept the fact that part of the aesthetic response is affective in nature.

Other measures.—Finally, objective records can be made of other reactions in aesthetic situations involving muscular movements, photographs of facial expressions while listening to music, or other records of general behavior.

Theories of the Aesthetic Response

During the nineteenth century the problems of art and beauty were considered the province of philosophy. Beauty was truth, devoid of the mundane complications of everyday life. It was a universal characteristic inherent in things, one which made them beautiful and was only to be appreciated by those persons endowed by nature with the proper perceptive powers. However, with the development of psychology, the prestige of the "eternal standard" idea of beauty in art has begun to wane and the recognition of the diversity of standards of beauty rather than

[2] K. Hevner, Tests for the aesthetic appreciation in the field of music, *J. appl. Psychol.*, 1930, **14**, 470–77.

one universal is beginning to be accepted. The solution of the problem involving the nature of the aesthetic response will not lie in understanding the *nature of the object alone* nor in any inherent perceptive powers of the organism but in an analysis of the interaction of the two, organism and stimulus object, which we have found to hold in other forms of behavior.

Hanslick's theory.—Shortly before the turn of the century (1891) Hanslick published a work, *The Beautiful in Music*,[3] which was concerned largely with combating the notion prevalent at the time that the significance of music lay in its power to provoke emotional expression. He claimed that the aesthetics of the day were describing the feelings that music aroused instead of inquiring into what was beautiful in music.

According to this view, the aim of music was *not* necessarily to arouse pleasurable emotions. Music has no aim or object other than *as a form*. Its aesthetic value and significance lie in its form, and the fact that feelings are aroused by aesthetic objects is only incidental to the fact. Hanslick did not deny the affective reaction to music, but he protested against the attitude that any aesthetic principles could be deduced from such feeling experiences. Feelings do not constitute the substance of the aesthetic response. Music is enjoyed only when it is *heard for its own sake*. The moment music is used as a means of inducing any emotion, imagination, or ideation experience, it ceases to be an aesthetic reaction. The meaning of music lies in the form itself and is inseparable from it.

Schoen's theory.[4]—More recently Schoen has set forth a view similar to that of Hanslick. For him the beautiful in music lies in the listening process and *not* in any associations, images, reflections or emotions as secondary or derived effects. The beauty is in the experiencing of the thing itself, the *musical form*. This ex-

[3] E. Hanslick, *The beautiful in music* (London: Novello & Co., Ltd., 1891).

[4] M. Schoen, *The psychology of music* (New York: The Ronald Press Co., 1940).

perience is direct, spontaneous, detached, not critical or analytical. Any critical attitude tends to destroy the aesthetic experience. So long as an individual attends to the music as music, he can maintain a high level of aesthetic enjoyment and associations will be barred from his consciousness. The meaning of music lies in the music itself and is inseparable from it. The person with the true capacity for the aesthetic response does not need to rely on his feelings or associations for aesthetic enjoyment. The less musical person may compensate for his lack of aesthetic capacity with extra musical matter.

The formulation of such a viewpoint is based on the following observations:

1. The constituents of a melody in the final analysis are merely sound waves whose properties are frequency, amplitude, length, and complexity of structure (number of overtones). When one hears a melody objectively, all he perceives is a sequence of tones varying in these four attributes. The melody is created by the listener out of the raw material supplied him. To *hear* a melody is to evolve a *form* out of the tonal material so that what may appear to be a melody for one person is nothing more than a conglomeration of tonal stimuli to another. At the bottom of the aesthetic response to music is the capacity to perceive this form or what Schoen terms *form-mindedness*.

2. When the form becomes significant to the listener, the experience may be described as aesthetic. The individual labels such an experience "beautiful." When a person derives his musical enjoyment from such extraneous factors as emotions, daydreams, or reminiscences, the experience is nonaesthetic.

Finally, in answering the question as to whether the aesthetic experience is primarily the result of training or is dependent on some native powers, Schoen reasons as follows: The degree of one's aesthetic response to music is in direct proportion to his sensitivity to pitch, intensity, duration, and timbre of the tones heard. Since the sensitivity to these characteristics of the musical stimulus is innate, it follows that the aesthetic response is also innate. Some possess this capacity for aesthetic appreciation and others lack it. Therefore, the unmusical person must derive his enjoyment from some other aspects of the stimulus because of his lack of native sensitivity to form. These other sources include familiarity and concreteness. An example of the latter might be the musical pattern explained to the listener which makes it possible for him to follow the course of the music much as one follows the play in a game of cards. Such appreciation can be taught. Concreteness may also imply that the piece tells a story. In this manner, enjoyment may also be had from the composition.

In order to discover the relation between one's attitude toward music and his sensitivity to tone, Schoen [5] believed he could experimentally demonstrate whether the aesthetic experience was dependent on training or the result of native endowment. In his investigation, each subject was given a questionnaire and an interview in order to evaluate his preferences, attitudes toward music, and the role music had played in his life. Subjects were also given four music tests. Finally, they listened to programs of music and recorded the degree of their enjoyment of the music on attitude scales. The judgments of how good or bad a selection was were recorded. The tests used were those of pitch, intensity, relative pitch, and tonal sequences devised by the author. The results indicated a high degree of relationship between the test scores and attitudes toward music. The conditions for artistic musical responses are the same as those for artistic musical rendition. The true music-lover possesses the capacity for aesthetic response and differs from the artist in degree, not in kind.

> What a person finds in music depends on his degree of susceptibility to musical form—his form-mindedness. Those who are least form-minded will find the value of music in what it suggests to them. Hence, their preference for program music and their interest in literary musical descriptions.[6]

[5] M. Schoen, The aesthetic attitude in music, *Psychol. Monogr.*, 1928, **29**, 161–83.

[6] M. Schoen, *The psychology of music*, p. 142.

Evaluation. Schoen's theory is only a modification of the older theory of Hanslick. The aesthetic response is described as a detached, subjective experience, completely within the individual. He has tried to demonstrate how such form-mindedness is inherent, a natural power, by relating it to the more simple discriminatory reactions to pitch, loudness, etc. This may follow if one accepts the inheritance of such sensory capacities. However, the foregoing chapters have demonstrated that such discriminatory responses are not inherent but acquired, so it follows that the aesthetic response is also learned. Whether such a detached, aesthetic response as Schoen has tried to describe exists can only be examined in terms of verbalizations. Certainly, it is not subject to any objective analysis or investigation. Finally, I know of no evidence to support the contention that the individual who depends on his associations, feelings, and imaginative reactions for part of the aesthetic enjoyment is the less musical or that such reactions are necessarily outside of the aesthetic experience. I believe they are just as much a part of the aesthetic response as is the perception of form in the object. The last section of this chapter will be devoted to an objective theory of the aesthetic response.

Seashore's theory.[7]—Although Seashore recognizes the characteristics of the sound wave (pitch, loudness, timbre, etc.), as well as the form of the musical stimulus, as being important attributes of the aesthetic object, he believes the aesthetic experience comes from the *meaning it conveys to the listener,* be it a feeling, ideation, craving, wish, or inspiration. The reader will immediately recognize that this idea is diametrically opposed to that of Schoen, who has considered these "meanings" as secondary and definitely auxiliary to the aesthetic experience. Whether the aesthetic experience is derived from the perception of form that is exemplified in pure music or from the feelings and associations for pro-

[7] C. E. Seashore, *Psychology of music* (New York: McGraw-Hill Book Co., Inc., 1938).

gram music is a moot question. Seashore doubts that there is any real feeling of pure beauty, as does the writer. The reaction expressed by the listener will depend largely on the intentions of the composer.

He argues *for* the affective reaction as part of the aesthetic response as well as the associative significance in music.

> One of the marks of great music is its purely affective appeal and freedom from discrete forms of meaning. In practice, however, the human mind tends irresistibly to give meaning to every experience. This meaning takes two general forms. First, the music may be light or heavy, frivolous or serious. Experiments have shown that musical chords may be matched against the principal types of human moods. Second, in hearing music, there is the irresistible tendency to visualize and dramatize it in concrete situations which acquire meaning through each and all of the senses. The famous psychological illustration of this is the sight of a beautiful apple. The apple is not only seen; it comes through associated imagery in all the other senses. This is the outstanding characteristic of the descriptive music, but the principle operates in various degrees in all forms of music.
>
> The esthetic significance of this lies in the fact that the imagery through which the listener lives in hearing music is the associated imagery aroused by it. In the love song, for example, he may not be aware of the harmonic and melodic movements which constitute the physical music, but he envisages and for the moment lives with his beloved. This principle is illustrated in all types of intensive emotional situations, such as love, hate, fear, tranquility, war, and peace. The value lies not only in the music itself, but in its effectiveness in arousing associated imagery which may, of course, occur in infinite variety and may furnish the dominant content of the feeling.[8]

Theory of Mueller and Hevner.[9]—These authors have set forth a theory of the aesthetic response to music which we might

[8] C. E. Seashore, *In search of beauty in music* (New York: The Ronald Press Co., 1947), p. 185.

[9] J. H. Mueller, *The American symphony orchestra: a social history of musical taste* (Bloomington, Ind.: Indiana University Press, 1951); see also K. Hevner, The aesthetic experience: a psychological description, *Psychol. Rev.*, 1937, **44**, 245–63.

call a *cultural theory of the aesthetic response*. With a few modifications, which involve stripping this theory of its mentalistic connotations, we may formulate a theory, modified from Hevner and Mueller, which seems most compatible with the data at hand and in keeping with the general direction of this book.

THE AESTHETIC OBJECT. It has been thought that beauty is an inherent characteristic of the object. Rather, it is a property which the organism has *imposed on* the object. Any object can be beautiful if it elicits a response of the organism which by its very characteristics may be labeled aesthetic.

Earlier, we discussed certain characteristics of the sound stimulus, the vibrational as well as the tonal. In a like manner there are other attributes of the musical object with which we may endow it. One of these may be labeled "beauty." This may be further reduced into a number of different qualities that may make an object beautiful. Perhaps it is the form, balance, harmony, melody, or pattern of the rhythm. On the other hand, for others the beauty may lie in its capacity to arouse certain feelings. When an object possesses many qualities capable of arousing aesthetic pleasure, the position of this stimulus as an object of art becomes more secure.

> The goodness or beauty of an object is, therefore, a superimposed quality with which an observer, according to his system of values, endows an object. If he confers beauty on an object, he also withdraws it after it has been conferred, or withholds indefinitely such a distinction.[10]

Individual differences exist among art objects. The strength of appeal of an art object depends on the number of responses it can stimulate within the individual. Any object may become a beautiful stimulus to some one individual. For that one person it has the significance and commands the special attention and feeling which elicit an aesthetic response. But we do not designate it as an object of art until many individuals find it beautiful.

[10] J. H. Mueller, *The American symphony orchestra*, p. 403.

Thus, the beautiful characteristic of the object has a cultural stimulus function. It is not typically idiosyncratic, to be enjoyed by only one person. Rather, it has the same significance for more than one person.

THE AESTHETIC RESPONSE. Such a reaction occurs in the behavior history of an individual when he remarks, "How beautiful that is!" The aesthetic response is a combination of many psychological activities. At any one time its main characteristics may be affective, at other times highly intellectual, and at still others almost entirely sensuous.

CHARACTERISTICS OF THE AESTHETIC RESPONSE. The aesthetic response is highly *attentional*. The entire response equipment of the organism is directed whole-heartedly toward the stimulus object. Such an intense attention reaction is going to require much of the organism's equipment. It is an active type of reaction involving muscular tension. The habits of attention which allow us to maintain this activity are a matter of practice and skill. Thus, the aesthetic response is a learned reaction.

The aesthetic response is also a *perceptual* reaction. Without this developed perceptual ability, the beauties of the objective world may be completely lost. It involves a keen perception of the qualities of the object. At one moment we may perceive the rhythmic progressions, the harmony, the melody, or all the elements combined. Acquiring such a perceptive ability means finding enough detail in the stimulus to engage all the organism's response equipment. Such perceptual habits are usually directed toward the formal aspect of the stimulus—the patterns, rhythms, melodic construction, etc.

The aesthetic response takes place with an *affective accompaniment*—thus giving the response importance and significance. The feeling act is not intense or disruptive so that the organism's attention is completely absorbed by it, for if this were the case, there would be no awareness of the aesthetic event. Instead, there is a feeling reaction which may be sustained over a long period of time. It might be a gentle visceral reaction, a slight lift of the head, or a faint tightening of the throat. The aesthetic response does not occur except with a background of these bodily and visceral responses. These body reactions are, of course, byplay reactions for the central responses are those of attention and perception of the aesthetic object. When the feeling reactions become so intense that the attention is directed toward them, the response ceases to be aesthetic and becomes merely an emotional or feeling self-reaction. Summarizing the affective response, Hevner writes:

> It is an attentive state, with musculature and all the senses alert and active, following every detail of the stimulus and making the experiencing of it a forceful and vivid awareness. With so much bodily activity in the perception of the stimulus, meaning is crowded into it richly, and these meanings are the unusual, impersonal, and abstract in contrast to the concrete and practical meanings of ordinary day-to-day activity. All of these activities are made more poignant because they occur on a background of widespread and unlocalized bodily sensations, especially from the involuntary muscles and viscera which give the experience affective and emotional qualities.[11]

Development of the aesthetic response. The aesthetic response, as an acquired reaction, must then be the product of learning. Such learning may, of course, be either casual or direct. These responses arise out of a background of previous contacts with the stimulus object. When new musical forms are confronted by us, there actually may appear a feeling of frustration on the part of the listener because he does not have the necessary response equipment to appreciate such innovations. A radically new musical form (atonality for example) will meet with delayed appreciation on the part of most listeners until they have developed the proper new responses with which to listen.

It is evident, therefore, that a new composition may bear sufficient resemblance to the past—e.g., the early Beethoven to

[11] K. Hevner, The aesthetic experience: a psychological description, *Psychol. Rev.*, 1937, **44**, 257.

Mozart and Haydn—to be readily assimilable and appreciated by the audience. . . . A small increment of novelty is essential; without it there is no interest to touch off attention and stimulate appreciation. It is for that reason that older compositions, having become too familiar through repeated hearings, are often greeted with apathy or boredom. From this danger of satiety, the greatest masterpieces are not exempt. Its onset will vary according to the background of the auditor; the intervals between hearings during which one may "forget" a part of what has been stored up, and the degree of variety within the composition itself.

Such an analysis partially explains the differences in the contours of the performance curves of Tchaikovsky and Brahms. Tchaikovsky, a prolific composer, whose melodic turns were easily grasped, provoked little controversy, and harvested quick popularity. But he has been on the wane from sheer saccharine monotony. On the other hand, the polyrhythmic and compact Brahms, whose name was once the synonym for all that is intellectual and esoteric, has only recently been generally apprehended after a vigorous campaign on the part of conductors.

There is, then, after repeated hearings, an optimum point of appreciation after which the law of diminishing aesthetic returns sets in. The attainment of which may be accelerated or delayed, but in the long run is psychologically inevitable. With the introduction of newer technological mechanisms for the dissemination of tonal pleasures—records and radio—familiarity with these compositions will be increased and the approach of satiety hastened.[12]

[12] Mueller, *op. cit.*, pp. 389–91.

Chapter 11

THE NATURE OF MUSICAL ABILITY

THE TERMS "musicality," "musical talent," "musical ability," and "musical capacity" are often used indiscriminately. Before we begin our discussion on the nature of musical ability, it seems wise to untangle some of these definitions.

Musicality and talent.—Schoen [1] distinguishes between musicality and musical talent. The latter refers to a capacity for musical performance and the former to musical reception. So one may be very musical, having considerable sensitivity toward, feeling for, and appreciation of music, without having any performance ability. This is musicality. One person may possess musicality and not necessarily any talent. Another may, on the other hand, perform in a fashion which is technically superior. He may have talent but not musicality. Ideally, one should possess both in abundance for the finest results. All psychologists interested in this field do not make such a distinction between the two terms. For example, when Seashore [2] refers to musical talent, he includes musicality as part of it.

Capacity and ability.—Capacity, for both Seashore and Schoen,[3] refers to inborn traits. It is the endowment of a potential talent for music. Musical capacity, then, refers to a something with which one is born that enables him to develop fine musicianship. For example, in 1919 Seashore wrote,

[1] M. Schoen, *The psychology of music* (New York: The Ronald Press Co., 1940), p. 151.

[2] C. E. Seashore, *Psychology of music* (New York: McGraw-Hill Book Co., Inc., 1938).

[3] Schoen, *op. cit.*

> Modern psychology distinguishes between capacity and ability. The term "capacity" has reference to the inborn or native power; the term "ability" is used to designate acquired skill in the use of a capacity. Thus, each of us has a certain native capacity for memory, but we develop various kinds and degrees of ability in the use of this capacity.[4]

Approximately twenty years later his attitude had not appreciably changed. We note in 1938,

> The investigator of inheritance is not interested primarily in the degree of achievement attained, which is usually a circumstance of fortune or misfortune in environment; he has to do exclusively with the valuation of inborn capacities. Skill or achievement is significant for inheritance only insofar as it gives evidence for native capacities. It is manifestly unjust to attempt to trace musical inheritance only in distinguished achievement in music. Whenever we find achievement, we count it as evidence of capacity . . .[5]

Unfortunately, these statements tell us very little—merely that something is inborn. This inborn "something" could be a gland, a structure, or a function or psychic potential. The problem of what actually is inborn bothers Seashore very little. To say that capacity is inborn is sufficient, without searching further.

If we are going to be objective psychologists, it seems prudent that we at least make an attempt to search for this "something." We have no objection to the concept of inheritance, per se, providing we try to discover what it is that we inherit. Since we know, by now, that the human organism's behavior, except for simple reflexes, is a product of learning, to say that musicianship is inherited is to go contrary to scientific evidence. Let us abandon this type of reference to inherited psychic powers of the mind and limit ourselves by defining capacity as the limiting influence of biological structure. For the modern psychologist, capac-

[4] C. E. Seashore, *The psychology of musical talent* (New York: Silver Burdett Co., 1919), pp. 14–15.

[5] By permission from *Psychology of music*, by C. E. Seashore, p. 332. Copyright by McGraw-Hill Book Co., Inc., New York, 1938.

ity for musical performance is possible. Our capacity includes, among other things, a sound nervous system, two hands, normal hearing structures, and other structures necessary for musical behavior. Capacity, then, is a biological potential which serves as a framework within which we develop musical actions. In referring to capacity, we mean biological capacity, not inborn behavior patterns or powers of the mind. Ability, on the other hand, refers to acquired skill. In speaking of musical abilities, we refer to such skills as the ability to discriminate different pitches, intensities, and intervals, or ability to harmonize melodies, sing at sight, or perform on an instrument. These abilities are learned to various degrees of proficiency. Just how these abilities are developed will be discussed later in this chapter.

What do we mean, finally, by the term "musical talent"? It is a term which has been used as some performance capacity with especial reference to artistic and creative things. One has a talent for singing, painting, or writing. Let us restrict use of the term to some acquired proficiency in these creative or artistic skills. Talents in music are not independent of each other and can be trained to various degrees of proficiency providing one has sound biological equipment. We do recognize that individual differences exist and that all people with similar training do not achieve the same degree of proficiency in musical tasks. The principle of individual differences operates in musical behavior as in other kinds of responses. However, these limitations are a function of both biological capacity and previous musical experiences, such as musical contact, either casual or deliberate, which have occurred throughout one's previous life history.

Having defined our terms, let us see what our musical psychologists have to say about the exact nature of talent, ability, or capacity. The problem of the nature of musical ability which confronts us actually has two aspects. The first concerns the matter of what is included in musical ability, and the second concerns how it comes about. First of all, what are the constituents of musical ability?

The elemental viewpoint or a theory of specifics.—A very common point of view concerning the nature of musical talent is set forth by Seashore. For him, musical talent consisted of a number of separate capacities which were fairly independent of each other. Work on the attributes of the sound wave gave him a start for his theory. In 1919 he wrote,

> Musical talent is not a single talent, it is a hierarchy of talents, many of which are entirely independent of one another. Therefore, a description of a musical mind reduces itself to the picturing of the relative prominence or latency of each musical talent. The talents naturally group themselves so that we have, for example, the tonal group, the rhythmic group, the motor group, the intellectual group, and others; and within each of these we may trace much detail.[6]

In the tonal group, we have pitch, the correlate of frequency of the sound wave; loudness, related to amplitude of the wave; time, related to the duration of the wave; and timbre, the correlate of the quality of the wave.

Here we have a perfect psychophysical parallelism. Each function of the mind has a physical counterpart. Wundt and Titchener,[7] the founders of structuralism, would have indeed been proud. Structuralism, as a mentalistic system of psychology, also followed an elemental viewpoint toward conscious experience. Its aim was the analysis of conscious experience into atoms and molecules of feelings and sensations. This is, of course, in direct contrast to a view which considers the mind as an integrated unanalyzable whole. Structuralism attempted to relate the mind and the body (physical) and came to the conclusion that they were parallel entities, quite separate from each other.

These various sensory talents for pitch, loudness, timbre, time, etc. are independent of each other. One may possess any or all in a high or low degree. In 1938 Seashore reported,

[6] Seashore, *The psychology of musical talent*, p. 6.

[7] For the structuralist approach to psychology see: W. Wundt, *Grundriss der Psychologie* (Leipzig: Engelmann, 1896); E. B. Titchener, *A textbook of Psychology* (New York: The Macmillan Co., 1909–10).

> On the sensory side we have recognized four branches of talent content as heard, namely pitch, time, intensity, and timbre, each forming a main division of the approaches to musicianship. Each one of these capacities runs as an independent branch, not only in sensation but through memory, imagination, thought, feeling and action. Each branch of this family tree throws out similar branches of capacities.[8]

Working on the hypothesis that an individual who can discriminate small differences in these qualities should also be a superior musician, Seashore set out to devise a set of tests which would measure individual differences in these discriminative capacities and thus predict success. He agreed that there were probably other talents as yet unmeasured, but this was at least a start.

> On the basis of our experiments in measuring these sensory capacities we find that the basic capacities, the sense of pitch, the sense of time, the sense of loudness, and the sense of timbre, are elemental, by which we mean that they are largely inborn and function from early childhood. After a comparatively early age they do not vary with intelligence, with training, or with increasing age, except as the exhibition of these capacities is limited by the child's ability to understand or apply himself to the task . [9]

Many years of investigation antedated Seashore's first *Measures of Musical Talent,* which came out in 1919. The first form of the test consisted of six subtests for that many talents: pitch, loudness, rhythm, time, consonance, and tonal memory. Even though the test of memory was more complex and less sensory than the others, he felt this to be an important part of the musical mind. He hoped to eliminate any effects of previous learning and training by presenting the tones isolated from any rhythmic or melodic configuration. In the 1939 revision, a test of timbre was substituted for the original test of consonance, which had

[8] By permission from *Psychology of music,* by C. E. Seashore, p. 332. Copyright by McGraw-Hill Book Co., Inc., New York, 1938.
[9] *Ibid.,* p. 3.

proved quite unsuccessful. As it stands today, Seashore's theory is little changed from the time it was first formulated in his *Psychology of Musical Talent* (1919). Later, in his *Psychology of Music* (1938), Seashore states his attitude as follows:

> Each of these six tests purports to measure one of the six capacities or abilities for the hearing of musical tones. There is little overlapping in these functions. They should not be validated in terms of their showing on an omnibus theory or blanket rating against all musical behavior, including such diverse and unreal situations as composition, directing, voice, piano, violin . . . because there are hundreds of other factors which help to determine job analysis in each of such fields.[10]

Seashore admits, of course, that musical talent is not limited to these six measurable capacities. There are actually four main trunks of the family tree of musical talent. There are the tonal, the dynamic, the temporal, and the qualitative. The tonal is made up of a sensitivity for pitch and timbre and relates to such musical forms as melody and harmony and all variations of pitch. The dynamic has reference to an acuity of hearing which distinguishes all forms and variations in loudness. The temporal includes aspects of rhythm, tempo, and time. Finally, the qualitative is particularly sensitive to timbre, with especial reference to the harmonic constitution of tone.

The presence of sensory capacities in an adequate degree is fundamental. But musical imagery, imagination, and memory are also important. In contrast to the innate sensory powers, musical imagery can be developed with training, and while a good memory is a great asset, it is not an essential condition. Finally, he adds musical feeling and performance. Feeling includes not only the aesthetic experience but also a "creative feeling" as it exists in the composer. But again, in dealing with the traditional structuralistic viewpoint, the expression of feeling comes through the sensory media. Musical performance is limited by certain "inherent and inherited" motor capacities: musical

[10] *Ibid.*, p. 383–84.

performance is limited by the limitations of the sensory capacity already discussed. For example, one low in rhythm discrimination will of necessity be low in rhythmic performance.

Seashore does not deny this atomistic viewpoint. He believes it gives us a basis for classification and makes possible an analysis and evaluation of musical talent.

A view which lies close to Seashore's and may be said to be a variation of the "theory of specifics" is set forth by Schoen. He agrees that musical talent is made up of a number of capacities but differs from Seashore as to what the capacities are and which are most important.

> . . . talent for music is not a single power or capacity but consists of several groups of talents, each group performing a specific and definite function in the making of the artist. In other words, when the musician works his miracles in his audience through the medium of his voice or instrument, he is exercising not one single power or capacity possessed by him, but a cluster of powers functioning together to produce the single effect.
>
> Musical talent as a whole, then, consists of scores of individual, elemental, specific capacities, each contributing its share to the making of the artist. These specific talents may be summarized under four heads, viz., Musical Feeling, Musical Understanding, Musical Sensitivity and Musical Virtuosity—forming the affective, the intellectual, the sensory, and the motor basis of musical artistry. . . . Where there is no technique there is no art, but where there is no feeling and understanding, that is, musicianship in general, technique is but an empty shell. Thus, it is only when the affective, the intellectual, the sensory, and the motor equipments exist to a marked and somewhat uniform degree in the same person that artistic accomplishment is possible.[11]

An inventory of musical talent is possible within these four areas. Musical talent consists of primary and secondary factors. The primary factors include auditory sensitivity (same as Sea-

[11] From M. Schoen, *The psychology of music*, p. 162. Copyright, 1940, by The Ronald Press Co., New York.

shore's sensory capacities: pitch, loudness, timbre, time), musical feeling and understanding (these include such "gifts" as absolute pitch, tonal memory, tonal and harmonic sequence, consonance, and rhythm), and musical virtuosity (inherited motor capacities).

Among the secondary factors Schoen includes intelligence, which he says should be above the average, musical memory, will power (persistence in music), self-confidence, and temperament. By "temperament" he means an acute sensitivity to things that are beautiful and need for a medium of emotional expression.

These two theories are strikingly similar. While both recognize the importance of sensory capacities, Seashore places a greater importance on them, whereas Schoen emphasizes the affective and intellectual side of the musical "mind." Just why Schoen emphasizes the importance of above-average intelligence is not at all clear. Finally, both follow an elemental analysis of various independent capacities, and both are completely dualistic.

Omnibus theory.—In contrast to this theory of specifics, Mursell has set forth what has been called an omnibus theory. He has criticized Seashore on the grounds that the latter's tests undertake to measure ". . . the responses of the ear as a receptor to certain differences in the sound wave."[12] He concludes, ". . . music depends upon our perception of the dynamic relatedness of tone." He does not believe in instinct, faculty, or special ability. Musicality is a combination of mental processes. There are three which are basic: (*a*) affective responsiveness to tone and tonal rhythmic patterns, (*b*) perceptual awareness of tonal relationships, and (*c*) perceptual awareness of rhythmic groupings. Thus, one individual may be more responsive, or capable of perceiving much more refined relationships, than another.

> We must not think of musicality as a faculty, or an instinct, or a special ability or trait marked off from all other mechanisms

[12] J. L. Mursell, *The psychology of music* (New York: W. W. Norton & Co., Inc., 1937), p. 300.

> of the mind and operated in isolation. Everything we know about the mind and its correlate, the central nervous system, indicates that it is not a congeries of separate faculties. (The popular term nowadays is "special ability," but substantially it is often used to mean exactly the same thing.) On the contrary, whenever it is performing any significant task, it operates as a unit . . .[13]
>
> Many different capacities are involved in dealing with music, and these may be combined in many ways. For instance, high ability to perform may be associated with a lack of musical memory. . . .[14]
>
> But the essential point is that musicality depends on and consists of an awareness of tonal-rhythmic configurations or tonal patterns and an emotional responsiveness thereto.[15]

These statements carry certain implications. First of all, according to Mursell, musicality does not depend directly on sensory abilities, as Seashore would have us believe. Secondly, psychological capacities, upon which musical behavior depends, are found in various degrees in widely differing combinations. The most fundamental of these is a general emotional responsiveness to tone which can manifest itself without any very clear apprehension of the structural elements. This emotional responsiveness involves no discrimination or selective awareness of music as a pattern where expressive significance depends upon its organization. However, a more massive undifferentiated response to tonal content is probably never found without some apprehension of the structural and relational factors.

Can we have individuals seriously defective in tonal apprehension who are still able to make good musical responses because of a refined perception of rhythmic groups? Mursell answers in the affirmative. He gives the case of a drummer in a jazz orchestra who is rhythmically effective but tonally inept.

This theory resembles the systematic point of view in psychology called "Gestalt." Advocates of this approach see things in terms of a whole or configuration. They are bitterly opposed to a structuralist's elemental view because, they argue, the whole

[13] *Ibid.*, p. 321. [14] *Ibid.*, p. 322. [15] *Ibid.*, p. 323.

is not equivalent to the sum of its parts. If Mursell's theory were not so completely packed with mentalism (musical mind), it would be an improvement over Seashore's. Its advantage lies in the author's recognition that musicality is more than a sum of special sensory abilities.

An interbehavioral view.—In view of the difficulties in the previous two theories, I would like to point out a third which stems from the school of psychology known as "interbehaviorism."[16] Our approach in this book so far has tended toward this particular psychological system. From the interbehavioral view, musical ability (note we say "ability" and not "capacity") is not a *single* trait possessed in various degrees by individuals. It consists of a number of acquired interrelated behaviors built up through a process of interaction of individual organisms with musical stimuli throughout the life history. When we speak of "behaviors," we refer to observable actions of the organism. Thus, a person interacts with various stimuli and acquires responses to them. Here we have no use for the "musical mind," because we are studying the actual responses a person makes and not some psychic capacities stored away in his head or his nervous system.

In any attempt to measure musical behavior, we attempt to select a number of possible behaviors for consideration. These will be discussed in more detail in the next chapter. Any set of measures, therefore, will not attempt to tell the whole story, because there are so many varieties of musicians, such as the performer (pianist, violinist, or vocalist), the composer, the theoretician, and the musicologist. The behavior equipment necessary for achievement will differ for each kind. Even among the performers, behaviors necessary for success will not always be the same for each. Ability to discriminate fine differences in pitch will be a prerequisite for the successful violinist or vocalist but

[16] J. R. Kantor, *Principles of psychology*, 2 vols. (New York: Alfred A. Knopf, Inc., 1924–26.)

not all-important for the pianist. Mursell has already pointed out that the drummer must have a good perceptual awareness for rhythm, but his sensitivity to tone is less important. Thus, it is impossible to state from our present knowledge just what behaviors are most important for each musical specialization. Again the most important behaviors will depend on the instrument on which one performs. There are, of course, some behaviors which musicians share. These are taught almost universally in music schools and usually are listed under the title of theory. Such behaviors include writing melodies and harmonies correctly after they have been produced audibly, harmonizing a single melodic line correctly after the rules set down by the older masters, ability to play and write rhythmic patterns correctly, and the ability to detect changes in sequential patterns.

The interbehavioral view approaches musical ability as devoid of any reference to mind, for we have explained our musical abilities in terms of actual responses and not powers or psychic entities. Musical responses are a function of an organism which has certain biological potentials and acquired behavior. The individual differences which do exist are based on what basic behavior equipment one has casually or deliberately acquired throughout his life, from a beginning shortly after birth. The development of proper basic behaviors early in life plus an adequate biological capacity adequately account for these individual differences.

Is musical ability inherited?—The second problem which confronts us concerning the nature of musical ability relates to its genesis. Schoen and Seashore have no doubt that one's talent is entirely a result of natural endowment. This may occur in various degrees, but it is something which is born within us or may be completely lacking.

According to Schoen,

> Musical talent is first an inborn capacity. Artistic musical performance rests ultimately on innate, inborn equipment. It is not something that is acquired in one's lifetime, but the per-

son is born with or without it. All that training can do is develop that which already exists potentially. We therefore speak of musical capacity and not of musical ability. [He does, we don't.] Ability is that which one has attained through training, practice, or experience; capacity is that which enables one to attain a certain degree of ability. . . .

Finally, talent for music is a gift bestowed by nature upon different persons very unequally. In the first place, we have the extremes of very marked talent, of the musical genius on the one hand and no talent at all on the other, and all the degrees of talent between the two extremes. Then again, there is the person who is equipped by nature with the sensory, the affective, and the intellectual basis for talent, but is deficient in the motor or technical requisites for effective musical production . . .[17]

Similarly, Seashore unquestioningly and dogmatically voices a strong argument for heredity.

Family pride, musical and social history, investments in musical education, the making or breaking of a career, hinge upon an adequate evaluation of talent; and talent, by definition, is an inherited trait. The world talks glibly of it in high praise and in deep disparagement, often without a glimmering of scientific insight or discriminating attitude. The concept of inheritance must have a place in the psychology of music.

Musical talent probably lends itself better than any other talent to the investigation of the laws of mental inheritance because it does not represent merely a general heightening of the mental powers but is specifically recognized as a gift which can be analyzed into the constituent elements, many of which may be isolated and measured with reasonable precision. The inheritance of musical talent may, therefore, be studied, not only for itself, but also for the bearing that it has on the inheritance of mental traits in general.[18]

And in 1947, despite inconclusive evidence from biology to support the theory of inheritance of musical talent, Seashore writes,

We may accept the Mendelian hypothesis as a general working basis and proceed to ascertain what determiners in the germ

[17] From M. Schoen, *The psychology of music,* pp. 161–63. Copyright, 1940, by The Ronald Press Co., New York.

[18] Seashore, *Psychology of music,* p. 330.

plasm function for musical talent; which are dominant and which are recessive; which musical dispositions are carried on the same determiner; and which are carried on determiners charged with nonmusical factors, etc. In psychology, these problems will be virgin soil for investigation.[19]

As an example of how a specific factor might be traced he refers to Scheinfeld's *You and Heredity* (1939) by saying: [20]

As an example of how a specific factor may be traced in studies of heredity, the author [Scheinfeld] shows the occurrence of *absolute pitch* in Kirsten Flagstad's family. Absolute pitch is a specific factor suitable for scientific measurement. But it may occur in vastly different degrees, ranging from the ability to name any note sounded on the piano to the ability to recognize a deviation of one vibration from international pitch without reference to any means of comparison. In the future the student of heredity will measure and indicate the *degree* of the possession of this factor.

The author [again Scheinfeld] makes a bold effort to apply the theory of genes in the chromosomes of the inherited cell to the inheritance of musical talent in the same way that it applies to the inheritance of stature, hair, blood type, or any other specific and measurable probable nature of the mechanism . . .

The author is undoubtedly right in holding that inheritance of musical talent eventually must be expressed in terms of mechanisms of genes as are other forms of heritage. But it remains to be shown that musical traits are as specific as the genes by which they are to be identified. Is the sense of *absolute pitch* one? Is the more general *sense of pitch* one trait? Is *ear-mindedness* a single trait? In a word, the difficulty now is not with the theory of heredity as a principle, but with the psychological description of the musical mind in terms of musical traits that may be inherited.

The example cited by Scheinfeld from Kirsten Flagstad's family indicates that in her genealogy were found a sister who was a singer; a brother who was a pianist, and another brother

[19] From C. E. Seashore, *In search of beauty in music*, pp. 248–49. Copyright, 1947, by The Ronald Press Co., New York.
[20] *Ibid.* pp. 257–58.

who was a cellist and a conductor; her mother, a pianist and oper atic coach and father, a violinist and conductor; her maternal grandmother, a singer, and grandfather, a violinist; and a maternal great-uncle, a cellist. On her paternal grandparents' side, things are not too clear. Of those mentioned, Mme. Flagstad and her mother, maternal grandfather, and maternal great-uncle all possessed so-called "absolute pitch." Is this evidence to support the inheritance of musical talent? The greatest difficulty with it is that it also supports, and equally well, the theory of the acquisition of musical behavior. Furthermore, the evidence for absolute pitch is somewhat anecdotal. Finally, if we accept this hypothesis, how are we going to account for musicians like Haydn, where no other musicians in the family exist?

Concerning the possibility that musical ability is acquired, Seashore states:[21]

> So long as we rate the presence of musical talent in terms of musical achievement, we shall be dealing mainly with the superficial, sociological, and pedagogical phenomena of opportunities and scope of musical training or with the effect of inhibiting circumstance on spontaneous self-expression in music.

Although leaning toward Seashore's view, Mursell at least does not state his position so finally and absolutely. Since the issue is not decided, statements such as those quoted from Seashore and Schoen are dangerous, because they are misinformative to the reader who does not have all the facts at hand and considers these statements as actual truths rather than the speculative opinions of their authors. Mursell writes:

> Our knowledge of the inheritance of mental traits is nowhere very exact or well established. . . . With regard to musicality, our uncertainty must be much greater, because no instruments in any way comparable with our best intelligence tests exist, and also because the total body of investigation is much smaller and in the main much more poorly controlled.[22]

[21] *Ibid.*
[22] Mursell, *op. cit.*, p. 331.

The most common argument for the inheritance of musical ability is that it "runs in families." Seashore makes a plea for a careful examination of family histories to prove this point. But if he cannot find this talent in family history, the hereditarian will advance some other hypothesis to account for those families in which it does not occur. If we are not careful, this argument may turn into a logical monstrosity. Concerning the matter of musical talent "running in families," Pronko and Bowles have pointed out this fallacy of attitude with great clarity.

> If we should then point out that both on his mother's and his father's side for two generations back there was not a single musician in Haydn's ancestry, but only blacksmiths, wheelwrights, and farmers, the defender of the heredity dogma would resort to statement-making that would involve further hypothetical assumptions leading to deeper obscurity.
>
> But let us take the Bach family, which did produce a succession of generations of able musicians. We do not need any additional principle to explain musical as opposed to other behaviors. These are not "out of this world" but of a piece with all other reactions.
>
> The argument that the musical ability of the Bachs was hereditary because it "ran in the family" should hold just as consistently for their German-speaking activity. By what criterion can one possibly discriminate what is hereditary and not when all "run in the family," including (in some families) Methodism, Catholicism, Buddhism, medical practice, weaving, skiing, voting, Republican, Whig, Tory, and so on. The argument is an obvious *reductio ad absurdum*.
>
> It is obvious that whether the Haydns or Bachs composed or performed, they were interacting with stimulus objects—pianos, organs, notes, teachers. Furthermore, they were not geniuses, from the very beginning. Their genius behavior was the culmination of a series of events of their reactional biographies involving long hours of practice and other labor.[23]

Let us take a different approach to the problem of inheritance in view of previous failures. We consider that musical behavior

[23] N. H. Pronko and J. W. Bowles, Jr., *Empirical foundations of psychology* (New York: Rinehart & Co., Inc., 1951), p. 26.

is acquired through a long process of individual interaction with musical stimuli. We do not need to accept the inheritance of capacity for music further than realizing that sound biological equipment for the reception of stimuli and for effective performances is inherited. The man born deaf is deprived of part of his biological equipment with which he may acquire musical responses. However, although Beethoven wrote some of his greatest work during his later years while deaf, we must consider that this equipment had already been acquired and developed before he became so stricken. Certain creative skills were important for composition, and their acquisition early in life was important and contributed to his later success.

Let us not suppose that musical ability is merely the result of classroom achievement. We realize that, before the onset of formal training, individual predispositions toward music will vary. Family stimulations early in life should not be ignored. Consider such great masters as Bach and Mozart. They came from musical surroundings and stimulation came early in life.

Evidence against the inheritance of musical behavior seems just as strong as that for it. Mursell mentions evidence for inheritance from two sources: the discriminative powers as measured by the Seashore tests, which do not seem to change, and the fact that musical talent runs in family groups. However, we have already seen in Chapter 2 that pitch discrimination, one of the responses measured by the Seashore tests, can be improved with training. This was previously thought to be a primary inherited talent. We have also seen how consonance and dissonance judgments are culturally determined, that these judgments depend on our social interactions rather than an inherited faculty.

Studies of family histories can support a view preferring the acquisition of musical behavior just as well as they can support the inheritance theory. In the field of intelligence, for example, the studies on the Jukes and Kallikaks usually have been reported as supporting a view that feeble-mindedness was inherited, since here were family histories of generation after generation where members were mentally deficient. However, recent interpretations have pointed out that the barren backwoods environment, poor structural stock, and incidence of disease are a few factors which could just as easily account for the line of feeble-mindedness as inheritance itself.

By saying that musical behavior is acquired, we are not denying biological inheritance of structure. Deficient structures will obviously be limiting factors for musical as well as other kinds of behavior.

Rate of maturation is also important. This is a function of heredity. Musically precocious children often have a head start because of early development. There will obviously be individual differences in musical reactions just as there are in other areas of behavior. These will be a function of the biological equipment one has as well as the presence or absence of musical stimuli at various stages in one's development. What we are arguing against is the inheritance of mental powers for musical reception and performance.

That musical talent is the result of previously acquired skills and not inherited genius should be clear by now. No great composer or performer ever achieved his goal without long hours of apprenticeship and struggle. Musical accomplishment is not the mere result of inherited inspiration but the product of hard work. This point is well illustrated by the following quotation from Siegmeister:

> What is true of today's composers was probably equally true of most of the great musicians of the past. We know that many of them toiled and struggled, often sweated blood over their music. We have only to look at Beethoven's sketchbooks to see how he chiseled and hammered away, wrote and rewrote most of his greatest compositions, before he got them right. Bach, asked what was the secret of his art, responded, "I have worked hard." There is no question that he and all the great masters labored constantly and with intense application—they had to in order to get all that work done.

Even Wagner, whose autobiography tends to give the impression that his life was one endless series of adventures, intrigues, love affairs, and his music the product of the famous *raptus*, must have spent years and years sitting stock-still at his desk or piano. The sheer labor of writing down the hundreds of thousands—if not millions—of notes contained in the orchestral scores of the "Ring" alone is appalling, and could never have been achieved without the months and years of patient, systematic work old Richard put in . . .[24]

[24] E. Siegmeister, *The music lover's handbook* (New York: William Morrow & Co., Inc., 1943), p. 56.

Chapter 12

THE MEASUREMENT OF MUSICAL BEHAVIOR: THE NATURE OF TESTS[1]

ONE VERY important and productive area in which the psychologist works is the measurement of behavior. Since the law of individual differences applies almost universally to behavior, we do not expect musical ability to be the same for all people. And it is not. The measurement of these individual differences in musical responsiveness is the main concern of this and the following chapter.

All sorts of tests have been devised to measure the various aspects of the musical personality. There are tests of musical knowledge which are of the purely informational sort; they might ask such questions as who composed *Lohengrin,* or what is a sonata form. More important are tests of musical ability, or what is sometimes called "capacity." These have as their aim the prediction of success in future musical performance. They attempt to answer the question, "Can this person profit from musical instruction?" If one appears to have no inclination toward musical performance, it would be useless to spend much time and money on this part of his education. But how are we going to find this out? Of course, we could buy him a musical instrument and start giving him lessons. If he succeeds, our investment is worth while, but if he fails we might sell the instrument and perhaps hope for better luck in some other area. However, a simpler method is to give him a standardized test which takes a relatively short

[1] This chapter is intended primarily as an introduction to the nature of musical tests for those people unacquainted with the general concepts involved in test construction and behavior measurement. It may be omitted by those already acquainted with psychometric principles.

time. Assuming the test is a good one, we might be able to tell from its results what chances our subject will have for success in his future musical activities. Notice the condition that the test must be good, for a poor test is no more valuable than guessing or flipping a coin, sometimes less. We know that musical behavior, like other kinds of activity, is acquired and that some people are more able than others to profit from learning because of their early history of contacts with specific stimuli. The problem of learning music has already been taken up in a previous chapter. The psychologist's job is to make up a test by which he can predict the future success of our aspiring musician. Although work on this problem of predicting musical success by means of tests has been going on for the last thirty-five years or more, the results so far have been far from what we might wish.

In considering the matter of a music test, a number of factors must be taken into account before we can judge the goodness of the test we have selected for study. What makes a good test? This question cannot be answered in a word. In choosing a test, one must recognize the purpose for which it is intended. Not all published tests are good. Many lack adequate research and refinement and are little better than chance as predictive measures. First of all, such practical considerations as cost, time, and ease in administration and scoring are necessary. Assuming our test meets these standards, we must next look into its reliability.

Reliability.—A good test must be reliable. The accuracy of a measurement is expressed in the reliability coefficient. Any test score is bound to be somewhat inaccurate because we are only taking a sample of a person's behavior at a particular time. We say that a test is reliable if it is consistent with itself.

Suppose today you take a test for musical ability and you get a score of 50. If next week we give you the same test or a comparable form, and, with other conditions the same, you receive a score of 90, the test is obviously unreliable. We cannot say that the improvement of forty points has been due to practice because you have done none of that. Reliability refers then only to the consistency of a test, regardless of what it measures. Take a test in the field of intelligence. Suppose today you receive an I.Q. of 70, about the level of a moron, and next week you end up with an I.Q. of 150, a genius. Who is to know which score is correct? True, we might have some preferences as to which score we would like to choose. At any rate, the test would be obviously unreliable. Reliability, then, is the first requisite of a good test. We want to be sure that the test, given on two different occasions under the same conditions, will yield about the same results. In other words, the score received is a true score, and the test an accurate measure of whatever it is testing.

The reliability of a test may be a function of a number of factors. First, reliability depends on the *length* of a test. Too short tests are not adequate samples of behavior, for on any given test, one might not "hit" any of the questions because the sample of what he knows or can do is too small. Secondly, a test might not be reliable for *all kinds of people*. A music test designed for adults might be useless for children. Items might be too difficult, or the directions might be aimed at an intellectual level too high for the child. To counteract this, many tests have forms for different age levels.

How are we able to find out the reliability of a test? First, we might give the test to the same group of people on two different occasions and compare the results. This method we have already referred to in explaining the nature of reliability. It is known as the *test-retest method*. As an alternative we might make up two equal forms of the test and give both forms to the same group. We then can compare the results. A practical modification of this method and one frequently used in checking reliability in any situation is to compare odd and even items of a test. Divide the test into two equal subtests and compare the odd and the even items. This method is called the *split-half method*.

In using any one of these methods to test for reliability, there is a statistical device which we can apply to determine the degree of reliability. This is known as the *coefficient of correlation* and is a statistical statement of the degree of relationship between any two sets of variables. In this case, the two variables are the two sets of test scores. A perfect correlation would give us a coefficient of 1.00. This means that everybody taking the test would have to get exactly the same relative score both times they took the test. This perfect correlation seldom happens, because there are so many factors which interfere. The best we can hope for will be an approximation of .90 or maybe .95. If we get a correlation this high, we may consider ourselves as having a very reliable test. On the other hand, let us suppose we all get completely different scores on two consecutive times. Compared to the first time, it is merely a matter of chance what score we get the second time. The correlation between these two testings would then be .00 or close to it, indicating no relationship. We may then have all degrees of correlation from .00 to a perfect 1.00. These are called *positive correlations,* because any relationship which is expressed between the two is a direct one. There are relationships of an inverse sort called *negative correlations,* but that need not concern us for the moment.

A good test, then, should have a high reliability coefficient. We do not expect perfect relationships and consider .90 or above very satisfactory. Many times one must be content with correlation coefficients of reliability much lower than that. The correlation coefficient is *not a percentage.* It is merely a statistical statement of the degree of relationship between any two sets of variables. The lower we go from 1.00 to .00 the less the two variables are related.

Validity.—Just as a good test must be reliable, so must it be valid. Validity means that the test measures what it purports to measure. In other words, a test that is reliable is an accurate measure, but this has no reference to *what it measures.* It might be anything from ability to play the bazooka to ability to count birdseed. If we have a test which we say measures musical ability of some sort, we want it to measure *that*, and not intelligence or some other behavior. How are we going to know whether this test we have selected really measures musical ability? A test may be validated in several ways.

INTERNAL CONSISTENCY. According to this check for validity, we see that each item on the test is measuring the same kind of behavior that all the other items are measuring. The internal consistency of a test may be arrived at by the process of constructing the test in its preliminary form and correlating every item of the test with every other item. It is then possible to make up a test which is quite internally consistent. All items intercorrelate highly and measure various degrees of the same behavior. Later we can name that behavior. A good example of this kind of validating is the Seashore Test of Pitch Discrimination.[2] The subject is presented various pitches by means of a phonograph. He hears two tones and tells whether the second is higher or lower than the first. From the point of internal consistency, the test is fairly valid. All items are alike in that they measure the same behavior, ability to discriminate fine differences in pitch. Whether or not this ability is related to all-round musical talent is another question. The fact remains that it does measure this particular kind of behavior, ability to discriminate pitch differences.

EMPIRICAL VALIDITY. If our test correlates with accepted evidence for the presence of certain abilities, we can say it in part measures these abilities. The validity of a test may be established by comparing test scores with some outside criterion, e.g., another measure. What are other possible criteria for checking validity of a music test? They often consist of ratings made by people who know the performance of the person rated. They might also be other tests already proved to be valid.

[2] C. E. Seashore, D. Lewis, and J. G. Saetveit, *Seashore measures of musical talents* (rev. ed.; Camden, N.J.: Education Department, R.C.A. Manufacturing Co., 1939).

Let us suppose that we want to make a test for singing ability. We would then choose to take the test a group of voice students who differ in ability. We assume their scores will also vary. As a criterion we might ask their teacher to rate them as to how good he thought the students were. He is a good judge of voice, and so we correlate his ratings of the persons and the actual test scores. If the correlation is high, we are led to believe that our test is valid; it is really measuring what it is supposed to measure, namely, singing ability. On the other hand, if our ratings correlate low with the test scores, we may wonder what the test measures; it may not be singing ability. Our ratings are accurate. This, of course, is not always a fair assumption, but there are also ways of checking on our raters.

By and large, validity coefficients are not as high as those for reliability. This is because there are so many more extraneous factors to be taken into account. Criteria are often ratings made by humans. Regardless of how careful and unbiased a rater tries to be, he cannot always be a perfect judge. Of course, a poor judge tends to lower the correlation. We might not know whether it was the poor judge or poor test which caused our low correlation. Ratings are often weak criteria because our judge may not know all the facts about the person he is rating. There are methods of improving ratings. One way would be to use more than one judge. Take several judges and average their ratings.

Grades in music subjects such as harmony, sight singing, performance on musical instruments, etc. are often used as criteria. Other possible means of validating might be to check the test with the performance of recognized musicians. Let us give the test to members of some major symphony orchestra. If they tend to do well, it is a positive check; if they do badly, we may assume, providing their playing is above question (a large assumption), that the test may be measuring something else beside musical talent. Finally, designers of new tests frequently validate their measurements by correlating them with existing established tests in recognized use. In the field of music, this is a difficult matter, as there is even now considerable disagreement as to the validity of our best existing devices. This is because musical ability is such a complex pattern of behavior.

It is important to keep in mind both the validity and the reliability of a test. If a test is unreliable, it cannot be valid, because if one cannot achieve consistency, he can hardly expect a high correlation with some other comparable factor. However, a test may be quite reliable and not valid. In other words, it is possible to develop a test which is quite reliable, but how well it measures musical ability is another matter. It might well be measuring intelligence instead. In interpreting a validity coefficient, we must keep in mind also the range of the group studied. A correlation is going to be lower for a very selected group than for one which has a wide range of abilities.

Objectivity.—Generally speaking, objective tests are considered more desirable than those where the opinions of the scorer influence the results. An objective test is one which yields exactly the same score regardless of who does the checking, excepting possible clerical errors which also may be eliminated by using scoring machines. In really objective tests, there is no doubt as to the rightness or wrongness of any given answer. Most of our current music tests are fairly objective. Consider again the Seashore Test of Pitch Discrimination.[3] Two tones are presented, one of which is either higher or lower than the other. Scoring keys with the correct answers are used and these are checked with any individual's record.

Norms.—Authors of most tests provide tables for interpreting a particular "raw score." These tables of norms are based on group scores and may be given as averages, percentiles, or standard scores, so that any one person's score can be compared with that of the group on which the test is standardized. There are, of course, different kinds of norms: age, grade, sex, and so forth.

[3] *Ibid.*

Age norms would indicate the average performance of individuals of a particular age group. One can also use grade norms, norms of high school seniors, college freshmen, college sophomores, etc. We might also have norms for musicians and non-musicians. Whether norms are satisfactory will depend on the size of the group on which the norms are based, the representation of the group selected, and the resemblance of the person in question to the group with which we are comparing him. The first two are checks on the adequacy of the published norms, the third depends on the use to be made of them. A recent criticism of the Seashore *Measures of Musical Talents* [4] has been the possibility that the norms actually published are based on people who are poorer than the average population.

With these facts in mind, let us proceed to the investigation of some of the current tests of music.

[4] *Ibid.*

Chapter 13

THE MEASUREMENT OF MUSICAL BEHAVIOR: CURRENT TESTS

For the purpose of convenience in discussion, the various measurements of musical behavior may be divided into three kinds: tests of aptitude or ability, tests of feeling and appreciation, and tests of musical knowledge. Although such a division is somewhat arbitrary, this classification will be the most useful for our analysis. Because musical behavior does not come already packaged in convenient little bundles, there is bound to be some overlap in our discussion. We have already considered the disagreement which exists among authorities as to the development of musical talent. Some say it is a function of previous learning, others say it is inherited. There is just as much disagreement as to what constitutes musical ability. So far, the existing measures of musical talent or ability have been largely of a sensory sort. Tests of feeling and appreciation have tried to sample the more aesthetic responses to music, while those of knowledge deal mainly with such admittedly acquired responses as the names of composers, notation, instruments, scales, etc. We shall begin our survey of the current tests with those of ability or talent. These have made the most serious attempt to predict musical success. They are based on the assumption that if an individual does well on these tests, he will be able to profit from training in musical accomplishment, particularly in the area of performance.

Because of the complexity of musical behavior, we will observe at the outset that little agreement exists among researchers as to the effectiveness of the existing tests in reaching their goal of the prediction of musical performance.

Tests of Musical Ability or Aptitude

The best known of the so-called musical aptitude tests are the Seashore Measures of Musical Talents.[1] Since their first publication in 1919, they have been given to many individuals and subjected to considerable research, so that at the present time we are able to evaluate them and formulate an opinion of their possible usefulness and limitations.

In the original form,[2] the Seashore tests consisted of six twelve-inch phonograph records, each devoted to a musical "sense." These included (*a*) pitch, (*b*) intensity, (*c*) time, (*d*) consonance, (*e*) rhythm, and (*f*) tonal memory. In a first revision,[3] the consonance test was supplanted by the sense of timbre test. The revised edition has two forms, A and B. Series A is designed for general testing purposes, while series B is intended for more intensive testing of musical groups and selected individuals and for research purposes.

Description of the Seashore Measures of Musical Talents (revised form).—PITCH. In the sense of pitch test, the subject listens to pairs of pitch comparisons. He is asked to tell whether the second pitch is higher or lower than the first. The source of the stimuli is a General Radio beat-frequency oscillator, the output of which is essentially tonally pure as far as frequency is concerned. By "pure" is meant that there is an absence of overtones or harmonics. By using this oscillating tone, the revised tests overcome the weakness of the original pitch test, in which tuning

[1] C. E. Seashore, D. Lewis, and J. G. Saetveit, *Seashore measures of musical talents* (rev. ed.; Camden, N. J.: Department of Education, R.C.A. Manufacturing Co., 1939).

[2] C. E. Seashore, *Seashore measures of musical talent* (Chicago: C. H. Stoelting & Co., 1919).

[3] J. G. Saetveit, D. Lewis, and C. E. Seashore, *Revision of the Seashore measures of musical talents,* Univ. Ia. Stud. Aims Progr. Res., 1940, No. 65, pp. 1–66.

forks were used, thus causing a lack of uniformity in intensity and duration of the tones. The cycle differences in frequency are 17, 12, 8, 5, 4, 3, 2, 1 for series A and 8, 5, 3, 2, 1 in series B.

LOUDNESS. The sense of loudness test (called intensity in the first version) contains pairs of tones which differ in physical intensity. Frequency is kept constant at 440 cps. The subject is asked to tell whether the second tone is louder or softer than the first. Decibel differences in intensity are 2.5, 1.5, 1.0, and 0.5 in series B and 4.0, 2.5, 1.5, 1.0, and 0.5 in series A.

TIMBRE. The timbre test supplants the original consonance test. It is designed to measure an individual's capacity to discriminate between complex sounds which differ only in their composition of overtones. A special generator has been devised for recording purposes which is able to produce as many as sixteen consecutive harmonics. The frequencies, intensities, and phases can be controlled. The actual tones used consist of six partials. Half of the pairs are different in harmonic structure; the other half are the same. The subject is asked to tell whether the two tones of the pair are the same or different in timbre. These changes in the structure of the tones are due to the reciprocal alternation of the third and fourth harmonics.

TIME. Two tones of different duration are presented in each item comparison, and the subject is asked to judge whether the second interval is longer or shorter than the first. Time differences in duration range from 0.30 sec. to 0.05 sec. in series A and 0.15 sec. to 0.025 sec. in series B.

RHYTHM. In the sense of rhythm test, the pairs of rhythmic patterns are determined by the number and temporal separateness of the pulses. In the construction of this test, the basic variable is time. Factors held constant are number of tones, the number and position of accents, tempo, and the temporal length of the rhythmic pattern. Series B consists of test items having notes in $\frac{3}{4}$, $\frac{4}{4}$, and $\frac{5}{4}$ time.

Tonal memory. A Hammond electric organ was used in recording the tonal memory test. Pairs of nonmelodic tonal sequences of increasing length are presented. The subject is to identify by number the tone in the second group which is different from the first. Items consist of three-, four-, and five-note spans. In both A and B series, items in each of the span groups are arranged approximately according to difficulty.

Reliability of Seashore Measures.—We will recall that the first necessary check on the goodness of a test is its reliability. Some studies reported to check the reliability of the Seashore Measures have been summarized in Table 2. These studies refer to the 1919 version. Examination of this table shows that the tests of pitch and tonal memory appear to be the most satisfactory, with those of consonance and rhythm decidedly the poorest. These latter coefficients are low enough to render questionable individual prediction on the basis of these tests. Farnsworth[4] concludes that only the pitch and tonal memory tests are sufficiently reliable for diagnostic value and that the other tests should be used with extreme caution. In commenting on the early version of the Seashore Measures, Farnsworth writes,

> The Seashore pitch and memory tests would appear to possess sufficient reliability for certain diagnostic purposes. The Kwalwasser battery [see below] and the remainder of the Seashore battery should be employed only with extreme caution.[5]

Saetveit, Lewis, and Seashore[6] report reliabilities by the split-half method for the revised version (1939), using adult subjects for Series A and B as follows: pitch, .88, .78; loudness, .88, .77; time, .75, .70; timbre, .74, .72; rhythm, .62, .72; tonal memory, .88, .89. We observe that these reliabilities are considerably higher than those reported by investigators on the 1919 version.

[4] P. R. Farnsworth, An historical, critical, and experimental study of the Seashore-Kwalwasser test battery, *Genet. Psychol. Monogr.*, 1931, **9**:5, 291–393.
[5] *Ibid.*, p. 384.
[6] *Op. cit.*

TABLE 2

TABLE OF STUDIES REPORTED ON RELIABILITY OF THE 1919 VERSION OF THE SEASHORE MEASURES OF MUSICAL TALENT

Investigator	*Method*	*Pitch*	*Intensity*	*Time*	*Rhythm*	*Tonal Memory*	*Consonance*
Brown [7]	Retest	.71	.65	.48	.29	.59	.43
Highsmith [8]	Retest	.76	.50	.52		.83	.53
Lanier [9]	Retest	.68	.60	.50	.43	.74	.54
	Split-Half	.84	.67	.64	.35	.60	.45
Stanton [10]	Retest	.54	.80	.45		.83	.62
		.64	.64	.58		.90	.54
	Split-Half	.60	.82	.67		.83	.46
		.51	.78	.66		.90	.58
Mursell [11]	Split-Half	.66	.86	.81	.64	.88	.52
Drake [12]	Split-Half	.72	.85	.68	.68	.94	
		.84	.88	.70	.48	.86	.30
Farnsworth [13]	Split-Half	.74	.72	.41	.43	.83	.33
		.75	.61	.46	.47	.81	.36

Validation of the Seashore Measures.—Seashore and his colleagues have insisted that the only real validation of their test is its internal consistency. Because an external criterion in a validation study may be itself *less reliable* than the test, they have insisted on this internal consistency of a test as the real criterion of the validity of their measure. Concerning the sense of pitch test, they write,

> It is not assumed that a good sense of pitch in itself is predictive of musical success. All that we have the right to assume on

[7] A. W. Brown, The reliability and validity of the Seashore tests of musical talent, *J. appl. Psychol.*, 1928, **12**, 468–76.

[8] J. A. Highsmith, Selecting musical talent, *J. appl. Psychol.*, 1929, **13**, 486–93.

[9] L. H. Lanier, Prediction of the reliability of mental tests and tests of special abilities, *J. exp. Psychol.*, 1927, **10**, 69–113.

[10] H. M. Stanton, Measurement of musical talent: the Eastman experiment, *Univ. Ia. Stud. Psychol. Music*, 1935, **2**, 1–140.

[11] J. L. Mursell, Measuring musical ability and achievement: a study of the correlation of Seashore test scores and other variables, *J. educ. Res.*, 1932, **26**, 116–26.

[12] R. M. Drake, The validity and reliability of tests of musical talent, *J. appl. Psychol.*, 1933, **17**, 447–58.

[13] Farnsworth, *op. cit.*

the positive side is that a person who has a fine sense of pitch ought to be capable of a corresponding control of pitch in musical achievement, other conditions being favorable. . . . In view of these demarcations, we must refuse to validate these measures against unanalyzed judgments about musical achievement and turn to the more technical analysis of the factors involved in the spirit of scientific method in the laboratory for the purpose of gaining insight into the nature of the processes involved, even at the sacrifice of broad generalizations and ultrapractical simplification.[14]

To the question as to whether the test does measure what it purports to measure, Seashore and his colleagues reply again regarding the sense of pitch test:

Pitch discrimination is measured in terms of the least perceptible difference in pitch under relatively optimum conditions. We have come to call this the "sense" of pitch because it is the basic measurement of the capacity for hearing pitch. Whether or not the measurement is valid from this point of view must be determined in terms of the extent to which pitch is isolated and varied for measurement and all other factors are kept constant.[15]

Mursell has sharply criticized this means of validating a test. He writes:

There is only one satisfactory method of finding out whether the Seashore tests really measure musical ability, and that is to ascertain whether persons rating high or low or medium on these tests also rate high and low and medium in what one may call *musical behavior*, that is, sight singing, playing the piano, getting through courses in theory and applied music, and the like.[16]

In defense of his position, Seashore replies:

The measures represent the theory of specific measurements insofar as they conform to the two universal scientific sanctions on the basis for which they were designated: namely, that (*a*)

[14] Saetveit, *et al., op. cit.*, pp. 42–43.
[15] *Ibid.*, p. 44.
[16] J. L. Mursell, What about music tests? *Music Educ. J.*, 1937, **24**:2, 16–18.

the factor under consideration may be known; (*b*) the conclusion must be limited to the factors under control.

The tests have been validated for what they purport to measure. This is an internal validation in terms of success in the isolation of the factor measured and the degree of control of all other factors in the measurement. When we have measured reliably the sense of pitch, that is, pitch discrimination, in the laboratory, and we know that pitch was isolated from all other factors, no scientist will question the fact that we have measured pitch. There would be no object in validating against the judgment of even the most competent musician. We would not validate the reading on a thermometer against the judgment of a person sensitive to temperature.

The tests should not be validated in terms of their showing on an omnibus theory or blanket rating against all musical behavior including such diverse and unrelated situations as composition, directing, voice, piano, violin, saxophone, theory, administration, or drums, because there are hundreds of other factors which help to determine job analysis in each of such fields.[17]

Seashore insists this is the only justifiable validation procedure. However, this leaves the prognostic value of the Seashore Measures still in the realm of speculation. Many others insist that *external criteria* are the real test of validity.

Validation studies based on empirical criteria have been summarized in Table 3. Examination of this table shows coefficients of correlation in general lower than those for reliability. Again *tonal memory* and *pitch* seem to be the only tests to show some promise. Our examination of the table shows most correlations below .50. This has risky predictive value. We must realize that criteria are also very likely to be defective, but despite the possible inadequacies, if the tests measured musical behavior to any marked extent, we should still expect higher coefficients. Again these studies are based on the 1919 version; little else is available on the 1939 version.

Mursell[18] found superiority of music school students on the

[17] C. E. Seashore, The psychology of music: XI, *Music Educ. J.*, 1937, **24**:3 25–26.

[18] Mursell, *op. cit.*

Seashore measures not sufficiently marked to warrant any educational advice. Both Highsmith [19] and More [20] found scores on intelligence tests to have a slight superiority over the Seashore Measures as means of predicting success in musical performance.

On the more positive side, let us consider Stanton's [21] extensive experiment at the Eastman School of Music. She administered five of the Seashore Measures over a period of ten years to entering students. On the basis of these scores and a test of tonal imagery, a case history, and an intelligence test (Iowa Comprehension Test), she was able to eliminate most of the people least likely to succeed. On the basis of this battery of tests, individuals were divided into five groups, "discouraged, doubtful, possible, probable, and safe . . ." The most convincing results are those using graduation as a criterion of success. Of the discouraged group, 17 per cent graduated, of the doubtful group 32 per cent graduated, of the possible group 33 per cent, of the probable 42 per cent, and of the safe group 60 per cent. Her method indicates relationships between ratings on the Seashore Measures and ratings on the Iowa test, arrived at by a special procedure, but no correlations are given or indications of the weightings attributed to each. Concerning this study, Mursell writes:

> But we cannot regard the results as in any way an adequate validation of the Seashore Measures of Musical Talent. It should be clearly understood that the groupings were formed not on the Seashore test alone, but on those tests combined with an intelligence test. And reports of the experiment nowhere separate out the influence of the two. . . . It is evident that from the results so presented we can draw no conclusions whatsoever as to the predictive value or validity of the Seashore battery. For all we know, quite as good or indeed better results might have been attained by using merely the intelligence test and the audition.[22]

[19] Highsmith, *op.. cit.*

[20] G. V. D. More, Prognostic testing in music on the college level, *J. educ. Res.*, 1932–33, **26**, 199–212.

[21] Stanton, *op. cit.*

[22] J. L. Mursell, *The psychology of music* (New York: W. W. Norton & Co., Inc., 1937), pp. 297–98.

TABLE 3

Validation Studies Done on the Seashore Measures of Musical Talent

Investigator	*Criterion*	*P*	*I*	*T*	*R*	*TM*	*C*	*Total*
McCarthy [23]	Voice grades	.43	.33			.40	.41	
Brown [24]	Ratings of teachers in musical aptitude	.15	.11	.15	.17	.41	.17	
Mursell [25]	Ratings of teachers in musical aptitude	.11	.07	.20	.35	.19	—.27	.08
	Piano grades	.01	.09	.10	—.15	.20	—.25	—.15
	Voice grades	.07	.08	—.14	.06	.05	.06	.08
Taylor [26]	Dictation grades	.02	.29	.27	.21	.26	.25	
	Sight-singing grades	.12	.33	.17	.14	.23	—.05	
	Harmony grades	.07	.02	—.05	.26	.15	.10	
More [27]	Average college grades in music	.41	.07	.13	.22	.45	.01	
Drake [28]	Teachers' ranking of music students	.27	.05	.14	.08	.33		
		.31	.14	.28	.36	.41	—.03	
Highsmith [29]	Grades in applied music	.80	.33	.26		.10	.04	
	Grades in music theory	.41	.35	.30		.14	.23	
Salisbury and Smith [30]	Sight singing	.60				.65		
Wright [31]	Piano performance							.45
	Music dictation							.51
	Music dictation at end of one year							.73
Mosher [32]		.44	.49	.36		.44	.29	
Brennan [33]	Teacher's ratings on performance	.17			.47	.47		
	Amount of training				.14		.02	

[23] D. McCarthy, A study of the Seashore measures of musical talent, *J. appl. Psychol.*, 1930, **14**, 437–55.

[24] Brown, *op. cit.*

[25] J. L. Mursell, Measuring musical ability and achievement: a study of the correlations of the Seashore test scores and other variables, *J. educ. Res.*, 1932, **26**, 116–26.

[26] E. M. Taylor, A study of the prognosis of musical talent, *J. exp. Educ.*, 1941, **10**, 1–28.

Except for tonal memory, the Seashore Measures deal with sensory acuities and do not touch on such functions as interval discrimination, harmonic sequences, tonality, or resolution. Thus, it would seem that these tests merely measure the ear's responsiveness to certain differences in sound waves. While sensory acuities may enter in as necessary equipment for certain types of special performance, this is not the whole story, and a different approach to the problem would seem advisable.

Kwalwasser-Dykema Music Tests.—The Kwalwasser-Dykema Music Tests[34] are in many ways similar to Seashore's but also contain a number of parts which measure admittedly trained abilities as well as sensory acuity to sound. We have already observed that Seashore believes he is measuring six innate capacities, so by eliminating the musical setting as much as possible he felt better able to measure these capacities.

Like the Seashore Measures, the Kwalwasser-Dykema battery contains measures of (*a*) pitch, (*b*) intensity, (*c*) time, (*d*) rhythm, (*e*) timbre (quality), and (*f*) tonal memory, plus tests of (*g*) tonal movement, (*h*) melodic taste, (*i*) pitch imagery, and (*j*) rhythmic imagery. These are also recorded on phonographic records. The first six tests resemble those designed by Seashore. However, in the test of *pitch discrimination,* a single tone is presented. If it does not fluctuate, the subject indicates it has remained the same by writing S. But if it rises or falls in

---

[27] More, *op. cit.*

[28] Drake, *op. cit.*

[29] Highsmith, *op. cit.*

[30] F. S. Salisbury and H. R. Smith, Prognosis of sight-singing ability of normal school students, *J. appl. Psychol.*, 1929, **13**, 425–39.

[31] F. A. Wright, The correlation between achievement and capacity in music, *J. educ. Res.*, 1928, **17**, 50–56.

[32] R. M. Mosher, *A study of the group method of measurement of sight singing* (New York: Bureau of Publications, Teachers College, Columbia University, 1925).

[33] F. Brennan, The relationship between musical capacity and performance, *Psychol. Monogr.*, 1926, **36**:167, 190–248.

[34] J. Kwalwasser and P. W. Dykema, *Manual of directions for Victor records* (New York: Carl Fischer, Inc., 1930).

pitch anywhere from 15 to 6 cps., returning to the original pitch, it is different. The *intensity discrimination* test is constructed in a manner somewhat similar to the corresponding test in the Seashore battery. It has thirty tones and chords which are repeated at different intensities. The record is taken from a Duo-Art reproduction which allows for a number of different degrees of loudness. In *time discrimination,* pairs of tones are compared as to duration. The subject gives corresponding reactions of same or different. The temporal variations range from 0.03 to 0.30 sec. *Rhythm discrimination* contains twenty-five items composed of two measures which form rhythmic patterns. The subject is to tell whether the second pattern is the same as or different from the first. The test of *quality discrimination* (timbre) includes thirty parts. Each part is composed of two notes played on one instrument. These are immediately followed by the same notes played on the same or a different instrument. Discriminations of same or different are made. The test of *tonal memory* has twenty-five pairs of melodic patterns which range from four to nine notes in length. These patterns are played twice on the piano, either in exactly the same or in changed form. The subject tells whether the second pattern is the same as or different from the first. These are the six tests which resemble those constructed by Seashore. They are supposedly measuring the same sensory capacities, but a comparison of test correlations between the two batteries makes this assumption questionable. This is partially due to the low reliabilities of some of the Kwalwasser tests, as we shall see later.

The Kwalwasser-Dykema battery includes four other tests, some of which measure admittedly learned behaviors. They attempt to measure the matter of musical feeling and appreciation. In the test of *melodic taste,* two melodies of two phrases each are played. The opening phrases of each pair of melodies are the same, but the concluding phrases are unlike. The subject tells which melody has the most appropriate ending. The test of *tonal movement* refers to the ability of the listener to indicate correct musical endings. The subject is asked to tell whether a final tone which would give the best possible resolution to the melody, according to musical theorists, would be higher (up) or lower (down) from the last tone given in the recorded melody. The final two tests, *pitch* and *rhythmic imagery*, are only useful with subjects who can read musical notation. The listeners are asked to compare the tonal and rhythmic patterns which they hear on the phonograph record with those presented in visual form on their answer sheets. They record S or D if the pitches or rhythms they hear on the record are the same as or different from those presented on the printed score before them.

Reliability of K.-D. tests.—Table 4 gives us a summary of studies on the reliability of the Kwalwasser-Dykema tests. We observe that these reliabilities are even lower than those reported for the Seashore Measures. From his investigations on the Seashore and Kwalwasser-Dykema tests, Farnsworth [35] concludes that with the exception of the test of tonal movement, the K.-D. tests are too unreliable for individual prediction. In another study Farnsworth [36] had compared the corresponding tests of the Seashore and K.-D. batteries. These include similar tests of pitch, intensity, time, rhythm, and tonal memory. He found that except for tonal memory these were not measuring at all perfectly the same behavior variables. The lack of correspondence, of course, in part may be accounted for by the low reliabilities of the tests. His correlations were for pitch .10, rhythm .24, intensity .03, tonal memory .62, and time .38. Tilson has verified these results, reporting correlations for pitch .14, rhythm .22, intensity —.12, tonal memory .32, and time .40. In a later study, Whitley [37] gives somewhat higher values: pitch .49, rhythm .43, intensity .38, tonal memory .71, and time .55. For both Whitley and Farnsworth, the two tonal memory tests correlate best.

[35] P. R. Farnsworth, Studies in the psychology of tone, *Genet. Psychol. Monogr.*, 1934, **15**:1, 1–91.

[36] Farnsworth, *Genet. Psychol, Monogr.*, 1931, **9**:5.

[37] M. T. Whitley, A comparison of the Seashore and K.-D. tests, *Teach. Coll. Rec.*, 1932, **8**, 731–51.

TABLE 4

Reliability Coefficients for the Kwalwasser-Dykema Battery of Music Tests

(*P*, pitch; *I*, intensity; *Q*, quality; *T*, time; *R*, rhythm; *TM*, tonal memory; *Tmo*, tonal movement; *MT*, melodic taste; *PI*, pitch imagery; *RI*, rhythmic imagery)

Investigator	*Method*	*P*	*I*	*Q*	*T*	*R*	*TM*	*Tmo*	*MT*	*PI*	*RI*	*Total*
Farnsworth [38]	Retest	—.05	—.10	.53	.42	.21	.73	.55	.53	.42	.40	
	Split-Half	.63	.60	.36	.63	.28	.63	.85	.28	.33	.20	
Sanderson [39]	Retest	.34	.07	.20	.19	.27	.43	.37	.10	.14	.31	
	Retest	.38	.12	.10	.11	.04	.53	.38	.06	.28	.27	
Manzer and Morowitz [40]	Retest	.18	.15	.32	.43	.48	.73	.69	.52	.45	.38	
Whitley [41]	Split-Half	.27	.27	.25	.33	.23	.46	.67	.19			
Drake [42]	Split-Half	.39		.39		.30	.57	.73	.40			
				.66			.55	.85	.61			
Beinstock [43]	Retest		.35	.45	.00	.39	.52					

[38] Farnsworth, *Genet. Psychol. Monogr.*, 1934, **15**:1.

[39] H. E. Sanderson, Differences in musical ability in children of different national and racial origin, *J. genet. Psychol.*, 1933, **42**, 100–20.

[40] G. W. Manzer and S. Morowitz, The performance of a group of college students on the K.-D. tests, *J. appl. Psychol.*, 1935, **19**, 331–48.

[41] Whitley, *op. cit.*

[42] Drake, *op. cit.*

[43] S. F. Beinstock, A predictive study of musical achievement, *J. genet. Psychol.*, 1942, **61**, 135–45.

TABLE 5

TABLE OF VALIDITY STUDIES REPORTED FOR K.-D. TESTS

Investigator	*Criterion*	*P*	*I*	*Q*	*T*	*R*	*TM*	*Tmo*	*MT*	*PI*	*RI*	*Total*
Chadwick [44]	Grades in sight singing	.01	.28	.19	.02	.08	.32	.31	.23	.32	.34	
		.18	—.11	.14	.27	.17	.14	.24	.31	.29	.46	
Drake [45]	Teachers' ranking in music school	.23		.17			.43	.15	—.13			
		.00		.14			.25	.23	—.10			
Beinstock [46]	Average theory grades		.02	—.01	—.13	—.02	.19					.02
			.16	—.10	—.06	.16						.16
	Music performance		.12	.05	—.12	.31	.26					
			—.09	.09	.01	.20	.28					
Tilson [47]	Grades in sight singing	—.12	.17	.21	.03	.19	.40	.23	—.19	.19	.39	
Taylor [48]	Marks in sight singing	—.18	.14	.10	—.07	.16	.28	.06	.06	.34	.08	
	Marks in dictation	.06	.29	.21	.06	.09	.45	.10	.12	.59	.25	
	Marks in harmony	.02	—.07	.00	.00	—.04	.02	.00	—.03	.00	.01	

[44] J. E. Chadwick, Predicting success in sight singing, *J. appl. Psychol.*, 1933, **17**, 671–74.
[45] Drake, *op. cit.*
[46] Beinstock, *op. cit.*
[47] L. M. Tilson, Music talent tests for teacher-training purposes, *Music Superv. J.*, 1932, **18**, 26.
[48] Taylor, *op. cit.*

Validity of K.-D. tests.—Table 5 gives an even more discouraging picture of validity than that shown for the Seashore battery. The number of negative correlations reported by all investigators mentioned seems to indicate that some of these tests have little to do with musical ability.

The superior reliability of the Seashore Measures is evident. Kwalwasser has forsaken reliability for brevity. In the 1939 revision of the Seashore Measures, two forms are given. These tests are shorter than the original ones but claim to retain their reliability in spite of the change. It is nevertheless true that the Seashore Measures are lacking in interest value because of their monotony. For this reason the test discriminates against younger subjects. Also, since items are not numbered, it is very easy for children to lose their place.

The low reliability of the K.-D. tests is unfortunate, for no matter how interesting a test may be, if it is unreliable, its value is open to question. Another disadvantage of the K.-D. tests is that they do not discriminate at the higher levels of talent. A college senior with adequate training in music is likely to get close to a perfect score.

One of the most extensive studies on the prognostic value of the Seashore and Kwalwasser tests was undertaken by Taylor[49] at the College of Music of Cincinnati, Ohio. Research was carried out over a period of five years, between 1930 and 1935. A group intelligence test (the Detroit Advanced Intelligence Tests, Forms V and W) was also given to all students taking the musical aptitude tests. The results showed that the batteries did not evidence sufficient predictive value to be used by themselves in guidance. However, it is also stated that the tests are not so bad that they should be discarded. The outstanding subtests found in both sets were the Kwalwasser-Dykema Tests of Pitch Imagery and Tonal Memory.

Beinstock[50] used the K.-D. tests in a predictive study with the subtests of the K.-D., which are similar to the Seashore bat-

[49] *Ibid.* [50] Beinstock, *op. cit.*

tery (Pitch, Intensity, Time, Rhythm, and Timbre). She found that the music test alone was not reliable in the prediction of individual success, and that intelligence measures were the best predictors of later success. The least effective criterion was the extent of previous training, and an actual performance test given each student. Her sample of 122 students were those enrolled in the High School of Music and Art in New York City. The external criteria were the grades and music courses.

Concerning the Seashore and Kwalwasser tests, Farnsworth concludes:

> This study clearly indicates that the Kwalwasser-Dykema battery is quite inferior to the older Seashore tests. The former tests do offer a few advantages. They are shorter and less tiresome. The stimuli are more musical and so, perhaps, more pleasing to the musical groups. As the items are announced by number, the testing procedure is made more fool-proof. The tests are recorded on small records and can be carried in neat cases. Certain of these improvements have been made at the expense of reliability.
>
> Several of the present writer's oldest subjects (with the best auditory limens) have claimed that the pitch test is very inaccurate (Kwalwasser). However, no definite study has been reported on the physical exactness with which the stimuli are given. . . . It is apparent that the K.-D. and Seashore tests are not measuring to any large extent the same behavior variables. And as to reliability one can clearly say they [K.-D.] are decidedly inferior to those constructed by Seashore. These newer tests should probably be employed solely in studies of group differences.[51]

The Drake tests.—The four subtests in the Drake battery are entitled *musical memory, interval discrimination, retentivity*, and *intuition*.[52]

The first of these, *musical memory*, contains twenty-four two-measure melodies. In each item a melody is presented as a stand-

[51] Farnsworth, *Genet. Psychol. Monogr.*, 1934, **15**:1, 83–84.

[52] R. M. Drake, Four new tests of musical talent, *J. appl. Psychol*, 1933, **17**, 136–47; *Drake test of musical talent* (Fredericksburg, Va.: The Author, 1932).

ard for comparison. It is then repeated with a change made in one of the following variables: key, time, note, or no change. In the last case, the original melody is simply repeated. Only one change occurs in any one of the variables. The subject is asked to identify the kind of change, if any, which occurs. As the test progresses, the standard melodies become more difficult. This test has been recorded and is available on phonograph records.

In the test of *interval discrimination*, the subject is asked to judge whether the second of two intervals is longer or shorter than the first. In this eighty-item test, the second interval is always played above the first and all intervals are ascending. During the first half of the test the intervals increase in difficulty, and they decrease in the second half.

The *retentivity* test refers to the memory for isolated tones, sometimes called absolute pitch. However, more than memory for pitch is involved. First of all, the subject hears a musical interval played on the piano; then he hears a metronome beating; finally, he listens to a three-note sequence. All of this constitutes the first part of the test. The subject is asked to remember these items. In the second portion, the listener hears a number of musical intervals and is asked to judge whether each of them is shorter or longer than the interval he heard in the first section. Following this, he hears the metronome beating again and is asked whether its beat is faster or slower than what he heard in the first section. Last of all, he hears a single note and judges whether it was the first, second, or third note he heard in the series in the first section. Drake has placed a great deal of importance on memory as a constituent of musical talent.

The last test, which Drake calls *intuition*, attempts to measure what he believes to be some of the more subtle aspects of musical talent which the musician reveals through his feeling for musical form. Such intuitive powers, Drake believes, are opposed to the intellectual and may be expressed musically in three ways—through a feeling for (*a*) key center, (*b*) phrase balance, or (*c*) time balance. This test contains seventy-two items, each consisting of two unharmonized phrases. The subject is to judge whether or not the second phrase makes a satisfactory answer to the first. Each answering phrase is supposed to test one of the "intuitions" for phrase balance, time balance, or key center.

Drake reports the following reliabilities for his tests: (*a*) musical memory, .93, .85; (*b*) interval discrimination, .74, .43; (*c*) retentivity, .76, .53. Using as the criterion teachers' rankings of students, validities reported are (*a*) musical memory, .67, .54; (*b*) interval discrimination, .58, .42; (*c*) retentivity, .54, .38; (*d*) intuition, .36, .35.

Other tests.—Madison [53] has investigated the effectiveness of interval discrimination as an index of musical ability. He believes that this sort of test is an achievement test, but it is indicative of success due to development through past experience, environment, and training. This ability is an important factor in predicting success of an individual because recognition of tonal relationships is a characteristic ability of musical persons. This relationship becomes the basic perceptual unit of larger patterns of musical thought which we recognize as melody and harmony.

Lundin tests.—In view of existing inadequate measures of musical behavior, Lundin [54] has constructed a series of tests of musical behavior which attempt to measure in an objective fashion some kinds of musical behavior not already considered by previous investigators. The five tests are called (*a*) *interval discrimination*, (*b*) *melodic transposition*, (*c*) *mode discrimination*, (*d*) *melodic sequences*, and (*e*) *rhythmic sequences*.

The test of *interval discrimination* consists of fifty pairs of tones or musical step intervals. For each item there are two sets of step intervals. The subject is asked to tell whether or not the second interval is the same as or different from the first. When an

[53] T. H. Madison, Interval discrimination as a measure of musical aptitude, *Arch. Psychol.*, 1942, No. 206, pp. 1–99.

[54] R. W. Lundin, The development and validation of a set of musical ability tests, *Psychol. Monogr.*, 1949, **63**:305, 1–20.

interval is the same, the number of steps or notes on the scale which lie between the first and second notes of each interval also is the same. This does not mean that the actual notes played are the same, but in some cases the intervals are. This test is divided into two parts; half of the intervals are ascending, and the other half are descending. In an upward-progressing interval, the second note always has a pitch higher than the first. In a downward-progressing interval, the pitch of the second note is lower than the first. In the preliminary investigation,[55] this test consisted of twenty-five items recorded on the piano, with no differentiation being made between upward- and downward-progressing intervals.

The second test, *melodic transposition*, consists of thirty pairs of simple melodies. The second melody is always played in a different key from the first. Sometimes the transposed melody is different, there being changes of one or more notes, so that if the second melody were transposed back into the original key, it would be different.

The test of *mode discrimination* consists of thirty pairs of single chords. If both chords in any item are of the same harmonic structure, i.e., in the same mode, for example both major or minor chords, the subject would respond with S, and if one chord is major and the second minor, the response would be D. The test is similar to the test of melodic transposition except that single chords are transposed rather than simple melodic lines.

The fourth test is called *melodic sequences*. *Grove's Dictionary of Music and Musicians* defines a sequence as ". . . the repetition of a definite group of notes or chords in different patterns of the scale like regular steps ascending or descending."[56] This test contains thirty sequential groups or patterns. Each item has four such groups. In all cases, the first three pat-

[55] R. W. Lundin, A preliminary report on some new tests of musical ability, *J. appl. Psychol.*, 1944, **28**, 393–96.

[56] *Grove's dictionary of music and musicians* (New York: The Macmillan Co., 1938).

terns follow the same melodic order, but sometimes the last group does not follow the same pattern as the first three. In such cases the subject should respond with D. If the entire sequence seems correct, he replies with S. All sequences are diatonic, that is "in key," and begin and end in the key of C. Here we speak of diatonic as opposed to modulating sequences which change key with each repetition of the pattern. In *rhythmic sequences* four rhythmic patterns are played as in the previous test of melodic sequences. The rhythmic pattern is set by the first three sequences, and the subject is asked to judge whether or not the last rhythmic group followed the same pattern as the first three. This measure is different from any previous rhythm test in that it does not isolate the rhythm from the melody. Tests 1 to 4 are recorded, using a Hammond electric organ, while Test 5 employs a piano. The tests were validated against criteria of six different ratings by professors for the music group alone. The behaviors rated were *melodic dictation, harmonic dictation, written harmonization, general ability in theory, performance ability*, and a sum of the first five ratings *constituting* a sixth category, *sum of ratings*.

Results indicate reliability coefficients, computed by the split-half method for groups separately, that are high enough to allow for general predictive purposes, particularly when total scores are used: interval discrimination, .79, .71; melodic transposition, .65, .71; mode discrimination, .65, .10; melodic sequences, .70, .77; rhythmic sequences, .60, .72; total scores, .89, .85. The reliabilities of the tests are superior to those found by previous investigators on the Seashore and Kwalwasser music tests. It should be noted, however, that Test 3 (mode discrimination) may be used to best advantage with people of previous musical training, since the reliability coefficient for this measure in the musician group does not drop as is the case with unselected subjects.

Individual tests correlate highly in general with the criteria used. When total test scores are validated by means of ratings, the results are .70 for melodic dictation, .70 for harmonic dictation, .43 for written harmonization, .65 for general ability in theory, .51 for performance, and .69 for sum of ratings. These coefficients are superior to those reported by previous investigators on other tests when similar external criteria are used. When the Seashore and Drake tests were validated against the same criteria, they showed lower coefficients almost without exception for any one criterion used.

Lundin found a statistically very significant difference between the means of music students and unselected groups for each test and for total scores. From this and other findings he concludes that the tests are measuring behavior more typical of a group of musicians than of a population of unselected people.

The relationship between the Lundin tests and the Seashore Measures for pitch, rhythm, and tonal memory is low (tonal memory only slightly higher than the others).

Relationship of musical ability to intelligence.—In general, reports[57] [58] support the assertion that performance on the Seashore Measures is not very closely related to general intelligence. Highsmith[59] in correlating scores on the Terman Group Test and the Thurstone Psychological Examination found correlations with the Seashore Measures as follows: pitch .58, intensity, .35, time .39, consonance —.14, tonal memory .30. Farnsworth[60] found the following correlations between the Thorndike Intelligence Examination and the Seashore Measures: pitch .14, intensity .11, time .10, consonance —.38, rhythm .17, tonal memory .11.

A number of studies already mentioned have shown intelligence examination scores to be better predictors of music success than the Seashore Measures. Highsmith found intelligence tests to show a slight superiority to the Seashore Measures as a means of predicting success in the performance of music. Farnsworth

[57] Highsmith, *op. cit.*
[58] Farnsworth, *Genet. Psychol. Monogr.*, 1931, **9**:5.
[59] Highsmith, *op. cit.*
[60] Farnsworth, *Genet. Psychol. Monogr.*, 1931, **9**:5.

found intelligence tests to be significantly superior in the prediction of academic grades in music appreciation. His correlations between these grades and the Thurstone tests were .44, grades and Iowa placement .32, grades and Seashore pitch test .14, and grades and Seashore tonal memory test .16. He found none of the tests to be superior in predicting grades in music theory.

In a résumé of studies on the relationship between musical ability and intelligence, Mursell[61] found that, in American studies where musical talent was generally measured by the Seashore method, very little relationship was reported between the two variables. In a more recent study, Lundin[62] reports similar results in using his own test with both unselected and musical subjects. Intelligence in his study was measured by the California Test of Mental Maturity. However, Mursell reports that in European studies where musical ability was measured by functional criteria, intelligence and musical ability showed a positive relationship. Schoen[63] insists that one of the attributes of musicianship is intelligence.

Dykema, using his own test with 5,840 European children between the ages of nine and eighteen, found a decided tendency for brighter children to rank higher than average for their age on his tests of musical ability. Beinstock also noted that students who ranked highest on intelligence tests were among the highest on the K.-D. tests.

It seems that the relationship between musical ability and intelligence is difficult to determine largely because of the inadequate existing measures of musical talent. Although many of our reports indicated low correlations, the relationship is a positive one. We should not necessarily conclude that no relationship exists between musical ability and intelligence. Our examination of the low validities of the Seashore Measures and Kwal-

[61] J. L. Mursell, Intelligence and musicality, *Education,* 1939, **59**, 559–62.
[62] Lundin, *Psychol. Monogr.*, 1949, **63**:305, 1-20.
[63] M. Schoen, *The psychology of music* (New York: The Ronald Press Co., 1940).

wasser tests shows us that these tests are rather poor measures of actual musical ability as judged by ratings of teachers and performers. Although the problem remains unsolved, we believe that where adequate measures of musical ability are used, it is positively related to intelligence.

Musical ability and race.—Using the Seashore Measures with 191 white and 191 Negro fifth-grade children in Gary, Indiana, Lenoire [64] reports Negroes superior in rhythm and tonal memory and *not* inferior on the other measures. Gray and Bingham,[65] using the Seashore Measures, found whites superior on all tests except consonance with sixth-, seventh-, and eighth-grade children. Johnson [66] found no difference between whites and Negroes in musical ability, and Peacock [67] has stated that whites surpass Negroes in the Seashore Measures. Woods and Martin [68] conducted a study among pupils in the sixth grade of a country school in the South, using the K.-D. tests. Negroes were found to be on the average superior to whites. Children who were most retarded in school showed the poorest results, and children with previous training in music did better than those with no training. They conclude that cultural determinants are the most significant factors in success on this particular aptitude test, and they believe the type of community from which the children came had a direct bearing on their scores.

Probably the most significant study on racial differences is reported by Farnsworth [69] with Oriental subjects. He tested

[64] A. D. Lenoire, Measurement of racial differences in certain mental and educational abilities (thesis), University of Iowa, 1925.

[65] C. T. Gray and C. W. Bingham, A comparison of certain phases of musical ability in colored and white school pupils, *J. educ. Psychol.*, 1929, **20**, 501–6.

[66] G. B. Johnson, Musical talent and the American Negro, *Music Superv. J.*, 1928, **15**, 81, 83, 86.

[67] W. Peacock, A comparative study of musical talent in whites and Negroes and its correlation with intelligence (thesis), Emory University, 1928.

[68] R. C. Woods and L. R. Martin, Testing in musical education, *Educ. and psychol. Meas.*, 1943, **3**, 29–42.

[69] Farnsworth, *Genet. Psychol. Monogr.*, 1931, **9**:5.

thirty-six Japanese and Chinese students at the University of California and Stanford University who were born and reared in America and fifty-three other students of similar nationalities who had lived in America for a considerably shorter time. These were compared with a third group of 200 white students. "All students understood English perfectly." Students were given tests of pitch, consonance, melody, and harmony. The white students scored higher on all but the melody test. His interpretations of these results are noteworthy. He believes the differences are generally a function of the varying acquaintance with Occidental music. For example, in pitch, ethnological evidence indicates that pitch differences are not stressed in the Orient as they are in the Western hemisphere.

> There is nothing to indicate that Oriental blood per se would predispose one to lower scores on the tests in question. It is conceivable, however, that lack of acquaintance with Occidental music may cause a lowering of scores.[70]

It seems that the data available to us are obviously confused. A number of factors could easily account for the apparent contradictions. Unreliability of the tests has already been noted. Different music and intelligence tests have also been used in the various studies reported. Samples in some cases are small. It is our belief that there are no inherent racial differences in musical ability. The differences which do exist certainly can be better accounted for by reference to cultural circumstances. Oriental and Occidental music are different, so that a Chinese may well not have acquired the appropriate response equipment for Western music. The superiority of Negroes in rhythm in the Lenoire study is not surprising, as it is well known that rhythm plays an important part in African music as well as in American Negro spirituals and folk songs. If the Negroes tend to be inferior to whites, we must recognize the fact that in many cases they have not had the same cultural opportunities to acquire adequate musical response equipment.

[70] *Ibid.*, p. 363.

Tests of Feeling and Appreciation

In 1925, Schoen [71] devised some tests which he called Tests of Musical Feeling and Understanding. The first test of *relative pitch* consisted of pairs of intervals. The object of the test is to see how accurately an individual can differentiate between compared musical intervals. His second test is called *tonal sequence*. Four two-phrase melodies are selected from standard compositions. This test is devised to reveal the individual's sensitivity to the fitness of tones in a melody. A musically good melody creates an impression of completeness. The criteria used in judging excellence were (*a*) balance, (*b*) coherence, (*c*) unity, (*d*) variety, and (*e*) finality effect. Each of these structurally perfect melodies had in the end an inferior alternative ending. The subject was to rate these various endings, starting with a rating of one (1) for the best. The third test measures one's sensitivity to slight variations in *rhythmic patterns*. This is similar to the corresponding tests in the Seashore and Kwalwasser batteries. Results on all three of these tests are reported by the author to correlate with musicality as a whole, which was measured by actual accomplishment. The author, however, gives no statistical evidence for these correlations.

Oregon music discrimination test.—Hevner has devised a *test of music discrimination* in which materials are taken from compositions of various styles and types written by established composers. In her first report,[72] published in 1930, each item of the test consisted of part of a composition by an accepted composer and was given in four versions. The correct version was the composer's own transcript. A second version was made by omitting many of the tones, so that the composition sounded bare and unexpressive. A third version was "elaborated" by introducing

[71] M. Schoen, Tests of musical feeling and understanding, *J. comp. Psychol.*, 1925, **5**, 31–52.

[72] K. Hevner, Tests for aesthetic appreciation in the field of music, *J. appl. Psychol.*, 1930, **14**, 470–77.

additional tones into chords and adding extra passing tones. In the fourth version the phrasing or melodic progression was changed. Items were included from such works as Bach's *B Minor Mass*, Brahms's *Sonata in F Minor*, and Chopin's *Prelude in B Minor* (*Opus* 28). In compiling the test, an attempt was made to find music of established merit but with little familiarity for the average listener. Because of the difficulty reported by subjects in considering four different versions of a melody and in suspending their judgments until all versions had been heard, a simpler form was devised [73] in which only two versions are presented, one correct and one mutilated. This was especially useful for younger listeners. Results on the two-version test show close correspondence with those on the four-version form in reliability and validity. The author believes these tests can be of use in measuring listeners' ability to discriminate good and bad music. These tests are now recorded on phonograph records.

Kwalwasser tests of melodic and harmonic sensitivity.—Kwalwasser [74] reported on what he called "feeling tests." The first, *melodic sensitivity*, consisted of various two-measure melodic fragments. The test attempted to measure the ability to discriminate good melodic progression from bad. Another test, *harmonic sensitivity*, consisting of three-chord progressions, attempts to measure the ability to judge good harmonic progression. In both harmonic and melodic sensitivity tests, the quality of progression is determined by established procedure for musical composition. Progressions that obey established "melodic and harmonic law are good, while those that violate established procedure are adjudged as bad." These tests have been recorded by the Victor Talking Machine Co.

[73] K. Hevner, A Study of tests for the appreciation of music, *J. appl. Psychol.*, 1931, **15**, 575–83. See also J. H. Mueller, E. G. Mill, N. B. Zane, and K. Hevner, Studies in the appreciation of art, *Univ. Ore. Publ.*, 1934, **4**:6.

[74] J. Kwalwasser, Tests and measurements in music, *Psychol. Bull.*, 1928, **25**, 284–301. See also *Kwalwasser Test of Melodic and Harmonic Sensitivity* (Camden, N. J.: Victor Talking Machine Co., 1926).

Tests of Musical Knowledge

Several tests of musical knowledge have been devised from time to time, and we mention only a few as samples. Probably the most widely known is the Kwalwasser-Ruch Test of Musical Accomplishment.[75] This test has several parts designed to measure various aspects of public school music. They consist of:

1. Knowledge of musical terms and symbols
2. Recognition of syllable names from notation
3. Detection of pitch errors in notation of a familiar melody
4. Detection of time errors in a familiar melody
5. Knowledge of pitch and letter names of bass and treble clefs
6. Knowledge of time signatures
7. Knowledge of key signatures
8. Knowledge of note values
9. Knowledge of rest values
10. Knowledge of familiar melodies from notation

The Torgerson-Fahenstock Tests[76] consist of two parts. In Part I a knowledge of note and rest values, time signature, pitch and syllable names, marks of expression, repeat bars, major and minor key signatures, and natural and harmonic minor scales is measured. Part II involves writing syllable names from oral dictation, writing time signatures, detecting pitch and time errors in notation, and writing notes on the staff from dictation.

The Kwalwasser Test of Musical Information and Appreciation[77] measures factual knowledge of music and is intended for high schools and colleges where music appreciation courses are offered.

[75] J. Kwalwasser and G. N. Ruch, *Kwalwasser-Ruch Test of Musical Accomplishment* (Iowa City, Ia.: University of Iowa, Bureau of Educational Research, 1924).

[76] T. L. Torgerson and E. Fahnestock, *Torgerson-Fahnestock Music Tests* (Bloomington, Ill.: Public School Publishing Co., 1926).

[77] J. Kwalwasser, *Kwalwasser Test of Musical Information and Appreciation* (Iowa City, Ia.: University of Iowa, 1927).

The subtests include:

1. Classification of artists
2. Nationality of composers
3. Composers of famous works
4. Classification of composers by types of composition
5. General historical and biographical knowledge
6. Production of tones of orchestral instruments
7. Classification of orchestral instruments
8. General knowledge of instrumentation
9. Knowledge of music structure and form

This latter group of tests is merely sampling acquired information about music and composers. They make no attempt at particular prediction of future success. In some cases an individual with performance ability will have considerable knowledge of things musical, but the reverse does not always hold. The tests are merely measures of knowledge accumulated and are not predictive of future success as the tests of ability or talent are intended to be.

Summary

In this chapter we have attempted to survey the most important tests of musical behavior, which include ability or aptitude tests, feeling and appreciation tests, and knowledge or achievement tests. The tests of ability make a serious attempt to predict future success. In that sense, they are often adjudged as aptitude tests. Seashore and Kwalwasser are the main leaders in this field. We have, however, considered the inadequacy of these tests as likely predictors of future success in music. Thus opportunities for research in the field are great. Music tests are notoriously unreliable and invalid. In comparison with comparable measurements in other areas of behavior such as intelligence, we realize that tests of musical ability have a long road ahead before they achieve any degree of perfection. Tests of appreciation and feeling have a particular difficulty in their lack of objectivity. There are no absolutes when it comes to deciding what makes a melody good or bad. These tests also attempt to predict musicianship potential, but they probably fall below the tests of musical ability. Finally, the tests of knowledge merely sample information acquired about things musical such as compositions, composers, and notation. They may be helpful aids to a teacher in separating the informed from the uninformed, but they make little attempt to do more than that.

Chapter 14

MUSICAL PERFORMANCE

In any consideration of musical responses, we cannot ignore the actual performance or "making" of music. These operative reactions may be either vocal, involving the entire human organism but in particular the mechanism of the voice, or they may be instrumental, where the manipulation of some musical instrument serves as a means of producing the musical sounds.

Most of the significant research on performance reactions to music has been related to three media: the voice, piano, and violin. We shall attempt to summarize some of the facts and principles of musical performance in these areas with the hope that the aspiring student can utilize them to his own advantage in his study.

The Voice

As a mechanism for the production of sound, the entire vocal apparatus may be divided into three main parts, the bellows, the vibrators, and the resonators, all three being involved in the proper production of vocal sound. The bellows refers to that division which serves as a source of supply and as a regulator of the flow and pressure of the air. This would include such body organs as the lungs, the trachea, and the bronchial tubes, which actually operate in the supply of air, as well as the diaphragm and the thoracic and abdominal muscles which serve to regulate the air pressure. By the vibrators we refer to the larynx and especially to the vocal chords. These take priority in importance because it is here that the musical sound originates. This does not mean that an artistic sound can occur without the proper air supply, since obviously the musical tone is created by the passing of air through the vocal mechanism. The bellows are all-important in *controlling* the sound which is created in the vibrators. Finally, the resonators serve to enhance the sound. These include the head cavities such as sinuses and nasal cavity, as well as such movable structures as the cheeks, lips, and jaw. Of the greatest importance in vocal training is the coordination of all three of these divisions as well as the accurate perception of pitch, loudness, rhythm, and other characteristics of the stimulus. All of the divisions of the voice mechanism are interdependent. Thus, we must stress the concept of coordination in proper vocal performance.

The tonoscope.—For the purposes of scientific analysis of musical performance, an instrument has been developed at the University of Iowa Laboratories known as the tonoscope.[1] It works on the principle of moving pictures, allowing the actual production of a certain pitch to be visualized. The sound vibrations are converted into pictures on a screen so a performer can actually "see" himself sing. The tonoscope produces a picture of tones which can reveal deviations in pitch even smaller than those which can be detected by the ear, since every pitch change is pictured on the screen. The screen covers one octave, and records changes in tenths of a tone. Finally, for purposes of permanent record and analysis, some kind of photographic recording can be made of the tonoscope changes. From these data and others obtained from a musical performance, a musical pattern score can be constructed. (See Figure 13.)

The musical pattern score.—A complete record of the entire performance is available on this score. It is a graphic record of how a singer (or player) actually performs a work. In this graphic record the score is divided into half steps indicated by alternating dotted and dash lines. If a note is steady and in per-

[1] C. E. Seashore, The tonoscope, *Psychol. Monogr.*, 1914, **17**:3.

fect pitch, the record would show a straight line superimposed on one of the interrupted lines. Any deviation from the true pitch as indicated on the original musical score is shown by an according deflection above or below the true pitch line. The distance between a dotted and dashed line is that of a half step. The musical notes in the figure are not a part of the photographic record of the performance but are inserted as an aid in comparing the

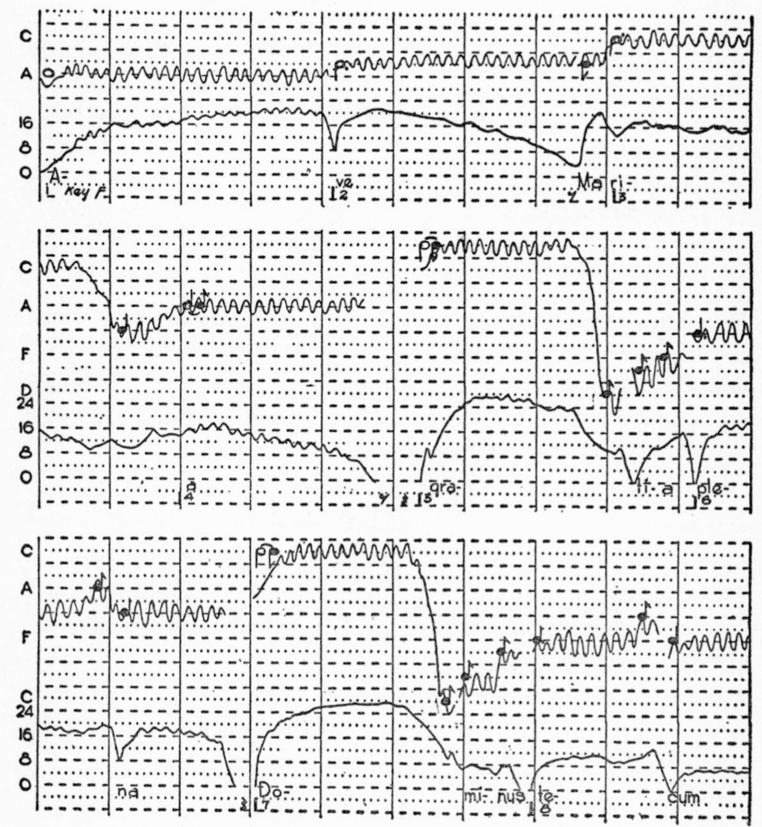

FIG. 13.—The Bach-Gounod *Ave Maria* as sung by Herald Stark. (From Seashore—see footnote 2.) Frequency (pitch) is represented by a graph for each note on a semitone staff; intensity, by the lower parallel graph in a decibel scale; and duration, by dots in tenths of a second. Measures are numbered at the bottom of the staff for ready reference.

pattern score with the original musical score. The vertical bars mark off the seconds, while the short, heavy bars at the bottom indicate the measures.

Harold Seashore[2] has attempted to analyze the musical performance of several vocal artists by means of this device. An example of this analysis of a musical performance appears in a portion of the *Ave Maria* sung by Stark (Figure 13).

The pattern score analysis reveals the following:

1. The mean pitch of the artist tends to correspond fairly well with that of the printed score.
2. The mean pitch is sharped and flatted to a surprising degree.
3. There is relatively more flatting in the upper than in the lower register.
4. Of the 107 notes analyzed, 48 were sung level, 37 rising, 6 erratic, and 9 falling.

In this interpretation of the performance score, the revelations may appear somewhat shocking. However, we need not condemn this singer, for the performance of famous artists analyzed in a similar fashion shows that they usually maintain a better than average level of achievement in intonation.

Seashore's studies indicate that all singers show a marked deviation from the true pitch. Thus, the desirable vocal tone is not one devoid of fluctuations, because these deviations from the rigid give aesthetic value to the performance. A rigid intonation and one without vibrato would be very uninteresting, perhaps intolerable to the listener.

Singers seldom remain as much as $\frac{1}{10}$ of a second on a true pitch. They tend to hover around it through the vibrato (see below) and other means of deviation. The pitch that we actually hear is a mean between the two pitches in the vibrato cycle. This is a "mean pitch" and should be distinguished from the "true pitch" which is represented in the printed score.

[2] H. G. Seashore, An objective analysis of artistic singing, *Univ. Ia. Stud. Psychol. Music,* 1935, **4,** 12–157.

Pitch intonation.—Schoen[3] has also studied the problem of pitch intonation in singing by means of the Seashore tonoscope. By means of this apparatus he analyzed the recorded voices of five famous opera singers performing the same composition, the Bach-Gounod *Ave Maria.* The voices recorded were those of Nellie Melba, Alma Gluck, Frances Alda, Emma Eames, and Emmy Destinn, all sopranos. The following aspects of the singing were studied: attack, release, predominant pitch, tonal movement including portamento, crescendo, and deviations above and below the predominant pitch. Space does not permit us to report the detailed analyses of each singer's voice. The interested reader might do well to consider the original study. However, Schoen draws the following conclusions on the basis of the voices analyzed:

1. A tone is almost invariably attacked below the pitch intended when it is preceded by a lower tone and in the majority of cases it is released above. The size of the error of attack depends on the distance below of the preceding tone—the greater the distance, the greater the error. The largest error occurs when the tone is sung after a rest . . . When the preceding tone is above the tone sung, the attack is accurate . . .
2. A tone is very rarely sustained on the same pitch for an interval of time beyond half a second, the number and extent of the deviations depending on the individual characteristics of the singer.
3. Two tones of the same pitch and of equal duration are never sung twice the same way, but vary in the number and the extent of fluctuation as well as the pitch of the predominant tones.
4. The vowel quality seems to have but an insignificant effect on the pitch of the tone . . .
5. The five singers are divisible into three classes in the matter of tonal steadiness and the number and extent of fluctuations: Melba and Gluck having the steadiest voices . . . Eames having a steady tone with few fluctuations . . . while Alda and

[3] M. Schoen, An experimental study of the pitch factor in artistic singing, *Psychol. Monogr.*, 1922, **31:**1, 230–59.

Destinn manifest unsteady tones with fluctuations large in number and extent.

6. The movement from tone to tone is predominantly in the form of glides, but varies in degree for the different singers . . .

7. A tendency for a rise in pitch with a rise in intensity is manifest throughout.

8. There exists a tendency for all the singers to sing sharp in the sense that the deviations above the predominant tone are more numerous than those below, the maximum deviations below the predominant tone are always larger than those above.[4]

In regard to attack, release, and portamento, Schoen reports:

The data from the studies made of numerous singers show that about 40 per cent of all intertonal movements are made with a continuous pitch glide, about 35 per cent are clearly attacked, and about 25 per cent are attacked with gliding pitch inflection, usually rising. In gliding attacks, 97 per cent begin below the proper tone and rise up to it, irrespective of the direction of the melodic line. . . . Of all the phrases investigated, almost 62 per cent were begun with gliding attacks . . .

The release of a tone is, in about 40 per cent of cases, that of a portamento glide to the succeeding tone, in another 55 per cent it is a level release followed by a pause, while only in 5 per cent does the tone end on a gliding release, usually falling, followed by a pause.[5]

The vibrato.—We have already had reference to the vibrato as a characteristic of artistic singing. Let us now consider a more detailed analysis of this vocal phenomenon. The vibrato has been the subject of much disagreement among musicians. However, as a result of the works of Schoen and Seashore we now have a fairly accurate understanding of this characteristic of music. Over a period of years Seashore and his associates have subjected the vibrato to scientific analysis and have written extensively on it. He defines a *good vibrato* as ". . . a pulsation of pitch, usually accompanied by synchronous pulsations of loud-

[4] From M. Schoen, *The psychology of music,* pp. 198–99. Copyright, 1940, by The Ronald Press Co., New York.

[5] *Ibid.*, pp. 200–1.

ness and timbre, of such extent and rate as to give a pleasing flexibility, tenderness, and richness to the tone."[6]

Although one might not agree precisely with this definition, it is generally accepted that the vibrato consists of a rapid series of pulsations in the tonal stimulus, most commonly in its pitch, but is frequently also accompanied by pulsations in loudness and timbre. A vibrato has been considered a desirable attribute of good singing, as it occurs most commonly in the human voice. Most successful players of stringed instruments also employ it, as do many other instrumentalists whenever possible.

Schoen[7] reported one of the first attempts in the analysis of the vibrato. He studied (1) monotones, (2) untrained non-musical voices, (3) untrained musical voices, and (4) trained musical voices on a tonoscope with regard to the vibrato. The voice of the monotone registered no vibrato. In the untrained and nonmusical voices, the tonoscope showed a tone which fluctuated irregularly *above and below a predominant pitch, but with no systematic vibrato*, whereas the musical voices showed pulsations of a marked periodicity, with a regular pitch fluctuation of from six to twelve pulsations per second. He concluded that the vibrato was a fundamental attribute of an effective singing voice.

Metfessel[8] has observed that, in celebrated singers, 95 per cent of the artistic tones, whether they be long or short, gliding or steady, high or low, loud or soft, register the vibrato. These observations are confirmed by Seashore, who has collected performance records of vibratos of singers under all sorts of conditions. He believes that the vibrato rests fundamentally upon the periodic innervation of paired muscles under emotional tension.

The vibrato may be one of pitch, intensity, or timbre and may not only occur in the human voice but in bowed stringed and

[6] C. E. Seashore, *In search of beauty in music*, p. 48. Copyright, 1947, by The Ronald Press Co., New York.

[7] M. Schoen, An experimental study of the pitch factor in artistic singing, *Psychol. Monogr.*, 1922, **31**:1, 230–59.

[8] M. Metfessel, The vibrato in artistic voices, *Univ. Ia. Stud. Psychol. Music*, 1932, **1**, 14–177.

other orchestral instruments. Seashore[9] reports that in objective measures the vibrato is universally present in good singing, even at times when the singer denies having used it and the listener has failed to hear it as such. He believes the vibrato to be an inherent mode of expression like a smile or frown, admitting, of course, that it can be imitated and learned. We could question the validity of the first part of this statement. Any violinist will bear witness to the desirability of the vibrato and its acquired nature by his careful cultivation of it at great effort.

CHARACTERISTICS OF A GOOD VIBRATO. Admitting that the vibrato is generally recognized as a part of artistic performance, we may ask ourselves what the characteristics of a "good" vibrato are. Again, Seashore believes that the most desirable vibrato is one which produces a flexibility of tone without giving undue prominence to the pulsating quality. A vibrato which is regular in extent is most artistic. Schoen also found this. However, a variation in extent and rate throughout a performance is needed. A uniform vibrato throughout a musical composition may become monotonous. Professional singers, as we have noted, will use a pitch vibrato in about 95 per cent of their tones. Well-trained singers have found it difficult to produce a tone without the use of any vibrato. On the other hand, many popular crooners have been known to use the vibrato in such an obvious and exaggerated way that it may give rise to an unpleasant reaction on the part of the listener.

What is the most effective rate and extent of the vibrato? The following table from Seashore[10] gives the average vibrato for singers. Most singers exhibit about 6.5 pulsations per second. The variations in pitch are on the average about one half of a tone step (0.48). Of course, each singer has his own characteristic rate. The intensity vibrato is often present, but Seashore finds it

[9] H. G. Seashore, The hearing of the pitch and intensity in vibrato, *Univ. Ia. Stud. Psychol. Music,* 1932, I, 213–35.

[10] By permission from C. E. Seashore, *Psychology of music,* page 43. Copyright 1938 by McGraw-Hill Book Co., Inc., New York.

only about 33 per cent of the time, as compared to the pitch vibrato, which is present 95 per cent of the time. The intensity vibrato is ordinarily less conspicuous and less frequent and pronounced than the pitch vibrato. Because of the changes in loudness and pitch which occur in the vibrato, a timbre vibrato is also often present and will usually take the same pattern as a pitch vibrato.

TABLE 6

THE AVERAGE EXTENT AND RATE OF PITCH VIBRATO FOR TWENTY-NINE SINGERS

Artists	Average Rate per Second	Average Extent of a Step
All artists	6.6	0.48
de Gogorza	7.8	0.46
Schumann-Heink	7.6	0.38
Galli-Curci	7.3	0.44
Macbeth	7.2	0.31
Caruso	7.1	0.47
Rethberg	7.0	0.49
Martinelli	6.9	0.44
Ponselle	6.9	0.48
Chaliapin	6.8	0.54
Jeritza	6.8	0.53
Lashanska	6.8	0.48
de Luca	6.8	0.58
Tetrazzini	6.8	0.37
Talley	6.7	0.54
Braslau	6.6	0.36
Marsh	6.6	0.52
Tibbett	6.6	0.55
Crooks	6.5	0.47
Gigli	6.5	0.57
Rimini	6.5	0.98
Stark	6.5	0.48
Onegin	6.4	0.41
Dadmun	6.3	0.46
Seashore	6.3	0.44
Baker	6.2	0.45
Hackett	5.9	0.47
Homer	5.9	0.51
Kraft	5.9	0.59
Thompson	5.9	0.53

One of the bases for the misconception that the vibrato is an undesirable aspect of artistic singing is its confusion with the tremolo, the pronounced wavering of the voice evident in some singers. This is often due to improper control of the muscles involved in vocal production and often makes its appearance when a singer is nervous or excited. Wagner[11] points out that one of the reasons artists and writers disagree on the value of the vibrato in singing is that they fail to distinguish it from the tremolo. Our previous discussion has indicated there may be many kinds of vibrato, but when the pulsations become conspicuously fast or slow in rate or wide in extent, the tremolo results. This is really an undesirable vibrato, since a good vibrato consists of regular and inconspicuous pulsations.

The trill.—Seashore[12] has investigated the characteristics of the vocal trill, using methods previously mentioned (tonoscope, etc.). Since the trill frequently resembles the vibrato, some distinction must be made. Its form is frequently the same as that of the vibrato but in the trill two distinct pitches are usually perceived instead of a modulated inflection.

Photographic analysis shows that the extent of the trill is always an overestimate of the actual pitches involved, so that when an artist is to sing a semitone, the vocalizations usually are exaggerated if a trill is indicated in the score. The singer must overreach the size of the interval in order to make it heard as indicated in the score, because there is a tendency on the part of the listener to underestimate the range. This is obviously the reason for augmenting the trilled interval for it to sound right. The actual rate of pulsation in the trill resembles very closely that of the vibrato, being about five or six pulsations per second.

Characteristics of good vocal quality.—Although there are many attributes which are characteristic of good voice quality,

[11] A. H. Wagner, Remedial and artistic development of the vibrato, *Univ. Ia. Stud. Psychol. Music,* 1932, **1**, 166–212.

[12] C. E. Seashore, The vocal trill, *Music Educ. J.*, Jan., 1942.

Bartholomew [13] has mentioned four outstanding ones which he has found in his analysis of male voices.

1. The first of these is the vibrato, which we have already discussed. A smooth, fairly even vibrato is inseparable from good vocal quality.

2. Absolute tonal intensity constitutes a second attribute. A singer with a good-quality voice is usually able to produce a tone of greater intensity than is one with poor quality. This is usually correlated with size of the throat. Physiological studies have shown that in poor voices there is either a constricted pharynx or a partly closed epiglottis, so that the sound is forced to escape through a very narrow opening.

3. A good male voice has a predominance of resonance at the low point. In records of good and poor voices singing middle C, Bartholomew found that the good voices emphasized the second partial, while poor voices shifted emphasis to the third, fourth, or fifth partial. This holds true for tenor as well as baritone and bass voices.

4. A good voice produces a predominance of resonance at a high point also. The data also showed that recorded voices judged to be good also showed a high formant, increasing in predominance with the better voices. However, this characteristic is not the most important attribute, as some poor voices also possess it. When it occurs along with the other three good attributes, the vibrato, intensity, and low resonance, it produces the effect of adding a very desirable "ring" or brilliance to the voice.

This discussion has obviously not considered all of the characteristics of a good voice. Obvious additions might include accurate pitch control, as well as stability of tone in terms of intensity, and proper attack and release. These, however, refer more to actual production of tones, whereas Bartholomew's analysis is limited to simple characteristics of tone quality.

[13] W. T. Bartholomew, A physical definition of "good voice quality" in the male voice, *J. acoust. Soc. Amer.*, 1934, 6, 25–33.

Piano

Certainly many theories have arisen on the technique of piano performance, some of which stress superfluous movements and gestures, while others actually violate man's anatomical patterns, resulting in all sorts of muscular aches and cramps. If teachers and artists would consider for a moment the actual importance of the studies available to us at this time, many fallacious teaching techniques would be eliminated and the technique of piano performance could be greatly simplified. We do not mean that piano playing should be reduced to a mere mechanical operation devoid of aesthetic expression—far from it. However, if many artists would consider the mechanics of the instrument they are playing, its possibilities and its limitations, much needless effort and anxiety could immediately be eliminated.

A theory of piano technique.—In 1926 Ortmann[14] observed that, of the four factors in music available to the pianist, only those of intensity and time are subject to his control, while pitch and timbre are determined by the composer and the nature of the instrument played. Although it is possible to modify the timbre of a tone through certain devices which we shall note, there is a great deal of truth in his observations.

The intensity of a tone produced on the piano depends on the stroking of the key. This is a function of the velocity of the hammer as it strikes the string. After this act the tone can be modified only by action of the dampers. On the basis of these simple observations, Seashore[15] has formulated a theory of piano touch well worth considering. Let us summarize a few of his observations.

[14] O. Ortmann, *Physical basis of piano touch and tone* (New York: E. P. Dutton & Co., Inc., 1925).

[15] C. E. Seashore, *In search of beauty in music* (New York: The Ronald Press Co., 1947). The quotation is from p. 138. Copyright, 1947, by The Ronald Press Co., New York.

1. It makes no difference whether a key is struck by an accelerating, retarding, even, or irregular hand movement. The important thing to realize is that the performer controls in his stroke the velocity of the key at the exact moment that it throws off the hammer.

2. The hammer has only one contact with the string, namely an instantaneous impact followed by an immediate release.

> The hammer is released just a trifle before the key reaches its bed. Like the bat and the ball, it has only one form of contact with the string, namely, an instantaneous impact followed by an immediate rebound. Therefore, no amount of waggling, vibrating, rocking, or caressing of the key after it has once released the hammer can modify the action upon the string. The only way in which the key can further affect the string is by a new stroke of the hammer. This can easily be verified by manipulating the key near its bed and looking at the action of the hammer.

3. Only indirectly can the pianist influence tone quality, and this is by his control of the intensity of the tone. Each piano may differ in tone qualities, but these are relatively fixed by the construction of the instrument. In general, the louder the tone, the richer the tonal quality.

4. Such tone qualities as change due to a modification of intensity are the result of resonance, reverberation, or the damping effects of the sounding board and the rest of the piano, the thuds and rattling of keys, and the acoustical characteristics of the room.

5. The most obvious change in tone quality comes through pedal action. The sostenuto pedal enables tones to be carried through a series of chords and keys and then released. Also the soft pedal or *una corda* allows the artist to eliminate strings. As a result, some partials are eliminated and the remaining strings may vibrate in sympathetic resonance. The effect of the damper pedal is obvious in enhancing the tonal quality.

The Iowa piano camera.[16]—In order to describe and analyze aspects of piano performance, some device is necessary which can accurately record an artistic interpretation with some degree of permanency. The tonoscope has already been found to be very helpful in recording the pitch variations of a vocal artist or string player. In the piano, however, pitch is fixed by the instrument, so intensity (loudness) and time are the variables of special interest to the investigator. The Iowa piano camera was devised for the purpose of studying these two aspects of piano performance. It registers the performance in minute detail on a photogram which later can be transcribed into a performance score. The two variables of intensity (loudness) and time are recorded to obtain an adequate picture of the piano playing in a manner quite similar to that for voice, which we have already noted.

Consistency in interpretation.—Although research on piano performance is not so extensive as that on the voice, some very interesting studies are available to us. One of these concerns the question often asked as to how consistent a particular artist is in his interpretation of a given work. One way of answering this question would be to ask an artist to play a composition several times and then study these renditions by means already at our disposal. Skinner[17] asked two piano artists, Harold Bauer and Philip Greeley Clapp, to perform a number of compositions, repeating them several times. In two successive renditions of Chopin's *Polonaise, Opus 40, No. 1,* Bauer took 49.1 and 49.7 sec. respectively for the first twenty-four bars. In terms of phrasing, the performance score revealed a great consistency in the two interpretations (Figures 14 and 15). The scores showed that the renditions were played with typical pianistic interpretation in phrasing, not merely in metronomic fashion. The second artist,

[16] M. T. Henderson, J. Tiffin, and C. E. Seashore, The Iowa piano camera and its use, *Univ. Ia. Stud. Psychol. Music,* 1937, 4, 252–62.

[17] L. Skinner, Some temporal aspects of piano playing (thesis), University of Iowa, 1930.

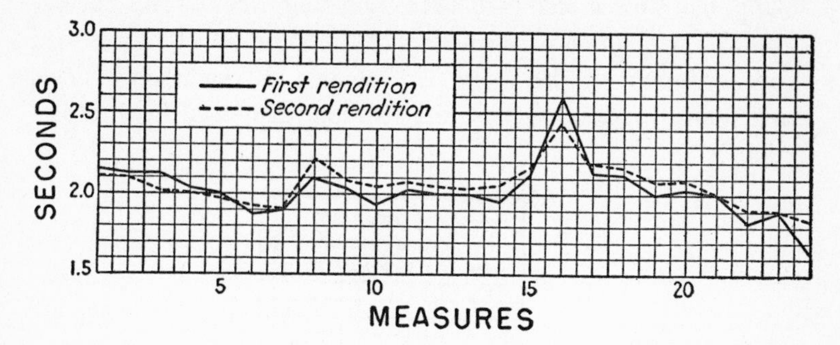

Fig. 14.—Duration of measures in two renditions of the first 24 measures of Chopin's *Polonaise, Op. 40, No. 1,* by Bauer (From Skinner—see footnote 17.)

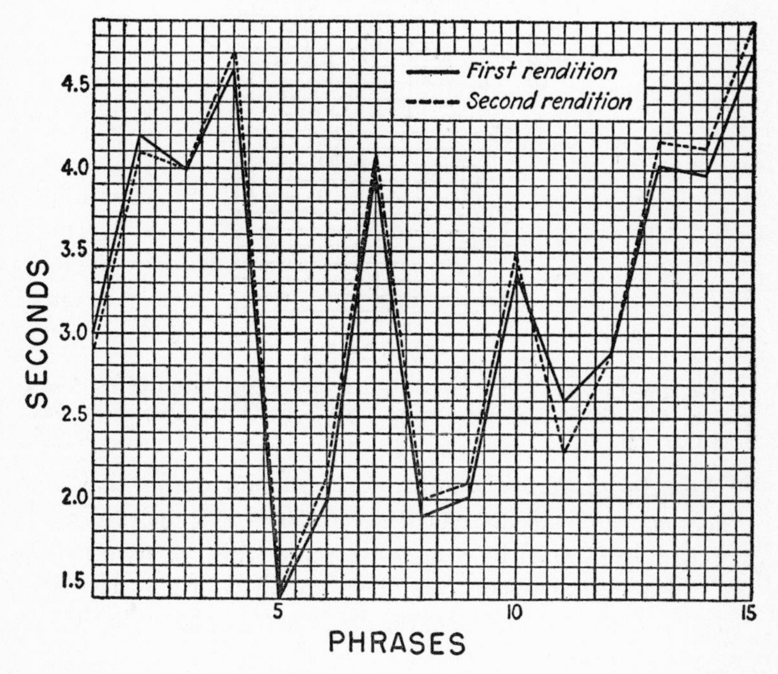

Fig. 15.—Duration of phrases in same performance as in Figure 14. (From Skinner—see footnote 17.)

Clapp, had similar results in a selection from Beethoven's *Sonata, Opus* 57, with three performances of the same unit (Figure 16). The agreement of the three performances is remarkably close, particularly in view of the great freedom expressed in interpretation.

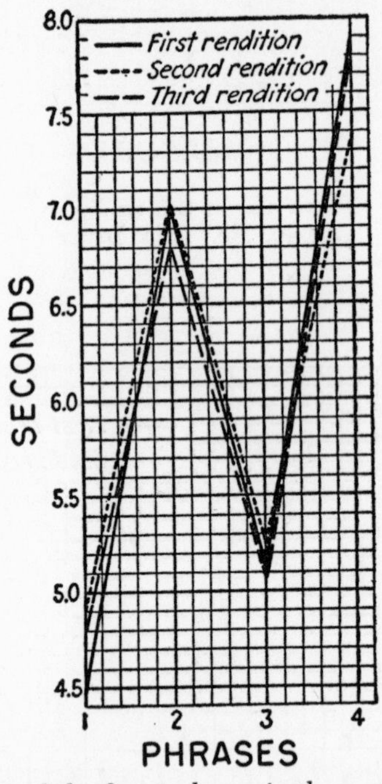

Fig. 16.—Duration of the first 4 phrases in three renditions of the first 4 phrases in Beethoven's *Sonata, Op. 57,* by Clapp. (From Skinner—see footnote 17.)

Asynchronization of chords.—In an attempt to study how well synchronized chords are when played, Vernon,[18] analyzed some selections performed by recognized artists which were available on Duo-art player piano recordings. Analysis of the selections from Beethoven and Chopin on the Duo-art yielded the following conclusions:

[18] L. M. Vernon, Synchronization of chords in artistic piano playing, *Univ. Ia. Stud. Psychol. Music,* 1937, 4, 306–45.

1. Pianists play as many as half their notes asynchronously.
2. Most of the deviations are probably intentional. He showed experimentally that the smallest deviations can be perceived easily by musicians, indicating that these deviations of performances undoubtedly were intentional and not due to lack of perception.
3. The frequency and extent of the deviations vary for artists and selections played. However, a player tends to be consistent in the degree of his deviations for a given selection.
4. More asynchronous chords occur in slow and changing tempos.
5. Melody notes are emphasized by playing them early or late in a chord.
6. Asynchronization is not related to beginnings or endings of phrases or to changes in tonality.

Sight reading.—The problem of reading a piano score at sight is one which confronts all aspirant artists. Any good musician desires to be able to read a piece of music the first time he sees it with ease and accuracy.

Lannert and Ullman [19] have undertaken a study to determine what factors are most important in the sight reading of piano music. For their subjects, they used nine advanced piano students. The subjects who participated in this investigation were not informed as to its purpose. They were presented with unfamiliar piano arrangements of orchestral compositions and asked to play these compositions at sight.

An analysis of the performances of these students indicated that the good sight readers, in approaching their task, showed certain behavioral characteristics in common. The good sight readers were the ones who took the least time and made the fewest errors in playing from the printed score at sight. Further, the *good* sight readers (1) read ahead of the measure being

[19] V. Lannert and M. Ullman, Factors in the reading of piano music, *Amer. J. Psychol.,* 1945, **58**, 91–99.

played, (2) perceived both the right- and left-hand scores at a single glance, (3) profited from a preliminary study of the score, and (4) had a good knowledge of the keyboard without looking at it. Factors *not* significant in distinguishing good from poor sight readers were (1) number of eye movements from score to keyboard, (2) ability to read ledger-line notes, and (3) amount of time taken for study. The students who read best had a previous history of a good deal of practice in reading at sight and had profited from this experience.

In order to study the eye movements of the pianist during performance, Weaver[20] took photographic records of these eye movements and the keyboard performances of fifteen trained musicians during the sight reading of short musical selections. The types of tonal arrangements used in the study were described as being of three kinds: melodic, harmonic, and accompanied melody. He found the average number of notes executed per reading pause to vary between one and two. The average reading pause varied between 0.27 and 0.33 sec.

A reading of the musical score typically progresses by rapid alternation of almost vertical movements of the eyes from one half of the staff to the other. There are also frequent horizontal movements on one half of the staff. Finally, the treble parts of chords are usually read before the bass parts and the eye-hand span is variable but never exceeds a separation of eight successive notes or chords between the eye and hand.

We have not attempted to cover all of the significant studies on piano performance. By means of the Iowa piano camera, a number of performance records of compositions played are available for analysis and the interested student may go to the original scores for the study of these records.[21] A detailed description

[20] H. E. Weaver, A survey of visual processes in reading differently constructed musical selections, *Psychol. Monogr.*, 1945, **55**:1, 1–30.

[21] M. T. Henderson, Rhythmic organization in artistic piano performance, *Univ. Ia. Stud. Psychol. Music,* 1937, **4**, 281–305. L. Skinner, A musical pattern score of the first movement of the Beethoven Sonata, Opus 27, No. 2, *Univ. Ia. Stud. Psychol. Music,* 1937, **4**, 263–80.

of these records would consume many pages and be of limited interest in a book of this kind.

Violin

By means of the musical performance score, Small [22] has made detailed analyses of violin performances. He has compared the performances of various violinists by recording photographically these violin performances in a manner similar to that described by Seashore and discussed earlier in this chapter with reference to vocal recorded performances. Some of the violinists studied were Busch, Elman, Kreisler, Menuhin, Slatkin, Small, and Szigeti.

A partial summary of Small's results follows.

Pitch intonation.—The violinists deviated over 60 per cent of the time from the actual scale notes, the average deviation being about 0.1 tone and predominantly in the direction of sharping. He accounts for these deviations as being due to anatomical difficulties in finger span for some intervals, accidental causes, use of the natural rather than tempered scale intonation, and diversion of attention.

Intensity.—The range of intensity between the softest and loudest tones for all records was about 21 db. The mean intensity differences for successive notes was 3.5 db.

Vibrato.—The pitch vibrato is a characteristic of the most competent players of stringed instruments. They usually employ the vibrato on stopped notes of sufficient duration. Of course, there are characteristic differences as to extent, just as for the voice vibrato. However, the average rate is about six and a half pulsations per second, which is about the same as that for the voice, but the degree of fluctuation in pitch is on the average much less than that for voice vibrato, being only about one fourth of a tone.

[22] A. M. Small, An objective analysis of artistic violin performance, *Univ. Ia. Stud. Psychol. Music,* 1937, **4**, 172–231.

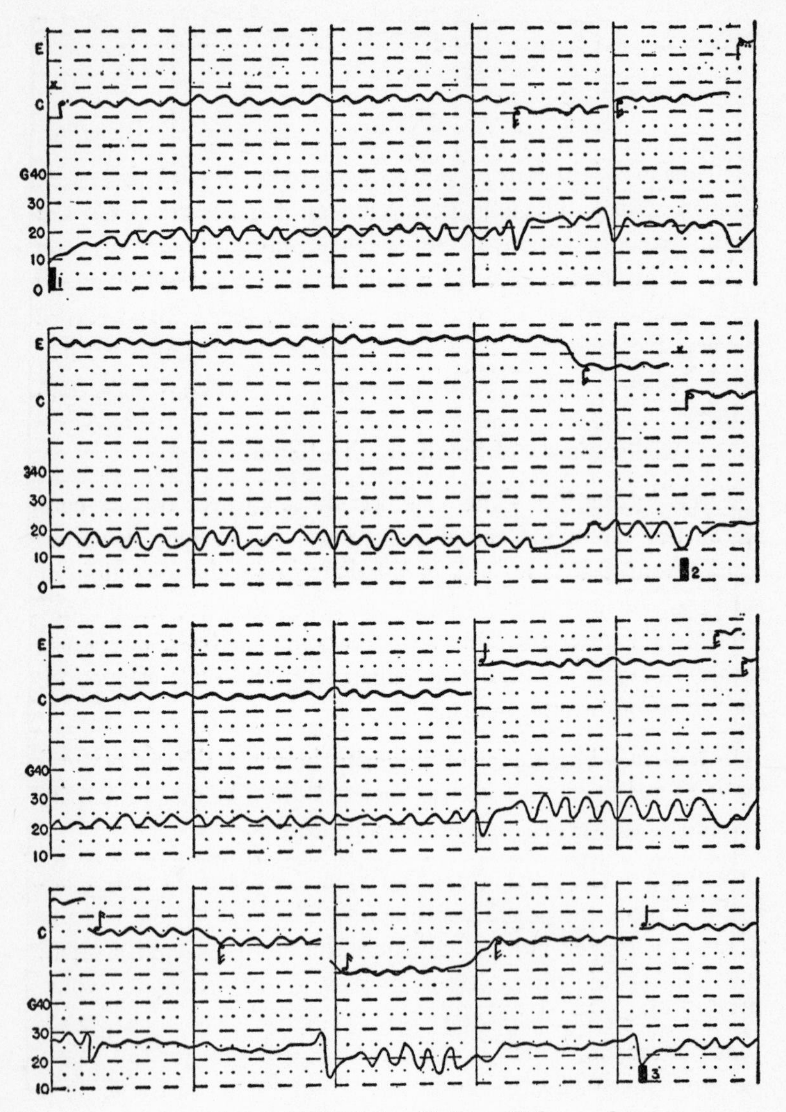

FIG. 17.–*Ave Maria* as played by Slatkin. Violin performance score.

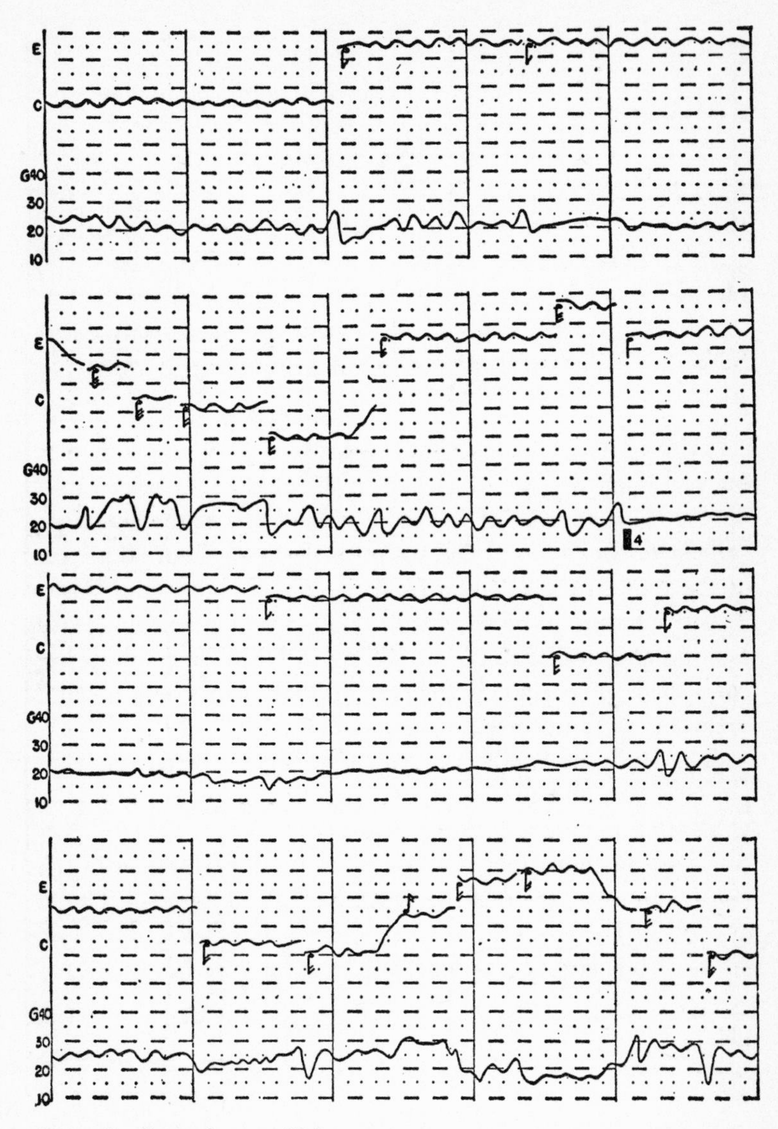

(From Small—see footnote 22.)

The number of cycles of deviation in vibrato is, obviously, a function of the particular frequency of the tone being played. The nature of the vibrato in terms of rate and fluctuation in pitch is about the same for the violin, viola, and cello.[23]

The intensity vibrato is also present. As with singing, the intensity vibrato for the violinist is present about 75 per cent of the time. It is not always continuous, nor does it necessarily appear throughout the entire duration of the tone. The average rate is about 6.3 pulsations per second, which is about the same as that of the pitch vibrato. The extent of the intensity change is about 4.4 db. and is relatively more important in violin playing than in singing.

Trill.—The violin trill closely resembles the vibrato when the interval is small. The distinction is difficult, being made largely on the characteristics of the score rather than of the actual performance. Small found that violinists deviated about 80 per cent of the time in their trilling from the actual note values, just as Seashore found in the vocal trill. There was a great deal of overholding and underholding in trilling so far as time values were concerned. The underestimation of time values was about as prevalent as the overestimation.

The study of Small is a most significant research on violin performance, and the interested student can go to the original work for a more detailed analysis.

This concludes our analysis of musical performance. The reader can easily see that the greatest effort has been in the field of vocal performance. However, significant studies in other areas are available, largely from the University of Iowa laboratories.

[23] C. E. Seashore (ed.), *The vibrato* (Iowa City, Ia.: University of Iowa, 1932).

Chapter 15

MUSIC IN INDUSTRY

UNTIL recently, few experimental data have been available dealing with the effects of music on our work. Despite this lack of experimental evidence, many of us recognize the fact that music does have an effect on our work. Students have been advised, for example, against playing their radios during study, and some college residences have regulations against it. But that, of course, is only one kind of work. The question we must ask ourselves is: Does music have any beneficial effects upon working? If so, what are they?

The use of music in work is certainly not an innovation of modern times. We read of how people long ago made use of music in their jobs. The "work song" is perhaps the best-known example. This type of song not only formed a part of a ritual, but was used by the workers in expressing their attitudes toward their jobs and their employers. Note especially some of the American Negro songs of the slave days. Singing served, in many instances, as a release from the toil and burdens they bore. Singing during work is supposed to have made the toil easier. So it appears that music may have some effect. Of course, these effects are bound to differ from one individual to another. First of all, we have different responsive equipment for listening to music and for different kinds of music (popular, classical, semiclassical, etc.). Secondly, we engage in so many different kinds of work and under such varying conditions that it is difficult to make broad generalizations as to the precise effects music will have. While the area of application of music to industry is relatively new, a few representative studies seem to be of significance. A fairly large number of studies are available, but a few significant ones will suffice for our discussion.

When we think of the effects of music in industry, two kinds of application confront us. First, there is the effect of music as a recreational measure where bands, orchestras, choruses, and so forth form a part of the general program along with baseball teams, bowling teams, etc. Many of our large companies have such programs, and their employees have developed abilities to such a degree that nation-wide broadcasts are made by the sponsoring company. Thus, industry has recognized the beneficial effect of such group participation on general work morale. It is difficult, however, to measure in any very objective fashion the exact improvement as far as rate of production is concerned or even attitude of workers. However, the fact that such institutions survive seems to be some indication of their effectiveness. The application of music to industry has been going on for some time and will probably continue.

The second kind of effect which we note is that which results when music is introduced into the work situation, that is, while a man is on the job rather than as an extracurricular activity. It is this type of application with which we wish to concern ourselves in this chapter.

Any experimental approach to the use of music in industry is comparatively new. For example, Thomas Edison tried recorded music in 1915 with factory workers in order to improve production, but nothing ever came of this attempt, probably because of the inadequate development of reproductive sound systems at that time.

Effect of music on work output.—One of the earliest studies which seems significant concerns the effect of music on fatigue and boredom in work, reported by Wyatt and Langdon [1] in Eng-

[1] S. Wyatt and J. N. Langdon, Industrial Health Research Board Report No. 77, Great Britain Medical Research Council, London, 1937; *Fatigue and boredom in repetitive work* (London: His Majesty's Stationery Office, 1937).

land. It had already been demonstrated by industrial psychologists that boredom in some types of work is most intense around the middle of the working period. This boredom is expressed in restless behavior and results in a lower rate of output. In the study reported, workers had tried to counteract this by singing, talking, and other varying activity. When phonograph records were played intermittently during the working period and particularly during the middle of the period, it was found that output increased from 6.2 to 11.2 per cent during the time when music was played. The total daily output showed a gain of from 2.6 to 6 per cent. The most obvious interpretation was that music is effective for those engaged in monotonous tasks largely of a manipulative sort and requiring little concentration once the task is learned. Of course, we must remember that this conclusion applied so far only to those tasks which become monotonous for a large per cent of the group studied. Obviously, if a man were solving a complicated engineering problem, it might be quite distracting for the radio to be blurting out some one of the current hit tunes, particularly if some sultry vocalist were augmenting the presentation.

It must be remembered that the rhythm and tempo should not be considered as necessarily stepping up working speeds but as a means of creating a cheerful and gay attitude. Langdon and Wyatt further report that the benefits seem to diminish when the music is applied in overdoses (all of the working time or close to it). This seems to be especially true in the case of women.[2]

This conclusion applies to averages for the group investigated, and individual cases are reported where music had little or no effect on production. It is of particular interest to note that the British Broadcasting Corporation made use of this study during the second World War when it introduced to 8,000,000 workers in Great Britain the daily program "Music While You Work." The BBC also found that the beneficial effects of music diminish

[2] D. Soibelman, *Therapeutic and industrial uses of music* (New York: Columbia University Press, 1948), p. 177.

if it is applied in overdoses and that the workers who seemed to benefit most were those who worked at the most monotonous tasks. By 1943 an estimated 90 per cent of British industries were using music.[3]

In England and the United States most of the programs merely appealed to the workers' preferences in music. The general impression has been that if the employees were given the music they wanted, it mattered little how the music was arranged in the programs presented to them.

Cardinell[4] has reported on studies done by the Muzak Corporation, the largest supplier of music service to industry. This organization supplies programs of music over transmission lines to various offices and industries over the country. The company has branch offices in major cities in the United States which furnish the same programs in each area. The music is recorded on transcriptions and arranged and interpreted for various organizations, such as offices, industries, and restaurants.

The musical programs played in offices are quite different from those played in factories. Nevertheless, the underlying principles are much the same in both cases. First of all, the promotion of industrial efficiency seems to be the main reason for playing music during work periods. Muzak has found that a maximum of two and one-half to three hours of music in any eight-hour work period gives the most beneficial results in factories. These effects of music increase in proportion to the amount of music played up to this point. Thereafter, the effects diminish as more music is played.

All the music should not be played in any single period. A period of twenty to thirty minutes at any one time seems to be sufficient. Thereafter, playing periods may be distributed throughout the day whenever they seem to be most effective. The average normal fatigue curve for the group should be deter-

[3] R. L. Cardinell, *Music in industry*, in D. Schullian and M. Schoen (eds.), *Music and medicine* (New York: Henry Schuman, Inc., 1948), p. 356.

[4] R. L. Cardinell, *Music in industry* (New York: American Society of Composers, Authors, & Publishers, 1944).

mined. Music is then played to counteract the points of fatigue just prior to and during the time when the fatigue peak is setting in. In industries where boredom is the chief ailment to be combated, it is more effective to use shorter playing periods at regular and more frequent intervals. This helps the passage of time and is a powerful aid in the relief of boredom induced by monotonous tasks.

Maximum stimulation is achieved when selections are arranged in order of ascending mood. Music should be non-attention-getting. Thus, abrupt changes in key and rhythm, loss of melodic line in background figures, vocals, and highly complicated modulations draw attention away from work and are to be avoided.

However, in highly monotonous work the degree of concentration required is extremely low, so that in many cases a distraction is favorable and does not interfere with the work. Moreover, pleasant music serves as an attention-getter and forestalls moodiness and worry into which a worker's fantasy might lead him. The factor of entertainment becomes more important than stimulation when boredom is the slowing-down factor.

Preferences for types of music can be easily determined through questionnaires, and both likes and dislikes must be noted. Through the questionnaire method, the Muzak Corporation has been able to set up patterns of programs in various geographic locations and for various age, sex, occupational, and educational groups.[5]

One of the most recent studies reported by Henry Clay Smith[6] involved a twelve-week period at a radio assembly firm. The aims of this study were (*a*) to discover employee attitudes toward music during work, (*b*) to discover what programming of music was most desirable, and (*c*) to determine the influence of music on piecework production and employee accidents.

[5] Cardinell, in Schullian and Schoen, *Music and medicine,* pp. 352–66.

[6] Henry Clay Smith, *Music in relation to employee attitudes, piecework production, and industrial accidents,* Appl. Psychol. Monogr., 1947, No. 14.

Employee attitudes.—A questionnaire was given to determine employee attitudes before the musical experiment began.

1. Results indicated that almost all of the employees (98 per cent) thought music would be mildly pleasant, and 74 per cent reported it would be extremely pleasant.
2. The intensity of interest in music while working decreased somewhat with age. Also, the oldest group preferred semiclassical, nonvocal, and quiet music more than the younger groups did.
3. There did not seem to be any sex differences in the intensity of interest in music shown by the workers or their preferences as to type of music.
4. Personal interviews with a sample of the group at the end of the twelve weeks indicated no decrease in the desire for music while working.

Piecework production.—The effects of music on production were observed in a highly repetitive assembly-line operation which was on incentive pay. Two separate shifts were observed simultaneously for a period of two weeks.

1. The results indicated that production under various conditions of music increased from 4 to 25 per cent. The average increase on the day shift was 7 per cent and on the night shift 17 per cent. These increases were statistically significant and were found large enough to be economically important.
2. Maximum production increases were found when music was played 12 per cent of the time on a day shift and 50 per cent of the time on the night shift.
3. With a large increase in the number of semiclassical selections played, the production tended to decline, but it did not change with a large increase in the number of vocal selections. Waltzes were more effective at the opening of the shift than were marches.
4. Production increases varied with the hour of the day at which music was played and were greatest during the hours of low production.

5. The more an employee wanted music as indicated by the attitude survey, the more music tended to increase that employee's production; the lower the previous production rate, the more music tended to increase production; the more the employees' job permitted conversation while working, the more music tended to increase production.

6. The greater effectiveness of large amounts of music on the night shift corresponded to a greater demand for music on that shift; the greater effectiveness of varied music corresponded to an expressed preference for varied rather than for special types of music; the greater effectiveness of certain distributions of music corresponded to an expressed preference for such distributions.

Industrial accidents.—No difference was found between the number of accidents on music days and on nonmusic days when all three shifts were combined. Separately, the day shift showed an increase in the number of accidents on music days, while the night shifts showed a slight decrease. Furthermore, accidents on the day shift tended to increase with increasing amounts of music, but this did not hold for the night shifts.

Conclusions from Smith study.—Smith concludes that music during working hours will generally improve production in a task where repetitive work is common. When properly administered in such situations, it will also provide employee satisfaction. Its major direct effect occurs when the individual's capacity for attention is not absorbed by his work. Under such circumstances, music seems to direct unused attention away from brooding and from talking on the job. Music, on the average, seemed to have little or no effect on the accident rate. The relation, if any, between music and accidents is not entirely clear in this study.

However, Hough,[7] in an earlier study, indicated a noticeable decrease in the number of accidents in certain shop work after the introduction of musical programs over a three-month period.

[7] E. Hough, Music as a safety factor, *J. acoust. Soc. Amer.*, 1943, **15**, 124.

Spears,[8] in a survey of 111 plants and offices which used some sort of music for employee work or recreation, found that in eight of the 111 plants surveyed, music tended to reduce fatigue and tension, which also reduced the accident rate. The remainder did not show any noticeable differences in accident reduction when music was used.

Kerr[9] conducted a series of experiments to test more rigorously the claims in favor of the effects of music on the quantity and quality of production. Four experiments were performed. These were designated as (*a*) naval capacitor manufacture, (*b*) quartz crystal, (*c*) radio tube experiment, and (*d*) Victor Orthacoustic experiment. The first three experiments attempted to test the effects of the amount and specific types of music on production. The fourth experiment dealt with the making of recordings used to produce the music.

Results are summarized as follows:

1. Quantity of output was greater on days when music was played than on days when no music was played.
2. There was a tendency for higher quality of output when *no* music or *less* music was used. The three cases in which music was favorable were hourly-rate-pay departments.
3. The net yield of goods was greatest on music days.
4. Experiments failed to point out any general type of music as being superior, except that music of a moderate or fast tempo seemed to be more beneficial to production than music of a slow, subjective tempo. The present evidence indicates that the best production is achieved when the music is of a moderate or brisk tempo. We observe that music in these experiments was associated with a greater percentage of production increase in those departments *not* having incentive wage systems. Also, it is noted

[8] E. M. Spears, *The use of music in industry,* Nat. Indust. Conference Board Reports, 1947, No. 78.

[9] W. A. Kerr, *Experiments on the effect of music on factory production,* Appl. Psychol. Monogr., 1945, No. 5.

that additional research is needed to determine the effects of specific musical factors on efficiency.

Further studies on employee attitudes toward music.—Since attitude toward one's work is a factor in building morale as well as gaining efficiency, several studies have undertaken to discover how the worker feels about having music played while he is on the job.

From his survey of the literature on music in industry, Kirkpatrick[10] reports (*a*) that workers generally believe that music has a beneficial effect during work and (*b*) that workers who perform repetitive, manual tasks seem to appreciate the music the most during their work. This observation is more specifically demonstrated by Kerr,[11] who surveyed several plants with regard to employee attitudes toward music. He recommends that music be provided in all work areas in which the tasks performed are manual and monotonous, provided the employees are agreeable to it.

Also Kirkpatrick[12] finds that workers report that music hinders work that demands a high degree of concentration. However, this is not a hard-and-fast principle, since Reynolds[13] has found that music may be beneficial during this type of work if the selections, style of playing, and reproduction are proper.

In another study of trainees in mechanic learner and junior repairman courses in a Signal Corps radio school, Kerr[14] found that workers' attitudes (as measured by attitude scales) indicated that music (*a*) helped their feelings toward their associates, (*b*) helped them when tired, (*c*) helped in performing wearisome tasks, and (*d*) helped them forget their worries.

[10] F. H. Kirkpatrick, Music in industry, *J. appl. Psychol.*, 1943, **27**, 268–74.

[11] W. A. Kerr, Psychological research in industrial music and plant broadcasting, *J. Psychol.*, 1944, **17**, 243–61.

[12] Kirkpatrick, *op cit.*

[13] W. Reynolds, Selecting music for the factory, *Personnel*, 1943, **20**, 95–98.

[14] W. A. Kerr, Psychological effects of music as reported by 162 defense trainees, *Psychol. Rec.*, 1942, **5**, 205–12.

Effect of music on absenteeism.—Another study by Spears,[15] made for the Industrial Conference Board, bears mentioning. Out of 111 plants surveyed which used music in some form, nine plants reported a lowered absentee rate which they believed due to use of music, fifteen plants reported reductions in turnover, and twenty-nine plants concluded that music improved production rates, reports varying from "a slight increase" to 30 per cent. A few others, however, showed a decrease in production, possibly due to the distracting effect of the music. The general quality of the work was reported improved in fifteen plants, and seven reported improvement in punctuality at work. Finally, 54 per cent of the managements surveyed believed that the music used in their plants promoted a greater harmony and good will among the workers.

General conclusions on music in industry.—From this review of the most significant research studies, what conclusions may we draw so far? First of all, it is obvious that the use of music does increase production, at least for certain types of factory work. The reason for this probably does not lie in any one factor. There is, of course, usually a reduction in both skeletal and visceral tension during music. The irritating din of factory noise contributes to fatigue. Noise, as we have already observed, is characterized by irregular pulsations and a lack of rhythmic form, whereas music has regular beats and sequences. In the midst of this industrial noise, pleasing rhythms and melodies are responded to in preference to unpleasant noises. Music can be adapted to most types of industrial work; only in those factories where noise is continuous and unusually intense is it impossible to play music.

Secondly, music tends to relieve monotony. The beneficial effects seem to have a direct relation to the degree of monotony caused by work. Simple mechanized work is most aided by music. As the complexity of the task increases and requires more intellectual activity, these effects become less perceptible.

[15] Spears, *op. cit.*

We note further that apparently too much music is not desirable. There seems to be an optimum amount for each operation, and this has to be determined for different types of jobs.

The beneficial effects are a function of the workers' attitudes. In the Smith study, we observed that favorable attitudes influenced the effectiveness of the music positively. Of course, generalized statements as to the effects of music must be qualified. We must realize that in order to lead to more efficient work, the music must be functionally effective. That is, it must turn the employee out at the end of the day's work a more desirable person psychologically than he would have been if no music had been played.

Cardinell and Burris-Meyer[16] state that, to be functionally effective, the music must be used to counteract natural degeneration which takes place in the individual during his normal working day. On the other hand, it must not seize and hold the attention of the individual to the detriment of his particular activity. A high degree of acceptability *to the worker* is also necessary.

Finally, to be most effective, the programs to be played must be arranged on a basis of proportional representation of musical tastes. In other words, music should be played which the workers like to hear. This is important. Musical tastes differ, so that the type of selections played ought to conform to the likes of the majority of the group listening. This is why it is rather difficult to determine in advance the kinds of music that are going to be most effective.

It has not been established precisely how much music should be played or what programs should be selected. Since there are thousands of different kinds of work done and people involved, the selections may be an individual matter. The selections which employees prefer will vary from industry to industry and location to location. It is deemed advisable for each company to determine by means of questionnaires the types of selections pre-

[16] R. L. Cardinell and H. Burris-Meyer, Music in industry today, *J. acoust. Soc. Amer.*, 1947, **19**, 547–49.

ferred by most workers. A sample tabulated by the RCA research staff revealed the following order of preferences:[17]

1. Hit tunes played in fairly straight arrangements
2. Waltzes
3. Semiclassical selections
4. Patriotic music
5. Marches
6. Classical selections
7. Sacred music
8. Hawaiian music
9. Humorous-novelty numbers
10. Hillbilly and Western music
11. Spirituals and blues
12. Polkas
13. Fast dances

Thus far we have been considering largely the effects of music in factories. How about other types of work? According to Soibelman:

> The benefits of music are not confined to factories. Several of the plants with large offices and firms that employ office help primarily, namely, banks and insurance companies, found that music was favorably received by the workers and often resulted in greater efficiency. However, for those doing mental work it is important that the volume be kept low and that the selections include only unobtrusive numbers.[18]

This conclusion is based on reports by Cardinell[19] and McDaniel.[20] It has been found that music can be used effectively in offices providing it does not *distract* the workers' attention where a high degree of concentration is involved. It is necessary

[17] *Music in industry* (Chicago: Industrial Recreation Association, 1944), p. 27.

[18] Soibelman, *op. cit.*, p. 191.

[19] R. L. Cardinell, A guide to music in industry, *Factory Management and Maintenance*, 1943, **101**:10.

[20] R. McDaniel, How music increases office production, *Amer. Business*, 1945, **15**, 22–26.

here also that the music be of an unobtrusive sort. This is reminiscent of what we said in the first part of the chapter to the effect that work on complicated engineering problems might be highly confusing if accompanied by the "Triumphal March" from *Aida* or "You've Got Everything, Baby" sung by Desirée L'Amour, sensuous torch singer direct from Paris. Just how effective music is in offices has not, as yet, been demonstrated.

Chapter 16

THERAPEUTIC USES OF MUSIC

> And it came to pass when the evil spirit from God was upon Saul that David took a harp and played with his hand; so Saul was refreshed and was well and the evil spirit departed from him.—I Sam., 16:23.

ACTUALLY, music is among the most ancient of all therapeutic devices. References to it as a healing aid appear in the Bible, Greek and Roman literature, and Egyptian records. Although little direct evidence is available concerning the behavior of primitive peoples, we may infer from our contemporary aborigines that music played an important part in treating the sick of early times, just as it does now among the less civilized.

Yet, today very few experimental studies relative to the therapeutic effects of music are available to us. Most of the evidence comes either from anecdotes or clinical observations, some of which are rather casual in nature. Nevertheless, the literature in this field is gradually growing, and our surveys show a wide use of music in many hospitals today.

The phrase "therapeutic uses of music" includes a variety of applications. Among these we may mention the use of music with the mentally ill, either in actual treatment or as part of the hospital situation. Occupational therapy, where patients learn to play some musical instrument as part of their rehabilitation, is another area of juncture between music and medicine. The use of music played in the sick-room of the general hospital, at mealtime, and as recreation indicates that music has a possible therapeutic value. Music's function therapeutically may be both active and passive. In an active sense it includes performances of groups, such as choirs or bands, as part of the program of recovery. The passive side is represented by listening to music in a casual manner. This may be beneficial for both the physically and the mentally ill. It can serve as a means of inducing relaxation and improving morale.

We must constantly be on our guard against exaggerating the effects of music as therapy by assuming results which are not present in the data. Because of the paucity of really experimental studies in this field, there is a tendency to overrate the positive effects of music. Perhaps because we are musicians or at least interested in music, we may have a prejudice in the direction of its beneficial effects.

Sear [1] has criticized those who accept music as therapy without questioning the validity of the reported cures. In most cases, he claims, the medical treatment is the determining factor in the cure. The patient's attitude toward the music has a greater effect on the individual than the music itself.

Early observations on the effect of music.—Music which accompanied drugs and other treatments among primitive people symbolized the power which a medicine man possessed. In this sense, songs as well as instrumental music (drums or rattles) were believed to be effective in driving away illness or healing wounds. The great function of music for primitive people, according to Radin,[2] was that it served as a symbol of the priest-practitioner's power, particularly with regard to his control of the spirits which caused illness. Music, then, was an emblem of his profession.

Much evidence on the use of music in healing comes from our studies of the American Indians. The Wallawalla Indians, for example, believe that song influences the cure of a patient; so

[1] H. G. Sear, Music and medicine, *Music and Letters,* 1939, **20,** 43–54.

[2] P. Radin, Music and medicine among primitive peoples, in D. Schullian and M. Schoen (eds.), *Music and medicine* (New York: Henry Schuman, Inc., 1948).

convalescents are ordered to sing for several hours each day.[3] Among the Ojibwa the medicine man simply sits near the patient and sings to the accompaniment of gourd rattles.

Many studies of other contemporary aboriginal cultures show the association of music with healing. Frequently, an individual's very existence is dependent on certain rites which have no necessary connection with disease. The dances, songs, and rituals are necessary preventives which serve to ward off or satisfy evil spirits. They are intended to preserve the well-being of the tribe and the individual. When sickness comes, it is either due to the wrath of the spirits or the enmity of those possessed. The function of the rituals is a preventive as well as curative one. However, once the spirits are angered, the remedies frequently will involve music and dancing.[4]

In her numerous studies of the American Indians, Densmore[5] found among the Sioux and Tetons, for example, a belief that the cure of a disease can be seen in the patient's dreams. As part of the ritual, the medicine man sings the patient's dream song as well as other songs addressed to sacred stones. Herbs are also often administered to accompany the music.

Among primitives, music is intensely pleasurable,[6] and its effect on a sick man will be to intensify his desire for recovery. The patient realizes he is part of the ritual-curing drama, according to Radin, and the successful priest-practitioner will be sure to stimulate an awareness of this fact.

The therapeutic effects of music also appear in ancient Greek and Roman literature. Plato, for example, refers to the healing power of song in his *Charmides*. A remedy consisting of a leaf and a magic song is suggested for a heavy head. The leaf, he believed, was ineffective by itself and had to be accompanied by music. Homer in the *Odyssey* relates the story of how the bleed-

[3] *Ibid.*
[4] *Ibid.*
[5] F. Densmore, Use of music in the treatment of the sick by American Indians, *Mus. Quarterly*, 1927, **13**, 555–65.
[6] Radin, *op. cit.*

ing of Odysseus' wound was stopped by music. What Homer probably did not know was that all wounds except those from a large artery will usually cease bleeding in twenty minutes regardless of what is done.[7] The great Greek physician Galen recommended music as an antidote for the bite of vipers and scorpions.[8]

One disease for which music was supposedly the only cure was tarantism. This was very prevalent in Italy during the seventeenth century. Although cases appeared throughout Italy and Spain, it tended to be localized in Apulia, a hot region in the heel of the Italian boot. The disease was attributed to the sting of a spider, the tarantula. This occurred usually at the height of the summer heat. People would suddenly jump up and run out of the house and start dancing in the street with great excitement. They would then be frequently joined by others also supposedly bitten. A whole mob might participate in this frenzied orgy until all were finally exhausted. It was believed that once one was bitten, the poison from the tarantula remained in his body, and although he might be temporarily cured, the poison remained and was reactivated each year by the summer heat. The only effective remedies seemed to be music and dancing. People were known to have died of this disorder if music was not accessible. The music, called a tarantella, was a piece played in a very fast tempo with frequently repeating melody.

Finally after having danced themselves into complete exhaustion, the people were at least temporarily cured. One August in 1695, so the story goes, a skeptical physician had himself bitten by two of the supposedly poisonous tarantulas. Except for the swelling, he felt no harmful effects. It seemed then that the disease must be due to the summer heat, which activated the poison. During the eighteenth century the disease gradually died out. It was eventually demonstrated that the Apulian tarantula

[7] S. Licht, *Music in medicine* (Boston: New England Conservatory of Music, 1946).

[8] *Ibid.*

was in no way different from the tarantula of any other country and its sting had no effect beyond theirs. Why then did this disease occur so frequently in such a localized area—this hysterical frenzy which appeared to have no organic basis?

Sigerist,[9] who relates the story of tarantism, explains it as a carry-over from an ancient pagan ritual. When Christianity came to Apulia, and this was relatively late, an adjustment had to be made in order to win over the population. As was a frequent practice in the early Christian era, the pagan holidays and rituals were preserved, but Christian events and symbols were substituted. The particular cult of Dionysos to which the Apulians adhered practiced orgiastic rites, and these the church could not assimilate. If the people continued to practice them, they were considered sinners, until one day, probably during the Middle Ages, the old rites took on the symptoms of a disorder. All of this wild, frenzied behavior became legitimized, and those who indulged in it were no longer sinners but poor victims of the bite of the tarantula.

Therapeutic uses of music have appeared in both sacred and secular writings. We have already made reference to David's use of the harp to ease Saul by driving away the evil spirit that afflicted him. The great religious reformer, Martin Luther, called the devil a saturnine spirit to whom music was hateful, and believed that it could be used to exorcise him as well as other evil spirits.[10]

In more recent times, Bacon prescribed music to be played every day to replenish the soul. More specifically, in his *Sylva Sylvarum,* he suggests that music might be tried for many disorders of the constitution. In 1634 Henry Peacham wrote in *The Compleat Gentleman* that music lengthened the life by stirring and reviving the spirits. It is an enemy to melancholy and dejection.

[9] H. G. Sigerist, The story of tarantism, in D. Schullian and M. Schoen (eds.), *Music and medicine* (New York: Henry Schuman, Inc., 1948).
[10] Licht, *op. cit.*

Use of music in general hospitals.—After this brief survey of early observations on the use of music for therapeutic purposes, we turn to some contemporary observations. The use of music in hospitals has varied, but Van de Wall[11] reports that most hospitals do employ some sort of music either therapeutically or as part of their entertainment program. As to its effects, surveys have varied from reports of negative effects through ineffective results to highly exaggerated claims. Probably one of the reasons for not using music more in hospitals lies in the physician's frequent prejudice toward consideration of the organic cause of a disorder by itself. Often, when musicians have used music in connection with the sick, there has been a tendency to exaggerate its benefits. It often hurts a doctor's pride to see results from anything but orthodox medical procedures. Obviously, if music is to be used in hospitals successfully, there must be an understanding developed between all of those persons involved. Most authorities agree that music should be under the direction of a medical man. They frown on the practice of giving a musician, untrained in any medical or biological field, a free rein in the hospital. The actual musical program may be under the direct supervision of a medical man who understands something about music and may be administered by a musician who is acquainted with the problems of medicine and knows something about the physiology and psychology of the human organism.

If music is to be successfully used in hospitals, a great deal of cooperation of hospital personnel is necessary. Both musician and doctor must show consideration for the musical tastes of the patients involved. Musicians must disregard at least momentarily their preconceived ideas of what constitutes good and bad music. Hillbilly music may be unpopular with the trained musician, but it may serve as a source of satisfaction and comfort for many distressed patients.[12]

[11] W. Van de Wall, Music in hospitals, in D. Schullian and M. Schoen (eds.), *Music and medicine* (New York: Henry Schuman, Inc., 1948).
[12] *Ibid.*

Ainlay,[13] from his study of music in military hospitals, has given us some specific suggestions concerning the use of music in our hospitals.

Programs for wards should not exceed forty-five-minute periods except under special circumstances.

Programs should not be planned generally for the forenoon, since this time is usually taken up with the necessary examinations and other hospital requirements.

The volume should be less than that for ordinary concerts. Too much volume may serve as an irritating factor, especially for those who do not wish to listen.

An orchestra or instrumental combination is preferred to single instruments by the majority of patients. But of those single instruments used, the piano is best liked and tolerated. Vocal music is least preferred, particularly sopranos.

Both classical and popular music are well received. Figures obtained by Ainlay in a survey of the Committee for the Surgeon General give patients' preferences as popular music 60 per cent and classical 40 per cent. Performers of classical music should follow the example of popular musicians by playing that which gives happiness and satisfaction to the listener rather than what *they think* is "good" for the patient.

Psychiatric uses of music.—In an earlier chapter, we observed that the affective reactions to music were both physiological and behavioral. Furthermore, music may have great associational value. For one person it can serve as a stimulus for a wide variety of imaginal reactions, both pleasant and unpleasant. If music can give rise to behavioral changes in the so-called normal person, then the question arises as to what its effect may be on the pathological individual who suffers from some form of behavioral disorder.

[13] G. W. Ainlay, The place of music in military hospitals, in D. Schullian and M. Schoen (eds.), *Music and medicine* (New York: Henry Schuman, Inc., 1948).

In this connection, one use of music has been as a means of gaining contact with the patient. In many mental disorders, particularly schizophrenia and to a lesser degree depressive psychosis, the patients become so insulated from the outside world that they are almost completely inaccessible to external stimuli. The patients have taken this withdrawal from reality as their only way of adjusting to a series of conflicts and frustrations. Because of such withdrawal behavior, they no longer have to face their problems. Such patients frequently develop autistic communities consisting of imagined behavioral relationships which are either partly or completely void of human contact.

Altshuler[14] has observed clinically that the mood of the music is a significant factor in eliciting a response from a depressed patient. The patient may be more readily attracted initially by music in the minor keys. This typical relationship between sadness and the minor key has been demonstrated by Hevner (see Chapter 9). Gay or happy music frequently irritates the depressed patient; contrariwise, the manic patient responds more readily to music in a fast tempo. The playing of such music has been suggested as an attempt to contact the patient who is otherwise inaccessible. However, music is not suggested as a substitute for other kinds of therapy, but as a supplement.

Care must be taken in using music with groups of psychotics. Altshuler has found stringed instruments to work best with depressed patients. The brass instruments are not suitable for patients sensitive to noise or suffering from anxiety states.

At the Eloise Hospital, Altshuler[15] has employed a method aimed at arousing the detached patient and changing his mood. With these patients he suggests beginning with music which is highly rhythmical and then continuing with music which normally arouses some affective reaction in keeping with the present mood, that is, sad music for the depressed. Finally shifting from

[14] I. M. Altshuler, The past, present, and future of musical therapy, *Educ. Music Mag.*, 1945, **24**, 16–17.
[15] *Ibid.*

sad to gay music (in this instance) may frequently have positive results. The temporary beneficial effects of using music can be lengthened by presenting it daily to the patients.

Further suggestions come from Ainlay[16] for using music to reach the withdrawn patient in order to make him more accessible to psychiatric treatment. From his experience with army neuro-psychiatric patients, he gives the following observations and suggestions. Groups of patients who listen to the music should be small and free from outsiders. The piano is the most acceptable instrument, with small string ensembles next. Vocal music is not usually desirable at first. Simple folk music is usually the safest in the early stages of treatment with soldiers. Shorter melodic numbers from the great masters may follow. Long numbers should never be used; the music should be simple and melodic. As improvement progresses, group participation should be encouraged. Singing in the wards is one of the first steps. Patients' orchestras, instrumental ensembles, music with calisthenics, and musical quiz and variety shows may follow as the patient improves, serving as supplementary aids in psychiatric treatment.

One of the few experimental studies of a psychiatric nature which used music comes to us from Altshuler and Shebesta.[17] They attempted to find a method whereby music could be used in conjunction with hydrotherapy in order to quiet the disturbed patients. It was believed that, for the psychotic as well as the normal, music often had associative value. We have already mentioned this fact. They hoped that through the use of certain kinds of music, the patients might become accessible because of the imaginal reactions which it might serve to stimulate.

Four chronically disturbed schizophrenic women were observed on whom hydrotherapy had previously been unsuccessful. Head movements and verbal output were measured with hydro-

[16] Ainlay, *op. cit.*

[17] I. M. Altshuler and B. H. Shebesta, Music (alone or with hydrotherapy); aid in management of psychotic patients, *J. nerv. ment. Dis.*, 1941, **94**, 179–83.

therapy alone and with music. These observations continued for five days per week for a period of two to three hours per day over a six-week period. Two patients were given continuous baths, and the other two had wet packs during the observation periods. The music consisted of a violin playing behind a screen. During the first ten to twenty minutes of the observation periods, little change in the behavior of the patients was noticed.

Soon familiar tunes attracted their attention, and the activity of the patients was changed from purposeless, irrelevant movements to singing and humming the familiar tunes. Popular waltzes were found to be the best type of music for quieting the patients. As a control, the patients were placed in dry sheets while music was played. Again after twenty to thirty minutes, activity in this situation diminished 50 per cent, indicating the possibility that music alone might possibly have the quieting effect. The experimenters conclude that music has been demonstrated to be useful in decreasing the restlessness of disturbed and inaccessible patients. This occurred while the music was played alone and in conjunction with hydrotherapy. They further found that the use of music with hydrotherapy patients eliminates the attitude that such treatments are punitive in nature.

In concluding this discussion we shall list the possible uses of music in psychiatry as suggested by Licht: [18]

1. Listening
   a) To improve attention
   b) To maintain interest
   c) To influence mood
   d) To produce sedation
   e) To release energy: foot-tapping, etc.
2. Participation (group singing, bands, etc.)
   a) To bring about communal cooperation
   b) To release energy
   c) To arouse interest

[18] Licht, *op. cit.*, pp. 71–72.

3. Creation of sound (playing an instrument, etc.)
   - *a*) To increase self-respect by accomplishment and success
   - *b*) To increase personal happiness by ability to please others
   - *c*) To release energy

Use of music as occupational therapy.—Up until the late eighteenth century, the mentally ill were considered to be rather helpless creatures, and the most humane treatment used was mere custodial care. However, the more violent patients were chained to the walls, often flogged, and generally mortified in an effort to keep them quiet. In 1797, the French physician Phillipe Pinel at the Salpêtrière Hospital in Paris attempted a more humane treatment of the mentally ill by having their chains removed. This treatment, rather unconventional for those times, stands as a milestone in the history of behavior disorders. But our concern with Pinel is that he was one of the first occupational therapists, for he introduced the use of activities to keep "the mind and the body occupied."

The term "occupational therapy" as we use it has a functional reference to muscle power, joint mobility, and coordination of movements. In this sense, music can be used as a means of exercise as well as a background interlude in inducing relaxation. Thus, the performance of music can be helpful in its effects on the joints, muscles, lungs, and larynx.

Licht [19] has pointed out that a number of different principles of occupational therapy can be applied to musical performance. For a complete account we refer the reader to his book, *Music in Medicine*.

From the viewpoint of interest and instruction, the piano, Licht believes, is probably the best instrument. It offers excellent opportunity for flexion of the fingers and thumb, extension, abduction, and adduction of the wrists and shoulders, and exercise of the neck and back. The piano is also an excellent medium for

[19] *Ibid.*, chap. iii.

the increase of joint motion. In striking the keys, the fingers are forcibly flexed. The exercise of coordination of particular fingers can be obtained better by particular musical arrangements and études than with most other crafts.

Licht, of course, recommends that such therapy be under the direction of a competent physician. In piano playing, the chief emphasis should be on the fingers needing the exercise. Flexion and extension of the wrist may be accompanied by staccato movements, by lateral motion of the wrists, and possibly by arpeggio work. Thumb motion, especially touching the last finger with the thumb, can be accomplished by playing arpeggios, particularly with the larger intervals played in legato style.

The violin is particularly recommended when flexion of the fingers of the left hand is desired, but its greatest value lies in the flexion and extension of the right elbow. It is also valuable as exercise in flexion and extension of the wrist and abduction and adduction of the shoulder. Heavier stringed instruments like the cello and double bass require greater motion of the shoulder.

The plectrum instruments (guitar, ukulele, banjo) offer excellent opportunities for exercise of the wrist of the right hand and the fingers of the left. They have the added advantage over the bowed instruments of being easier to learn, so that the performer will be able to play simple accompaniments in a relatively short time.

For foot exercises, such instruments as the parlor organ or pianola are adaptable. The foot-pumped organ offers excellent ankle exercise. Although the bass drum with foot pedal is not a solo instrument, when used in ensemble with a full set of traps and snare drum, it may be of benefit to those suffering from ankle as well as various wrist and hand disorders.

The reed and brass instruments are not usually suitable for exercise. Their use is limited to the chronic patient. Wind instruments, of course, can be employed for patients with pulmonary disorders which have cleared up enough that the physician feels lung exercise may be helpful. The wind instruments may also be helpful in exercising the facial muscles during recovery from facial palsy.

Singing has also been used for treatment of speech disorders and for exercise of the jaws, larynx, lungs, and diaphragm. With proper instruction it is an excellent exercise for muscles of the chest and abdomen.

The following table from Licht [20] gives a summary of the motions and exercises possible with the various instruments.

Part	*Action*	*Instrument*
Fingers	All	Piano
Fingers	Extension	Ukulele
Thumb	All but adduction	Piano
Wrists	Flexion—extension	Piano
Elbow	Pronation—supination	Guitar
Elbow	Flexion—extension	Violin
Shoulder	Abduction—adduction	Piano
Neck	All motions	Xylophone
Back	All motions	Bass viol
Hips	Abduction—adduction	Organ
Knees	Flexion—extension	Pianola
Ankles	Flexion—extension	Parlor organ

Use of music with anesthesia.—A number of hospitals use music in their operating rooms as an adjuvant to local anesthesia. In 1930 McGlinn [21] found it especially effective during spinal anesthesia because it reduced the possibility of complete loss of consciousness. It also masked noises in the room but did not interfere with the operating technique.

Rusca [22] fitted his patients with a set of earphones during spinal anesthesia. Thus the patient heard only music chosen to suit his tastes. Not only was the operation painless, but it became associated with a pleasurable experience.

[20] *Ibid.*, p. 57.

[21] J. A. McGlinn, Music in the operating room, *Amer. J. Obstet. Gynaec.*, 1930, **20**, 678–83.

[22] Rusca, Rachianaesthesie mit Tutocain und Percain, *Schweiz. med. Wschr.*, 1935, **65**, 637–38.

Music has also been used as a diversion during local anesthesia. Burdick [23] has found that if music is played during the induction of anesthesia, it is accomplished with less resistance.

Music has also been used with dentistry. Cherry and Pallin [24] report the following procedure. From the time the patient enters the waiting room, everything is done to minimize his anxiety. In the dental chair, the conversation is directed to the music, and the patient is allowed to manipulate the volume control. Such popular classical selections as Beethoven's *Moonlight Sonata,* Wagner's "Evening Star" from *Tannhäuser*, and Debussy's *Clair de Lune* were used with success. After the music has started, the anesthetic is administered (75 per cent nitrous oxide, 25 per cent oxygen). They conclude that music is found to render anesthesia adequate for all types of dental office procedure. Further advantages include (*a*) smooth induction of the anesthesia without excitement, struggling, or delirium; (*b*) absence of retching or vomiting; (*c*) rapid emergence from the anesthesia, so that the patient requires no assistance or support when leaving the chair; (*d*) minimum chair occupation time, and (*e*) no undesirable effects on the poor-risk patient.

Music and digestion.—The actual positive effects of music during mealtime have not been satisfactorily demonstrated. All we are sure of is that in some cases music produces a feeling of well-being, and this may have positive effects when associated with eating, which by itself usually elicits feelings of satisfaction and gratification.

However, the custom of eating to music stems from ancient times. The masters of the classical period wrote divertimentos and sarabands which were frequently intended as background music for feasts. Voltaire once said that the purpose of going to the opera was to aid digestion. In past years and still today in

[23] W. P. Burdick, The use of music during anesthesia and analgesia, *The American Yearbook of Anesthesia and Analgesia,* 1916, **1,** 164–67.

[24] H. Cherry and I. M. Pallin, Music as a supplement in nitrous oxide-oxygen anesthesia, *Anesthesiology*, 1948, **10.**

fashionable eating places, dinner music accompanies the meal. This music usually consists of light classical and semiclassical selections played softly by some string ensemble in a slow tempo. Most recently the jukebox, radio, and such specialized methods as Muzak are frequently in evidence.

If music can serve to elicit a pleasurable response while eating and give a feeling of repose, it stands to reason that such effects should be beneficial.

Licht [25] mentions some facts which he believes are important if music is to aid digestion. Mealtime music should be unobtrusive. It should lack the stimulating qualities which attract attention. Perhaps the most suitable dinner music is that played by a string ensemble, piano, or harp. Dinner music should be soft and slow. The level of intensity should not interfere with normal conversation. If the music is so loud that one must raise his voice, it defeats its purpose of relaxing the person by avoiding any demand for increased exertion. There should be nothing abrupt about the selection played. Unusual sequences and novelties should be avoided. Vocalizations, either announcements or singing, should also be avoided. The music played should be of the light classical and semipopular sort. Such selections as those from Johann Strauss and his contemporaries, Victor Herbert, Rudolph Friml, and Sigmund Romberg, as well as such popular favorites of the recent past as Jerome Kern, Cole Porter, George Gershwin, and Irving Berlin, are considered the best.

This concludes our survey of the therapeutic uses of music. Much needs to be learned, as this field is only in its infancy. There is a tremendous need for objective experiments which will either substantiate or refute the observations here reported.

The reader interested in further information may consult the references cited in this chapter. Also, an extensive bibliography in this field appears in Schullian and Schoen, *Music and Medicine*.

[25] Licht, *op. cit.*, chap. vi.

This also concludes our objective psychology of music. This survey has not been the most complete one possible; such was not our intention. We believe that we have succeeded in reporting enough objective evidence to support our general thesis that musical behavior, like other forms of psychological activity, is subject to the same laws and principles as other human activity.

We have tried to be systematic in our approach. This has not been an eclectic viewpoint. Our approach has aimed at being both practical and theoretical and preparing a book useful to both the psychologist and the musician. It is our hope that such an attempt will serve as a stimulus for further objective investigation in this field.

BIBLIOGRAPHY OF REFERENCES CITED

AINLAY, G. W. The place of music in military hospitals. In D. M. Schullian & M. Schoen (eds.), *Music and medicine.* New York: Henry Schuman, Inc., 1948.

ALLPORT, G. W., VERNON, P. E., & LINDZEY, G. *A study of values.* Boston: Houghton Mifflin Co., 1951.

ALTSHULER, I. M. The past, present and future of musical therapy. *Educ. Music Mag.*, 1945, **24,** 16–17.

ALTSHULER, I. M. & SHEBESTA, B. H. Music (alone or with hydrotherapy): aid in management of psychotic patients. *J. nerv. ment. Dis.*, 1941, **94,** 179–83.

ANDREWS, T. G. *Methods in psychology.* New York: John Wiley & Sons, Inc., 1949.

BACHEM, A. Various types of absolute pitch. *J. acoust. Soc. Amer.*, 1937, **9,** 146–51.

BACHEM, A. Genesis of absolute pitch. *J. acoust. Soc. Amer.*, 1939–40, **11,** 434–39.

BAIRD, J. W. Memory for absolute pitch. In *Studies in psychology: Titchener commemorative volume.* Worcester, Mass.: Louis H. Wilson, 1917.

BARTHOLOMEW, W. T. A physical definition of "good voice-quality" in the male voice. *J. acoust. Soc. Amer.*, 1934, **6,** 25–33.

BEINSTOCK, S. F. A predictive study of musical achievement, *J. genet. Psychol.*, 1942, **61,** 135–45.

BEKKER, P. *The story of music.* New York: W. W. Norton & Co., Inc., 1926.

BINGHAM, W. V. D. Studies in melody. *Psychol. Monogr.*, 1910, **12:**3 (Whole No. 50), 1–88.

BORING, E. G. *Sensation and perception in the history of experimental psychology.* New York: Appleton-Century-Crofts, Inc., 1942.

BORING, E. G., & STEVENS, S. S. The nature of tonal brightness. *Proc. nat. Acad. Sci.*, Wash., 1936, **22,** 514–21.

BORING, E. G., *et al. Introduction to psychology.* New York: John Wiley & Sons, Inc., 1939.

BRENNAN, F. The relation between musical capacity and performance. *Psychol. Monogr.*, 1926, **36:**1 (Whole No. 167), 190–248.

BRITAIN, H. H. *The philosophy of music.* New York: Longmans, Green & Co., Inc., 1911.

BROWN, A. W. The reliability and validity of the Seashore tests of musical talent. *J. appl. Psychol.*, 1928, **12,** 468–76.

BROWN, R. W. A comparative study of "whole" and "part" and "combination" methods of learning piano music. *J. exp. Psychol.*, 1928, **11,** 235–47.

Brown, R. W. The relation between two methods of learning piano music. *J. exp. Psychol.,* 1933, **16,** 435–41.

Bugg, E. G. An experimental study of factors influencing consonance judgments. *Psychol. Monogr.,* 1933, **45:**2 (Whole No. 201).

Bugg, E. G. An analysis of conditions influencing consonance judgments. *J. exp. Psychol.*, 1939, **24,** 54–72.

Burdick, W. P. The use of music during anesthesia and analgesia. *Amer. Yearb. of Anesth. & Analges.*, 1916, **1,** 164–67.

Cameron, E. H. Effects of practice in the discrimination and singing of tones. *Psychol. Monogr.*, 1917, **23:**3 (Whole No. 100), 159–80.

Capurso, A. A. The effect of an associative technique in teaching pitch and interval discrimination. *J. appl. Psychol.*, 1934, **18,** 811–18.

Cardinell, R. L. A guide to music in industry. *Factory Management and Maintenance*, 1943, **101:**10.

Cardinell, R. L. *Music in industry.* New York: Amer. Soc. Composers, Authors and Publishers, 1944.

Cardinell, R. L. Music in industry. In D. Schullian & M. Schoen (eds.), *Music and medicine.* New York: Henry Schuman, Inc., 1948.

Cardinell, R. L., & Burris-Meyer, H. Music in industry today. *J. acoust. Soc. Amer.*, 1947, **19,** 547–49.

Chadwick, J. E. Predicting success in sight singing. *J. appl. Psychol.*, 1933, **17,** 671–74.

Chandler, A. R. *Beauty and human nature.* New York: Appleton-Century-Crofts, Inc., 1934.

Cherry, H., & Pallin, I. M. Music as a supplement in nitrous oxide-oxygen anesthesia. *Anesthesiology*, 1948, **10.**

Coffman, A. R. Is rhythm subject to training? *Sch. Musician* 1949, **21:**14, 45.

Densmore, F. Use of music in the treatment of the sick by American Indians, *Mus. Quarterly*, 1927, **13,** 555–65.

Downey, J. E., & Knapp, G. E. The effect on a musical programme of familiarity and of sequence of selections. In M. Schoen (ed.), *The effects of music.* New York: Harcourt, Brace & Co., Inc., 1927.

Drake, R. M. Four new tests of musical talent. *J. appl. Psychol.,* 1933, **17,** 136–47.

Drake, R. M. The validity and reliability of tests of musical talent. *J. appl. Psychol.*, 1933, **17,** 447–58.

Drake, R. M. *Drake Test of Musical Talent.* Fredericksburg, Va.: The Author, 1942.

Dreher, R. E. The relationship between verbal reports and galvanic skin responses to music. Unpublished doctor's thesis, Indiana University, 1947.

Farnsworth, P. R. Atonic endings in melodies. *Amer. J. Psychol.,* 1925, **36,** 394–400.

FARNSWORTH, P. R. Ending preferences among three positions of the tonic chord. *J. comp. Psychol.*, 1926, **6**, 95–102.

FARNSWORTH, P. R. The effect of repetition on ending preferences in melodies. *Amer. J. Psychol.*, 1926, **37**, 116–22.

FARNSWORTH, P. R. A modification of the Lipps-Meyer law. *J. exp. Psychol.*, 1926, **9**, 253–58.

FARNSWORTH, P. R. An historical, critical and experimental study of the Seashore-Kwalwasser test battery. *Genet. Psychol. Monogr.*, 1931, **9**:5, 291–393.

FARNSWORTH, P. R. Studies in the psychology of tone, *Genet. Psychol. Monogr.*, 1934, **15**:1, 1–91.

FARNSWORTH, P. R. *Musical taste: its measurement and cultural nature.* Stanford, Calif.: Stanford University Press, 1950.

FECHNER, G. T. *Vorschule der Aesthetik.* 1st ed.; Leipzig: Breitkopf und Haertal, 1876.

FLETCHER, H. Loudness, pitch, and timbre of musical tones and their relation to the intensity, the frequency, and the overtone structure. *Jour. acoust. Soc. Amer.*, 1934, **6**, 59–69.

FLETCHER, H., & MUNSON, W. A. Loudness in definition, measurement, and calculation. *J. acoust. Soc. Amer.*, 1933, **5**, 82–108.

Fundamentals of acoustics. Encyclopaedia Britannica Films, Inc.

GAMBLE, E. A. M. & FOSTER, J. C. The effect of music on thoracic breathing. *Amer. J. Psychol.*, 1906, **17**, 406–14.

GARDNER, P. A. D., & PICKFORD, R. W. Relation between dissonance and context. *Nature*, 1943, **152**, 356.

GILLILAND, A. R., & MOORE, H. T. The immediate and long-time effects of classical and popular phonographic selections. In M. Schoen (ed.), *The effects of music.* New York: Harcourt, Brace & Co., Inc., 1927.

GRAY, C. T., & BINGHAM, C. W. A comparison of certain phases of musical ability in colored and white school pupils. *J. educ. Psychol.*, 1929, **20**, 501–6.

Grove's dictionary of music and musicians. New York: The Macmillan Co., 1938.

GURNEY, E. *The power of sound.* London: Smith, Elder, 1880.

HALVERSON, H. M. Tonal volume as a function of intensity. *Amer. J. Psychol.*, 1924, **35**, 360–67.

HAMILTON, C. G. *Outlines of music history.* Bryn Mawr, Pa.: Oliver Ditson Co., Inc., 1924.

HAMPTON, P. J. The emotional element in music. *J. genet. Psychol.*, 1945, **33**, 237–50.

HANSLICK, E. *The beautiful in music.* London: Novello & Co., Ltd., 1891.

HEINLEIN, C. P. The affective characters of major and minor modes in music. *J. comp. Psychol.*, 1928, **8**, 101–42.

Heinlein, C. P. A brief discussion of the nature and function of melodic configuration in tonal memory with critical reference to the Seashore Tonal Memory Test. *J. genet. Psychol.*, 1928, **35,** 45–61.

Heinlein, C. P. A new method of studying the rhythmic responses of children, together with an evaluation of the method of simple observation. *J. genet. Psychol.*, 1929, **36,** 205–28.

Helmholtz, H. L. F. von. *On the sensations of tone*, 1862. Trans. Ellis. 4th ed.; London: Longmans, Green & Co., 1912.

Henderson, M. T. Remedial measures in motor rhythm as applied to piano performance. Thesis, University of Iowa, 1931.

Henderson, M. T. Rhythmic organization in artistic piano performance. *Univ. Ia. Stud. Psychol. Music*, 1937, **4,** 281–305.

Henderson, M. T., Tiffin, J., & Seashore, C. E. The Iowa piano camera and its use. *Univ. Ia. Stud. Psychol. Music*, 1937, **4,** 252–62.

Hevner, K. Tests for aesthetic appreciation in the field of music. *J. appl. Psychol.*, 1930, **14,** 470–77.

Hevner, K. A study of tests for appreciation of music. *J. appl. Psychol.*, 1931, **15,** 575–83.

Hevner, K. The affective character of major and minor modes in music. *Amer. J. Psychol.*, 1935, **47,** 103–18.

Hevner, K. Expression in music: a discussion of experimental studies and theories. *Psychol. Rev.*, 1935, **47,** 186–204.

Hevner, K. Experimental studies of the elements of expression in music. *Amer. J. Psychol.*, 1936, **48,** 246–68.

Hevner, K. The affective value of pitch and tempo in music. *Amer. J. Psychol.*, 1937, **49,** 621–30.

Hevner, K. The aesthetic experience: a psychological description. *Psychol. Rev.*, 1937, **44,** 245–63.

Highsmith, J. A. Selecting musical talent. *J. appl. Psychol.*, 1929, **13,** 486–93.

Hough, E. Music as a safety factor. *J. acoust. Soc. Amer.*, 1943, **15,** 124.

Howes, F. *The borderland of music and psychology*. London: Kegan Paul, Trench, Trubner & Co., Ltd., 1926.

Hughes, E. Musical memory in piano study. *Mus. Quart.*, Oct., 1915.

Hyde, I. M. Effects of music upon electrocardiograms and blood pressure. In M. Schoen (ed.), *The effects of music*. New York: Harcourt, Brace & Co., Inc., 1927.

Jacobson, E. Electrophysiology of mental activities. *Amer. J. Psychol.*, 1932, **44,** 677–94.

Jaques-Dalcroze, E. *Rhythm, music and education*. Trans. Rubinstein. New York: G. P. Putnam's Sons, 1921.

Johnson, G. B. Musical talent and the American Negro. *Music Superv. J.*, 1928, **15:**81, 13, 86.

KANTOR, J. R. *Principles of psychology.* 2 vols. New York: Alfred A. Knopf, Inc., 1924–26.

KANTOR, J. R. *A survey of the science of psychology.* Bloomington, Ind.: The Principia Press, Inc., 1933.

KELLEY, N. A. A comparative study of the response of normal and pathological ears to speech sounds. *J. exp. Psychol.*, 1937, **21,** 342–52.

KERR, W. A. Psychological effects of music as reported by 162 defense trainees. *Psychol. Rec.*, 1942, **5,** 205–12.

KERR, W. A. Psychological research in industrial music and plant broadcasting. *J. Psychol.*, 1944, **17,** 243–61.

KERR, W. A. *Experiments on the effect of music on factory production.* Appl. Psychol. Monogr., 1945, No. 5, pp. 1–40.

KIRKPATRICK, F. H. Music in industry. *J. appl. Psychol.*, 1943, **27,** 268–74.

KOFFKA, K. Experimental-Untersuchungen zur Lehre von Rhythmus. Z. *Psychol.*, 1909, **52,** 1–109.

KOVACS, S. Untersuchungen über das musikalische Gedächtnis. Z. *angew. Psychol.*, 1916, **11,** 113–35.

KRUEGER, F. Die Theorie der Konsonanz. *Psychol. Studien*, 1910, **5,** 294–409.

KRUGMAN, H. E. Affective responses to music as a function of familiarity. *J. abn. soc. Psychol.*, 1943, **38,** 388–93.

KURTZ, E. B., & LARSEN, M. J. An electrostatic audio generator. *Elec. Eng.*, Sept., 1935.

KWALWASSER, J. *Kwalwasser Test of Melodic and Harmonic Sensitivity.* Camden, N. J.: Victor Talking Machine Co., 1926.

KWALWASSER, J. *Kwalwasser Test of Music Information and Appreciation.* Iowa City, Ia.: Bureau of Educational Research and Service, University of Iowa, 1927.

KWALWASSER, J. Tests and measurements in music. *Psychol. Bull.*, 1928, **25,** 284–301.

KWALWASSER, J., & DYKEMA, P. W. *Kwalwasser-Dykema Music Tests.* New York: Carl Fischer, Inc., 1930.

KWALWASSER, J., & DYKEMA, P. W. *Manual of directions for Victor records.* New York: Carl Fischer, Inc., 1930.

KWALWASSER, J., & RUCH, G. N. *Kwalwasser-Ruch Test of Musical Accomplishment.* Iowa City, Ia.: Bureau of Educational Research and Service, University of Iowa, 1924.

LANDIS, C., & HUNT, W. A. The conscious correlates of galvanic skin response. *J. exp. Psychol.*, 1935, **18,** 505–29.

LANIER, L. H. Prediction of the reliability of mental tests and tests of special abilities. *J. exp. Psychol*, 1927, **10,** 69–113.

LANNERT, V., & ULLMAN, M. Factors in the reading of piano music. *Amer. J. Psychol.*, 1945, **58,** 91–99.

LARSON, D. L. An experimental critique of the Seashore Consonance Test. *Psychol. Monogr.*, 1928, **38**:4 (Whole No. 176), 49–81.

LENOIRE, A. D. Measurement of racial differences in certain mental and educational abilities. Thesis, University of Iowa, 1925.

LICHT, S. *Music in medicine.* Boston: New England Conservatory of Music, 1946.

LIPPS, TH. Zur Theorie der Melodie. Z. *Psychol.*, 1902, **27**, 225–63.

LIPPS, TH. *Psychologische Studien.* Leipzig: Durr'sche Buchhandlung, 1905.

LUNDIN, R. W. A preliminary report on some new tests of musical ability. *J. appl. Psychol.*, 1944, **28**, 393–96.

LUNDIN, R. W. Toward a cultural theory of consonance. *J. Psychol.*, 1947, **28**, 45–49.

LUNDIN, R. W. The development and validation of a set of musical ability tests. *Psychol. Monogr.*, 1949, **63**:305, 1–20.

MCCARTHY, D. A study of the Seashore Measures of Musical Talent. *J. appl. Psychol.*, 1930, **14**, 437–55.

MCDANIEL, R. How music increases office production. *Amer. Business,* 1945, **15**, 22–26.

MCDOUGALL, R. The relation of auditory rhythm and nervous discharge. *Psychol. Rev.*, 1902, **9**, 460–80.

MCGEOCH, J. A. *The psychology of human learning.* New York: Longmans, Green & Co., Inc., 1942.

MCGLINN, J. A. Music in the operating room. *Amer. J. Obstet. Gynaec.*, 1930, **20**, 678–83.

MADISON, T. H. *Interval discrimination as a measure of musical aptitude.* Arch. Psychol., 1942, No. 206, 1–99.

MANZER, C. W., & MOROWITZ, S. The performance of a group of college students on the K.-D. tests. *J. appl. Psychol.*, 1935, **19**, 331–48.

MAX, L. W. Action-current responses in the deaf during waking, kinaesthetic imagery, and abstract thinking. *J. comp. Psychol.*, 1937, **24**, 301–44.

METFESSEL, M. The vibrato in artistic voices. *Univ. Ia. Stud. Psychol. Music,* 1932, **1**, 14–177.

MEYER, M. Elements of a psychological theory of melody. *Psychol. Rev.*, 1900, **7**, 241–73.

MEYER, M. *Contributions to a psychological theory of music.* Columbia, Mo.: University of Missouri, 1901.

MEYER, M. Experimental studies in the psychology of music. *Amer. J. Psychol.*, 1903, **14**, 456–78.

MEYER, M. Experimental studies in the psychology of music: III. Quartertone music. *Amer. J. Psychol.*, 1903, **14**, 207–14.

MEYER, M. Unscientific methods in musical esthetics. *J. Phil. Psychol. sci. Meth.*, 1904, **1**, 707–15.

MILLER, D. C. *The science of musical sounds.* New York: The Macmillan Co., 1926.

Miles, W. R. Accuracy of the voice in simple pitch singing. *Psychol. Rev. Monogr.*, 1914, **17**:3 (Whole No. 69), 13–66.

Misbach, L. E. Effect of pitch of tone-stimuli upon body resistance and cardiovascular phenomena. *J. exp. Psychol.*, 1932, **16**, 167–83.

Moore, H. T. The genetic aspect of consonance and dissonance. *Psychol. Monogr.*, 1914, **17**:2 (Whole No. 73), 1–68.

More, G. V. D. Prognostic testing in music on the college level. *J. educ. Res.*, 1932–33, **26**, 199–212.

Mosher, R. M. *A study of the group method of measurement of sight singing.* New York: Bureau of Publications, Teachers College, Columbia University, 1925.

Mueller, J. H. *The American symphony orchestra: a social history of musical taste.* Bloomington, Ind.: Indiana University Press, 1951.

Mueller, J. H., Mill, E. G., Zane, N. B., & Hevner, K. Studies in the appreciation of art. *Univ. Ore. Publ.*, 1934, **4**:6.

Mueller, J. H., & Hevner, K. *Trends in musical taste.* Ind. Univ. Publ., Humanity Series, 1942, No. 8.

Mull, H. K. The acquisition of absolute pitch. *Amer. J. Psychol.*, 1925, **36**, 469–93.

Mursell, J. L. Psychology of music. *Psychol. Bull.*, 1932, **29**, 218–41.

Mursell, J. L. Measuring musical ability and achievement: a study of the correlation of the Seashore test scores and other variables. *J. educ. Res.*, 1932, **26**, 116–26.

Mursell, J. L. What about music tests? *Music Educ. J.*, 1937, **24**:2, 17–18.

Mursell, J. L. *The psychology of music.* New York: W. W. Norton & Co., Inc., 1937.

Mursell, J. L. Intelligence and musicality. *Educ.*, 1939, **59**, 559–62.

Music in Industry. Chicago: Industrial Recreation Association, 1944.

Neu, D. M. A critical review of the literature on "absolute pitch." *Psychol. Bull.*, 1947, **44**, 249–66.

O'Brien, C. E. Part and whole methods in memorization of piano music. *J. educ. Psychol.*, 1943, **34**, 552–60.

Ogden, R. M. A contribution to the theory of tonal consonance. *Psychol. Bull.*, 1909, **6**, 297–303.

Ogden, R. M. *Hearing.* New York: Harcourt, Brace & Co., Inc., 1924.

Ortmann, O. *Physical basis of piano touch and tone.* New York: E. P. Dutton & Co., Inc., 1925.

Ortmann, O. On the melodic relativity of tones. *Psychol. Monogr.*, 1926, **35**:1 (Whole No. 162), 1–35.

Ortmann, O. Tonal intensity as an aesthetic factor. *Music Quart.*, 1928, **14**, 178–91.

Ortmann, O. Some tonal determinants of melodic memory. *J. educ. Psychol.*, 1933, **24**, 454–67.

Ortmann, O. Interval frequency as a determinant of melodic style. *Peabody Bull.*, Dec., 1937, pp. 3–10.

Papinski, A. The nature of rhythm response. *Proc. Mus. Teach. nat. Assn.*, 1946, pp. 321–29.

Peacock, W. A comparative study of musical talent in whites and Negroes and its correlation with intelligence. Thesis, Emory University, 1928.

Peterson, J., & Smith, F. W. The range and modifiability of consonance in certain musical intervals. *Amer. J. Psychol.*, 1930, **42,** 561–72.

Phares, M. L. Analysis of music appreciation by means of the psychogalvanic response technique. *J. exp. Psychol.*, 1934, **17,** 119–40.

Pronko, N. H., & Bowles, J. W., Jr. *Empirical foundations of psychology.* New York: Rinehart & Co., Inc., 1951.

Radin, P. Music and medicine among primitive peoples. In D. M. Schullian & M. Schoen (eds.), *Music and medicine.* New York: Henry Schuman, Inc., 1948.

Reynolds, W. Selecting music for the factory. *Personnel*, 1943, **20,** 95–98.

Rich, G. J., A preliminary study of tonal volume. *J. exp. Psychol.*, 1916, **1,** 13–22.

Rich, G. J. A study of tonal attributes. *Amer. J. Psychol.*, 1919, **30,** 121–64.

Rigg, M. G. An experiment to determine how accurately college students can interpret intended meanings of musical compositions. *J. exp. Psychol.*, 1937, **21,** 223–29.

Rigg, M. G. Speed as a determiner of musical mood. *J. exp. Psychol.*, 1940, **27,** 566–71.

Rigg, M. G. The effect of register and tonality upon musical mood. *J. Musicology*, 1940, **2,** 49–61.

Riker, B. L. The ability to judge pitch. *J. exp. Psychol.*, 1946, **36,** 331–46.

Rubin-Rabson, G. The influence of analytical prestudy in memorizing piano music. *Arch. Psychol.*, 1937, **31:**220, 1–53.

Rubin-Rabson, G. Studies in the psychology of memorizing piano music: I. A comparison of unilateral and coordinated approaches. *J. educ. Psychol.*, 1939, **30,** 321–45.

Rubin-Rabson, G. Studies in the psychology of memorizing piano music: II. A comparison of massed and distributed practice. *J. educ. Psychol.*, 1940, **31,** 270–84.

Rubin-Rabson, G. Studies in the psychology of memorizing piano music: III. A comparison of whole and part approaches. *J. educ. Psychol.*, 1940, **31,** 460–76.

Rubin-Rabson, G. Studies in the psychology of memorizing piano music: IV. The effect of incentive. *J. educ. Psychol.*, 1941, **32,** 45–54.

Rubin-Rabson, G. Studies in the psychology of memorizing piano music: V. A comparison of prestudy periods of varied lengths. *J. educ. Psychol.*, 1941, **32,** 101–12.

RUBIN-RABSON, G. Studies in the psychology of memorizing piano music: VI. A comparison of two forms of mental rehearsal and keyboard overlearning. *J. educ. Psychol.*, 1941, **32**, 593–602.

RUBIN-RABSON, G. Studies in the psychology of memorizing piano music: VII. A comparison of three degrees of overlearning. *J. educ. Psychol.*, 1941, **32**, 688–98.

RUBIN-RABSON, G. The influence of age, intelligence, and training on reactions to classic and modern music. *J. genet. Psychol.*, 1940, **22**, 413–29.

RUCKMICK, C. A. The role of kinaesthesis in the perception of rhythm. *Amer. J. Psychol.*, 1913, **24**, 303–59.

RUCKMICK, C. A. A new classification of tonal qualities. *Psychol. Rev.*, 1929, **36**, 172–80.

RUSCA. Rachanaesthesie mit Tutocain und Percain. *Schweiz. med. Wschr.*, 1935, **65**, 637–38.

SAETVEIT, J. G., LEWIS, D., & SEASHORE, C. E. Revision of the Seashore Measures of Musical Talents. *Univ. Ia. Stud. Aims Progr. Res.*, 1940, No. 65, pp. 1–66.

SALISBURY, F. S., & SMITH, H. R. Progress of sight-singing ability of normal school students. *J. appl. Psychol.*, 1929, **13**, 425–39.

SANDERSON, H. E. Differences in musical ability in children of different national and racial origin. *J. genet. Psychol.*, 1933, **42**, 100–20.

SCHOEN, M. An experimental study of the pitch factor in artistic singing. *Psychol. Monogr.*, 1922, **31**:1 (Whole No. 140), 230–59.

SCHOEN, M. Tests of musical feeling and understanding. *J. comp. Psychol.*, 1925, **5**, 31–52.

SCHOEN, M. (ed.). *The effects of music.* New York: Harcourt, Brace & Co., Inc., 1927.

SCHOEN, M. The aesthetic attitude in music. *Psychol. Monogr.*, 1928, **29**:2 (Whole No. 178), 161–83.

SCHOEN, M. *The psychology of music.* New York: The Ronald Press Co., 1940.

SCHOEN, M., & GATEWOOD, E. L. Problems related to the mood effects of music. In M. Schoen (ed.), *The effects of music.* New York: Harcourt, Brace & Co., Inc., 1927.

SCHOEN, M., & GATEWOOD, E. L. The mood effects of music. In M. Schoen (ed.), *The effects of music.* New York: Harcourt, Brace & Co., Inc., 1927.

SCHULLIAN, D. M., & SCHOEN, M., (eds.), *Music and medicine.* New York: Henry Schuman, Inc., 1948.

SEAR, H. G. Music and medicine. *Music and Letters,* 1939, **20**, 43–54.

SEASHORE, C. E. The tonoscope. *Psychol. Monogr.*, 1914, **17**:3 (Whole No. 69).

SEASHORE, C. E. *The psychology of musical talent.* New York: Silver Burdett Co., 1919.

SEASHORE, C. E. *Seashore Measures of Musical Talent.* Chicago: C. H. Stoelting & Co., 1919.

SEASHORE, C. E. *Manual of instructions and interpretations for Measures of Musical Talent.* New York: Columbia Gramophone Co., 1919.

SEASHORE, C. E. (ed.). *The vibrato.* Iowa City, Ia.: University of Iowa, 1932.

SEASHORE, C. E. The psychology of music: XI. *Music Educ. J.*, 1937, **24**:3, 25–26.

SEASHORE, C. E. *Psychology of music.* New York: McGraw-Hill Book Co., Inc., 1938.

SEASHORE, C. E. *Why we love music.* Bryn Mawr, Pa.: Oliver Ditson Co., Inc., 1941.

SEASHORE, C. E. Critical training by specific practice. *Educ. Music Mag.*, Sept.-Oct., 1941, pp. 4–5.

SEASHORE, C. E. The vocal trill. *Music Educ. J.*, Jan., 1942.

SEASHORE, C. E. *In search of beauty in music.* New York: The Ronald Press Co., 1947.

SEASHORE, C. E., LEWIS, D., & SAETVEIT, J. G. *Seashore Measures of Musical Talents.* Rev. ed.; Camden, N. J.: Education Department, R.C.A. Manufacturing Co., 1939.

SEASHORE, H. G. The hearing of the pitch and intensity in vibrato. *Univ. Ia. Stud. Psychol. Music*, 1932, **1**, 213–35.

SEASHORE, H. G. An objective analysis of artistic singing. *Univ. Ia. Stud. Psychol. Music*, 1935, **4**, 12–157.

SEASHORE, R. H. Improvability of pitch discrimination. *Psychol. Bull.*, 1935, **32**, 546.

SEASHORE, R. H. Studies in motor rhythm, *Univ. Ia. Stud. Psychol. Music,* 1926, No. 9, pp. 149–99.

SHOWER, E. G., & BIDDULPH, R. Differential pitch sensitivity of the ear. *J. acoust. Soc. Amer.*, 1931, **3**, 275–87.

SIEGMEISTER, E. *The music lover's handbook.* New York: William Morrow & Co., Inc., 1943.

SIGERIST, H. G. The story of tarantism. In D. M. Schullian & M. Schoen (eds.), *Music and medicine.* New York: Henry Schuman, Inc., 1948.

SKINNER, L. Some temporal aspects of piano playing. Thesis, University of Iowa, 1930.

SKINNER, L. A musical pattern score of the first movement of the Beethoven Sonata, Opus 27, No. 2. *Univ. Ia. Stud. Psychol. Music,* 1937, **4**, 263–80.

SMALL, A. M. An objective analysis of artistic violin performance. *Univ. Ia. Stud. Psychol. Music,* 1937, **4**, 172–231.

SMITH, F. O. The effect of training on pitch discrimination. *Psychol. Monogr.*, 1914, **16**:3 (Whole No. 69), 67–103.

SMITH, H. C. *Music in relation to employee attitudes, piecework production, and industrial accidents.* Appl. Psychol. Monogr., 1947, No. 14.

SOIBELMAN, D. *Therapeutic and industrial uses of music.* New York: Columbia University Press, 1948.

SPEARS, E. M. *The use of music in industry.* Report No. 78. New York: Industrial Conference Board, 1947.

STANTON, H. M. Measurement of musical talent: the Eastman experiment. *Univ. Ia. Stud. Psychol. Music,* 1935, **2,** 1–140.

STANTON, H. M., & KOERTH, W. Musical capacity measures in adults repeated after musical education. *Univ. Ia. Stud. Aims Progr. Res.,* 1930, **31.**

STANTON, H. M., and KOERTH, W. Musical capacity measures in children repeated after musical training. *Univ. Ia. Stud. Aims Progr. Res.,* 1933, **42:**259.

STETSON, R. B. A motor theory of rhythm and discrete sensation. *Psychol. Rev.,* 1905, **12,** 250–70, 293–350.

STEVENS, S. S. Tonal density. *J. exp. Psychol.,* 1934, **17,** 585–92.

STEVENS, S. S. The attributes of tone. *Proc. nat. Acad. Sci.,* Wash., 1934, **20,** 457–59.

STEVENS, S. S. Are tones spatial? *Amer. J. Psychol.,* 1934, **46,** 145–47.

STEVENS, S. S. The volume and intensity of tones. *Amer. J. Psychol.,* 1934, **46,** 397–408.

STEVENS, S. S. The relation of pitch to intensity. *J. acoust. Soc. Amer.,* 1935, **6,** 150–54.

STEVENS, S. S., & DAVIS, H. *Hearing: its psychology and physiology.* New York: John Wiley & Sons, Inc., 1938.

STREEP, R. L. A comparison of white and Negro children in rhythm and consonance. *J. appl. Psychol.,* 1931, **15,** 53–71.

STUMPF, C. *Tonpsychologie.* 2 vols. Leipzig: S. Hirzel, 1883–90.

TAYLOR, E. M. A study of the prognosis of musical talent. *J. exp. Educ.,* 1941, **10,** 1–28.

THOMAS, G. J. Equal-volume judgments of tones. *Amer. J. Psychol.,* 1949, **62,** 182–201.

TILSON, L. M. Music talent tests for teacher training purposes. *Music Superv. J.,* 1932, **18,** 26.

TITCHENER, E. B. *A textbook of psychology.* New York: The Macmillan Co., 1909–10.

TORGERSON, T. L., & FAHNESTOCK, E. *Torgerson-Fahnestock Music Tests.* Bloomington, Ill.: Public School Publishing Co., 1926.

UNDERWOOD, B. J. *Experimental psychology.* New York: Appleton-Century-Crofts, Inc., 1949.

UPDEGRAFF, R. A preliminary study of the nature of finality in melody. *Proc. Ia. Acad. Sci.,* 1926, **23,** 279–82.

VALENTINE, C. W. The aesthetic appreciation of musical intervals among school children and adults. *Brit. J. Psychol.*, 1913, **6**, 190–216.

VALENTINE, C. W. The method of comparison in experiments with musical intervals and the effect of practice on the appreciation of discord. *Brit. J. Psychol.*, 1914–15, **7**, 118–35.

VAN ALSTYNE, D., & OSBORNE, E. Rhythm responses of Negro and white children two to six. *Monogr. Soc. Res. Child Developm.*, 1937, **2**:4.

VAN DE WALL, W. Music in hospitals. In D. Schullian & M. Schoen (eds.), *Music and medicine.* New York: Henry Schuman, Inc., 1948.

VAN NEUYS, K., & WEAVER, H. E. Memory span and visual pauses in reading rhythms and melodies. *Psychol. Monogr.*, 1943, **55**, 33–50.

VERNON, L. M. Synchronization of chords in artistic piano playing. *Univ. Ia. Stud. Psychol. Music*, 1937, **4**, 306–45.

VERVEER, E. M., BARRY, H., JR., & BOUSEFIELD, W. A. Changes in affectivity with repetition. *Amer. J. Psychol.*, 1933, **45**, 130–34.

WAGNER, A. H. Remedial and artistic development of the vibrato. *Univ. Ia. Stud. Psychol. Music*, 1932, **1**, 166–212.

WAKEHAM, G. Query on a revision of the fundamental law of habit formation. *Science*, 1928, **68**, 135–36.

WASHBURN, M. F., CHILD, M. A., & ABEL, T. M. The effects of immediate repetition on the pleasantness or unpleasantness of music. In M. Schoen (ed.), *The effects of music.* New York: Harcourt, Brace & Co., Inc., 1927.

WASHCO, A. The effects of music upon pulse rate, blood pressure, and mental imagery. Philadelphia: Temple University, 1933.

WEAVER, H. E. A survey of visual processes in reading differently constructed musical selections. *Psychol. Monogr.*, 1945, **55:1**, 1–30.

WEBER, E. H. *De pulsu, resorptione, auditu, et tactu.* 1834.

WECHSLER, D. *The measurement of emotional reaction: researches on the psychogalvanic reflex.* Arch. Psychol., 1925, No. 76.

WEDELL, C. H. The nature of the absolute judgment of pitch. *J. exp. Psychol.*, 1934, **17**, 485–503.

WEDGE, G. H. *Rhythm in music: a textbook.* New York: G. Schirmer, Inc., 1927.

WEGEL, R. L., & LANE, C. E. The auditory masking of one pure tone by another and its probable relation to the dynamics of the inner ear. *Physiol. Rev.*, 1924, **23**, 266–85.

WELD, H. P. An experimental study of musical enjoyment. *Amer. J. Psychol.*, 1912, **23**, 245–308.

WHIPPLE, G. M. Studies in pitch discrimination. *Amer. J. Psychol.*, 1903, **14**, 289–309.

WHITLEY, M. T. A comparison of the Seashore and K.-D. tests. *Teach. Coll., Rec.*, 1932, **8**, 731–51.

WHITLEY, P. L. The influence of music on memory. *J. genet. Psychol.*, 1934, **10**, 137–51.

WIEBE, G. The effect of radio plugging on students' opinions of popular songs. *J. appl. Psychol.*, 1940, **24**, 721–27.

WOLNER, M., & PYLE, W. H. An experiment in individual training in pitch-deficient children. *J. educ. Psychol.*, 1933, **24**, 602–8.

WOODROW, H. The role of pitch in rhythm. *Psychol. Rev.*, 1911, **18**, 54–77.

WOODS, R. C., & MARTIN, L. R. Testing in musical education. *Educ. and psychol. Meas.*, 1943, **3**, 29–42.

WRIGHT, F. A. The correlation between achievement and capacity in music, *J. educ. Res.*, 1928, **17**, 50–56.

WUNDT, W. *Grundriss der Psychologie.* Leipzig: Engelmann, 1896.

WYATT, R. F. A new instrument for measuring pitch discrimination. *Amer. J. Psychol.*, 1936, **48**, 335–41.

WYATT, R. F. The improvability of pitch discrimination. *Psychol. Monogr.*, 1945, **58**:267, 1–58.

WYATT, S., & LANGDON, J. N. Industrial Health Research Board Report No. 77, Great Britain Medical Research Council, London, 1937.

WYATT, S., & LANGDON, J. N. Fatigue and boredom in repetitive work. London: His Majesty's Stationery Office, 1937.

INDEX OF NAMES

INDEX OF SUBJECTS